Easy Diabetic Cookbook

800 Quick, Healthy and Delicious Diabetes Recipes for Smart People on a Budget

Dr Shone Blardon

© Copyright 2020 Dr Shone Blardon- All Rights Reserved.

In no way is it legal to reproduce, duplicate, or transmit any part of this document by either electronic means or in printed format. Recording of this publication is strictly prohibited, and any storage of this material is not allowed unless with written permission from the publisher. All rights reserved.

The information provided herein is stated to be truthful and consistent, in that any liability, regarding inattention or otherwise, by any usage or abuse of any policies, processes, or directions contained within is the solitary and complete responsibility of the recipient reader. Under no circumstances will any legal liability or blame be held against the publisher for any reparation, damages, or monetary loss due to the information herein, either directly or indirectly.

Respective authors own all copyrights not held by the publisher.

Legal Notice:

This book is copyright protected. This is only for personal use. You cannot amend, distribute, sell, use, quote or paraphrase any part of the content within this book without the consent of the author or copyright owner. Legal action will be pursued if this is breached.

Disclaimer Notice:

Please note the information contained within this document is for educational and entertainment purposes only. Every attempt has been made to provide accurate, up-to-date and reliable, complete information. No warranties of any kind are expressed or implied. Readers acknowledge that the author is not engaging in the rendering of legal, financial, medical or professional advice.

By reading this document, the reader agrees that under no circumstances are we responsible for any losses, direct or indirect, which are incurred as a result of the use of information contained within this document, including, but not limited to, errors, omissions, or inaccuracies.

Table of contents

Introduction 8
Chapter 1: Overview 9
    What is Type 2 Diabetes? 9
    Signs and Symptoms 9
    Prevention 9
    The Link between Diet and Type 2 Diabetes 10
    Foods that You Can Eat and Cannot Eat 10
    Tips for Eating Out 11
    Tips for Changing Your Diet 11
Chapter 2: Breakfast and Brunch Recipes . 13
    Cucumber & Quark Toast 13
    Baked Banana Oatmeal 13
    Toasted Bread with Goat Cheese & Beet Slices 13
    Oatmeal with Pears & Ginger 14
    Fruit Bread 14
    Cucumber Yogurt 14
    Mexican Scrambled Eggs 15
    Breakfast Fruit Medley 15
    Whole Grain Pancakes 16
    French Toast with Banana 16
    Pear Salad 17
    Scrambled Eggs with Spinach 17
    Classic Oatmeal 17
    Oatmeal with Blueberries 18
    Banana Choco Chip Muffins 18
    Oatmeal Pancake with Fruits 19
    Baked Oatmeal with Cinnamon & Pears 19
    Sweet Potato Hash Browns 19
    Waffle with Avocado & Salsa 20
    Cauliflower Hash 20
    Egg Peppers with Avocado Salsa ... 21
    Baked French Toast 21
    Banana Pancake 22
    Breakfast Cereal 22
    Cinnamon Overnight Oatmeal 22
    Vegan Crepe 23
    Yogurt with Vanilla & Dried Apples 23
    Cereal Mix 23
    Oatmeal Pancake with Sauteed Apples .. 24
    Cheesecake Toast with Kiwi & Strawberry 24
    Italian Breakfast Sandwich 25
    Toasted Bread with Peaches & Pistachios 25
    Avocado Toast with Eggs 25
    Breakfast Casserole 26
    Spiced Oatmeal 26
    Honey & Apple Pancakes 27
    Breakfast Pizza Bread 27
    Breakfast Cookie with Yogurt 28
    Toasted Bread with Jam 28
    Trail Mix Cereal 28
    Turkey Breakfast Strata 28
    Zucchini & Cheese Frittata 29
    Yogurt & Granola Sundae 29
    Cantaloupe Breakfast Smoothie in a Bowl 30
    Oat Bran Pancake 30
    Egg & Veggie Muffin 31
    Cheesy Spinach Strata 31
Chapter 3: Main Course Recipes 33
    Veggies & Grains with Turmeric ... 33
    Artichoke with Shredded Chicken 33
    Asian Chicken With Cabbage 33
    Roasted Chicken & Veggies with Hummus 34
    Corned Beef & Cabbage 34
    Sweet & Spicy Flank Steak 35
    Chicken with Broccoli 35
    Chicken Stew 36
    Baked Chicken with Tomato & Basil ... 36
    Chicken Thighs with Orange & Fennel 36
    Balsamic Beef & Mushrooms 37
    Chicken with Kale & Sweet Potato ... 37
    Bacon & Green Beans 38
    Fried Chicken with Collard Greens 38
    Oven Fried Chicken 39
    Sausage Pasta with Kale 39
    Kung Pao Chicken 40
    Beef Stir Fry with Bok Choy 40
    Beef Picadillo 41
    Turkey Burger 41
    Pork Carnitas 42
    Sweet Pot Roast 42
    Cinnamon Pork Tenderloin 43
    Italian Pork 43
    Barbecue Brisket 44
    Rosemary Turkey Roast 44
    Balsamic Chicken with Herbs 45
    Italian Meatballs 45
    Mustard Pepper Steak 46
    Italian Chicken 46

Lettuce Wraps 47
Beef & Veggie Soup 47
Beef Brisket with Wine 47
Barbecue Beef Sandwich 48
Beef Stew 48
Mediterranean Beef 49
Shredded Beef Sandwich 49
Garlic Chicken with Thyme 50
Moroccan-Style Pot Roast 50
Pork Pot Roast 51
Garlic Beef & Broccoli 51
Chicken Kebabs 52
Grilled Beef & Veggies 52
Pork & Rice Noodles 53
Chicken with Peanut Sauce 53
Chicken With Jerk Sauce 54
Grilled Pork Tenderloin 54
Chicken with Tomatoes & Capers 55
Sweet & Sour Pork Tenderloin 55
Sweet & Spicy Sirloin 56
Turkey Kebab 57
Chicken with Mango Chutney 57
Smoky Paprika Pork 57
Pot Roast with Mashed Potatoes 58
Lemon Chicken 58
Pork Tenderloin with Blackberry Sauce 59
Pork Chops with Grape Sauce 59
Roasted Pork & Apples 60
Lime Pork Piccata 60
Philly Chicken Sandwich 61
Lamb with Apples & Onions 61
Steak Rice Bowl 62
Fruit Glazed Meatballs 62
Zucchini Lasagna with Turkey Sausage 63
Spicy Pork Tenderloin 63
Persian Chicken with Rice 64
Eggplant with Lamb 64
Chicken & Sweet Potatoes 65
Chicken & Squash Bake 65
Thai Chicken 66
Cranberry Pork Medallions 66
French Dip Sandwich 67
Mustard & Maple Pork 67
Meatball Soup 68
Italian Beef Pasta 68
Chicken Rice Bowls 69
Pork Stew 69
Grilled Curry Burgers 70
Pork Burger 70
Grilled Lamb & Veggies 71
Savory Chicken 71
Jambalaya 72
Pork Chops with Cider Sauce 72
Spicy Pot Roast 72
Aromatic Steak Dinner 73
Mexican Chicken & Rice 73
Beef with Tomato & Wine 74
Chicken Teriyaki 74
Pork & Rigatoni Stew 75
Pork Stew with Beer 75
Chicken Vera Cruz 76
Beef & Mushroom Stew 76
Bloody Mary Pork 77
Asian Pork with Cabbage 77
Cheesy Chicken 78
Chicken & Veggie Curry 78
Sausage & Potatoes 79
Cajun Pork 79
Creamy Beef Pasta 80
Shawarma Rice 80
Chapter 4: Fish and Seafood Recipes 81
Baked Tuna Steak with Mustard Sauce 81
Miso Glazed Salmon 81
Mediterranean Cod 81
Baked Halibut 82
Turkish Tuna 82
Seared Scallops with Lemon 83
Greek Salmon 83
Spicy Salmon 84
Garlic Salmon 84
Roasted Salmon & Asparagus 85
Baked Fish with Mushrooms 85
Baked Salmon with Ginger & Veggies 86
Swordfish With Tomatoes & Capers 86
Barbecue Shrimp 86
Moroccan Cod 87
Shrimp Boil 87
Grilled Fish with Peppers 88
Salmon with Pineapple Salsa 88
Fish with Tomato Relish 89
Salmon Burgers 89
Halibut with Eggplant 90
Baked Trout 90
Lemon Trout 90
Sesame Tuna 91
Roasted Tilapia 91
Salmon with Pumpkin Pie Spice 92
Salmon with Yogurt 92
Popcorn Shrimp 93
Cod with Caramelized Onions 93

Fish with Squash & Peppers 93
Fish Curry 94
Fish & Salsa Medley 94
Shrimp Kebab 95
Salmon with Spring Veggies 95
Fish with Blueberry Sauce 96
Basil Shrimp 96
Tuscan Tuna 96
Grilled Salmon with Herbs 97
Salmon with Sauteed Kale 97
Lemon Shrimp 98

Chapter 5: Soup Recipes 99
Sweet Potato Soup 99
Turkey & Veggie Soup 99
Mushroom Soup 100
Creamy Tomato Soup 100
Strawberry Soup with Thyme 101
Nacho Soup 101
Onion & Mushroom Soup 101
Cucumber Soup 102
Tomato Soup with Italian Bread 102
Potato Soup 103
Barbecue Meatball Soup 103
Squash Soup 104
Sweet Potato Soup 104
Tofu & Veggie Soup 105
Beef & Root Veggie Soup 105
Carrot Soup 106
Mexican Beef Soup 106
Beef & Veggie Soup 107
Roasted Tomato Soup 107
Cauliflower Soup 107
Spinach Soup 108
Salmon Chowder 108
Curry Veggie Soup 108
Chilled Melon Soup 109
Carrot & Squash Soup 109
Chilled Cucumber Soup with Lemon . 110
Tomato & Zucchini Soup 110
Ginger & Melon Soup 110
Strawberry Soup with Rhubarb 111
Moroccan Chicken Soup 111
Caribbean Pork Soup 112
Creamy Cod Chowder 112
Mexican Style Soup 113
Turkey Soup 113
Italian Egg-Drop Soup 114
Pesto Chicken Soup 114
Seafood Gumbo 115
Garlic Tofu Soup 115
Turkey Posole 115
Squash Soup with Lentils 116

Chapter 6: Salad Recipes 117
Kale & Avocado Salad 117
Chicken Salad with Yogurt 117
Broccoli & Pasta Salad 117
Cucumber & Tomato Salad 118
Citrus Salad 118
Spinach Salad with Sweet Potatoes 119
Shrimp Salad 119
Vibrant Fruit Salad 119
Spinach & Strawberry Salad 120
Strawberry, Avocado & Spinach Salad 120
Arugula Salad with Citrus 120
Spinach & Apple Salad 121
Green Bean Salad 121
Garden Salad 121
Watermelon & Tomato Salad with Feta
 122
Grapefruit & Fennel Salad 122
Potato Salad with Cucumber 123
Asparagus Salad 123
Spinach & Peach Salad 123
Corn & Raspberry Salad 124

Chapter 7: Vegetarian Recipes 125
Basil Pesto 125
Kale & Avocado with Blueberries 125
Potato with Green Beans 125
Green Beans with Crispy Garlic 126
Balsamic Mushrooms 126
Veggie Wraps 126
Eggs with Corn & Black Beans 127
Tofu & Veggie Wrap 127
Potato Curry 128
Mashed Parsnip 128
Mashed Cauliflower & Potatoes 129
Salsa Stuffed Potatoes 129
Veggie Stew 129
Grilled Tomatoes & Eggplant 130
Vegetable Lasagna 130
Zucchini Lasagna 131
Veggie Burgers 131
Spicy Tomato Pasta 132
Garlic Carrots with Pistachios & Spices
 132
Grilled Broccoli 132
Green Beans with Rosemary & Garlic 133
Grilled Zucchini with Avocado Salsa .. 133
Mango & Cucumber Relish 134
Lettuce Cups 134

Tofu Kebab 134
Stuffed Zucchini 135
Cinnamon Oats................................ 135
Cucumber Salsa 135
Sautéed Zucchini 136
Corn & Avocado 136
Chickpea Curry 137
Cauliflower Parmesan 137
Grilled Veggies in Foil Packet........... 138
Roasted Mushrooms with Butter & Parmesan 138
Garlic Butter Mushrooms 139
Pasta Salad with Pesto 139
Beet Burger 139
Kale with Grapes 140
Black Rice with Tofu & Asparagus 140
Cheesy Baked Potato 140

Chapter 8: Side Dish Recipes 142
Orange Broccoli Rabe 142
Baked Zucchini Rounds with Herbed Cream Dip 142
Baked Potato Stuffed with Salmon 143
Parmesan Spiralized Onions 143
Roasted Mushrooms with Shallots...... 143
Grilled Eggplant 144
Packet Potatoes 144
Potato & Bacon Hash 144
Mixed Veggies with Lemon 145
Pickled Zucchini 145
Squash & Zucchini with Anchovy Paste 146
Spicy Root Veggies.......................... 146
Green Beans with Garlic & Mushrooms 146
Zucchini with Couscous 147
Mashed Veggies 147
Zucchini & Squash with Green Chili .. 148
Peas with Celery 148
Mustard & Parsley Potatoes 148
Ginger & Miso Kale 149
Collard Greens with Mushrooms 149
Mashed Potato Casserole 150
Zucchini Fries with Buttermilk Dip 150
Roasted Veggies with Gremolata......... 151
Apples & Pea Pods 151
Roasted Mixed Mushrooms 152
Steamed Carrots & Cabbage 152
Baked Potato with Cheese & Broccoli 152
Potatoes with Rosemary 153
Honey Balsamic Parsnips & Carrots... 153
Balsamic Squash & Beans................. 154
Lemon Mustard Baby Veggies 154
Cheesy Acorn Squash 155
Roasted Carrots with Honey............... 155
Parmesan Leeks 155
Zucchini Fritters 156
Roasted Brussels Sprouts with Parmesan Cheese 156
Baked Beans with Bacon 156
Spicy Brussels Sprouts 157
Sautéed Spinach 157
Smoky Mashed Potatoes....................158

Chapter 9: Appetizers and Snacks Recipes 159
Cauliflower Gnocchi with Marinara Dip 159
Goat Cheese Crostini......................... 159
Black Bean Dip..................................159
Cheesy Apple Bites........................... 160
Baked Cheesy Broccoli 160
Grilled Figs with Goat Cheese & Honey 161
Deviled Eggs with Rosemary 161
Rainbow Salsa 161
Spicy Pecans..................................... 162
Tomato Dip 162
Chives Dip 162
Tuna Canapes 163
Wasabi Snack Mix 163
Spicy Appetizer Mix 164
Roasted Vegetable Spread 164
Sugar Snap Peas with Dip 164
Pumpkin & Avocado Salsa 165
Chicken Wings 165
Roasted Pears with Bacon 165
Zucchini Rolls................................... 166
Bruschetta with Cranberry & Pomegranate 166
Mushrooms with Pesto 167
Chicken Fingers 167
Spicy Cauliflower 167
Onion Rings 168
Chips & Salsa 168
Zucchini Chips 169
Cheesy Deviled Eggs......................... 169
Pickle Chips 169
Spinach Feta Dip & Crackers 170
Turkey Nachos 170
Caprese Skewers 171
Antipasto Skewers 171

Beet Hummus 171
Cocoa Pumpkin Seeds 172
Buffalo Wings 172
Garlic Olives 172
Stuffed Mushrooms 173
Cauliflower Nachos 173
Garlic Chicken Wings 173

Chapter 10: Drinks Recipes 175
Pineapple & Strawberry Smoothie 175
Green Smoothie 175
Berry Smoothie With Mint 175
Berry & Spinach Smoothie 176
Banana, Cauliflower & Berry Smoothie
.... 176
Peach & Apricot Smoothie 176
Peanut Butter Smoothie with Blueberries
.... 177
Banana & Strawberry Smoothie 177
Tropical Smoothie 177
Watermelon & Cantaloupe Smoothie 178
Cantaloupe & Papaya Smoothie 178
Avocado Green Smoothie 178
Peach, Strawberry & Green Tea Smoothie
.... 179
Peach & Nectarine Smoothie 179
Carrot & Orange Smoothie 179
Grapefruit & Pineapple Smoothie 180
Avocado & Raspberry Smoothie 180
Strawberry, Watermelon & Lime Shake
.... 180
Honeydew Melon Smoothie 180
Orange Lemon Juice 181
Pomegranate Cooler 181
Fruit Tea 181
Cherry & Spinach Smoothie 182
Frozen Lemonade 182
Watermelon Juice 183
Pineapple Smoothie 183
Banana & Cranberry Shake 183
Strawberry Frappe 183
Banana & Coffee Smoothie 184
Strawberry Smoothie With Almonds & Tofu 184
Mint Melonade 184
Pear Tea 185
Green Tea & Fruit Smoothie 185
Melon & Kiwi Smoothie with Ginger . 186
Hawaiian Smoothie 186
Mango Smoothie with Yogurt 186
Vegan Fruit Smoothie 187
Watermelon & Turmeric Smoothie 187
Sage Tea 187
Green Tea with Honey 188

Chapter 11: Desserts Recipes 189
Brûléed Oranges 189
Pumpkin & Banana Ice Cream 189
Peanut Butter Choco Chip Cookies 189
Frozen Lemon & Blueberry 190
Strawberry & Mango Ice Cream 190
Watermelon Sherbet 190
Lemon Custard 191
Blueberry Pudding 191
Vanilla Pudding Pops 192
Strawberry & Orange Cupcakes 192
Choco Chip Balls 192
Baked Rice Pudding 193
Tiramisu Shots 193
Peanut Butter Cups 194
Ice Cream Brownie Cake 194
Choco Peppermint Cake 195
Fruit Pizza 195
Cocoa Popcorn 195
Chocolate Cookies 196
Orange & Pumpkin Custards 196
Apricots & Vanilla Yogurt 197
Berry & White Chocolate Pops 197
Apricot Pizza 197
Choco Pretzels 198
Vegan Cookies 198
Roasted Plums 198
Roasted Mango 199
Berries with Vanilla Yogurt 199
Figs with Honey & Yogurt 199
Berries with Creamy Orange Topping 200
Baked Apples 200
Berries with Lime Syrup 200
Cranberry Pears 201
Grilled Peaches 201
Fruit Salad 201
Balsamic Melon 202
Honey Strawberries 202
Fruit Kebabs 202
Strawberry & Watermelon Pops 203
Spiced Apples 203

Chapter 12: 30-Day Meal plan 204
Week 1 204
Week 2 204
Week 3 204
Week 4 205

Conclusion 206

Introduction

Diabetes is one of the most serious health conditions that can have severe negative effects in one's quality of life.

But if you are diagnosed with diabetes, it doesn't mean that you can no longer live a happy and fulfilling life.

One thing that can help you in managing this condition is by adopting a healthy and well-balanced diet, which is what this book is exactly here for.

This provides you with delicious and healthy recipes that are suitable for diabetics.

Aside from that, it provides an overview of this health condition so you can get to know more about it, as well as tips on how to manage it more efficiently.

Do not let this condition get in the way of a rewarding and healthy lifestyle.

Chapter 1: Overview
What is Type 2 Diabetes?

Type 2 diabetes is the most common type of diabetes that affects 400 million people around the world, according to the World Health Organization.

It is a chronic disease that was previously called adult-onset diabetes since most people diagnosed in the past are 45 years and older. However, cases in children and teens became prevalent over the years, mainly due to obesity and diet.

Our body requires glucose, a type of sugar we get from the foods we consume, to function properly. This serves as our body's fuel and energy and is absorbed by the cells with the excess being stored in the liver for future use.

Our pancreas produces a hormone called insulin that is responsible for the absorption of glucose in the blood to the cells.

When communication between cells and organs become erratic, problems such as diabetes, arise. Once the body becomes resistant to the insulin or when it is not using it properly, glucose accumulates in the blood, that is why people suffering from type 2 diabetes need medication or insulin shots to correct this.

Signs and Symptoms

Early testing and diagnosis are crucial to effectively keep diabetes away.

Some of the signs and symptoms may be so mild that individuals hardly notice it.

It is essential to talk to your doctor or a diabetes educator to know more about type 2 diabetes, especially if you are experiencing any of the symptoms below.

- Fatigue
- Need to hydrate and urinate frequently
- Increased hunger
- Unintended or unexplained weight loss
- Wounds and sores that take a long time to heal
- Darkened areas in folds of skin usually around the neck and armpits called acanthosis nigricans
- Susceptibility to infections
- Numbness of the hands and feet
- Headache
- Irritability
- Blurred vision

Prevention

The easiest way to prevent diabetes or manage its symptoms is to watch what you eat and maintain a healthy weight and lifestyle.

Keeping a waist circumference of 40 inches and below for men and 35 inches and below for women is not only helpful in avoiding excess fat but is also effective in lowering the risks of diabetes, high blood pressure, and heart problems. If you are overweight, losing 5-10% of your body weight will significantly improve your blood sugar levels.

Start eating healthy and consider exercising at least 30 minutes per day, if possible. Health issues may arise when we become sedentary for extended periods.

Keep yourself moving throughout the day either by doing household chores, using a standing desk, walking or biking instead of commuting when you're out running errands, skipping the elevator to take the stairs, keeping daily alarms to remind you to take a break and move around, and stretching every after a few hours of inactivity.

Physical activity will help use up the excess glucose in your bloodstream.

Lifestyle changes such as quitting smoking and getting enough sleep each night will positively impact your health in the long run.

Smoking not only increases your risk of getting lung disease but will also increase the risk of contracting diabetes, stroke, and heart problems, among others.

The Link between Diet and Type 2 Diabetes

Diet has the biggest impact on maintaining healthy levels of sugar in the blood since we source our glucose primarily through the food we eat. Diabetic or not, we all need to eat more than once each day to have sufficient energy to perform daily tasks.

The good news is diet is highly modifiable to meet the nutritional needs of our body. Therefore, we can have complete control over what we consume.

The modern comforts we enjoy from breakthroughs in technology gives us more reason to become physically inactive. Nowadays, we can get more work done by sitting or lying down and clicking away at our laptops.

Foods are loaded with so many sugars that whenever we feel stressed out, we find ourselves reaching for a dessert or even a cigarette to de-stress. The combination of unhealthy diet and lifestyle leads to obesity, and obesity is the main risk factor in developing diabetes.

Millions of people around the world have already been diagnosed with type 2 diabetes. This number keeps on rising each year with the ages of patients getting younger and younger.

Several studies have shown that a diet poor in fruits and vegetables and the frequent consumption of sugary drinks causes high blood sugars that develops into diabetes.

Foods that You Can Eat and Cannot Eat

A good diet for people with type 2 diabetes consists of a healthy balance of carbohydrates, fats, and proteins. By understanding which type of foods your body needs and should avoid, it will be easier for you to look after your health.

Carbohydrates are the primary sources of sugar and are classified between complex and simple carbohydrates. Complex carbohydrates, especially those high in fiber, are ideal for diabetics since they also contain nutrients that slow down the release of sugars in the blood attributing to more stable blood sugar levels. Look for foods made from 100% whole wheat and consume lots of vegetables and plant-based fats and proteins.

Artichoke, berries, barley, chia seeds, brown rice, oatmeal, and other grains are exceptional sources of fibers, proteins, and essential nutrients. These types of foods makes you feel full and help prevent overeating.

People with diabetes can get the dose of their needed proteins through legumes, beans, peas, lentils, lean meat, eggs, tofu, fish, and seafood. Starchy vegetables that are rich in vitamin C such as squash, corn, potato, sweet potato, and other root crops may be consumed moderately.

Avoid animal fat and aim for fats sourced from plants such as olive, canola, and avocado oils. Nuts and seeds are also good sources of plant-based fat. Animal fats that support a healthy heart are sourced from fish like wild salmon, herring, lake trout, sturgeon, anchovies, and mackerel.

These types of fishes, along with nuts and seeds, are rich in omega-3 fatty acids that are anti-inflammatory and are important in combatting health problems such as stroke, arthritis, and asthma.

Simple carbohydrates usually found in processed foods and cause blood sugar to spike should be completely avoided. Steer away from processed meats such as hot dogs, sausages, and deli meats. Moreover, refrain from foods such as white sugar, flour, pasta, pastries, white bread, white rice, trans fat, soft drinks, sodas, high fructose corn syrup, and other artificial sweeteners. Remember to limit your consumption of red meat and animal and dairy products that are high in fat.

Tips for Eating Out

It is vital to let your family know what foods you are trying to avoid. Talk to them about how important it is for you to keep yourself healthy. You may also tell them your goals diet-wise so they can also help you.

If possible, know the restaurant you are going to in advance. Search for their food offerings online if they have a website. A lot of food businesses these days publish their menus online and even have chat support. From here, you can plan on what to order. If you can, choose specialty restaurants that offer a lot of vegetable dishes such as Thai, Korean, Japanese, or Indian.

If there is no way for you to know the restaurant in advance, just remember to exercise portion control. Not everyone likes to eat as healthy as you need to, but that does not have to get you down.

Do not hesitate to ask about the portion sizes and how the food was prepared. It might even be useful to let the servers know about your condition for them to know how they can prepare the food, especially if most of the choices on the menu can cause dangerous surges in your blood sugar.

You can look for lean meat like skinless chicken and turkey, tofu, steamed/broiled fish and seafood, or vegetable salads with olive oil. Pick grilled, steamed or baked dishes instead of fried. You may also skip dessert and sugary drinks and sodas and opt for plain water instead.

There may be times when you might get pressured by family members to indulge. You can respectfully decline, or better yet, share the dish or dessert with them, so you do not end up eating an entire serving.

Tips for Changing Your Diet

If you are someone with type 2 diabetes, you may consider drastically changing your diet. Although this seems intimidating at first, as with all major changes in our lives, know that this type of change is beneficial and highly necessary.

Just because you will not be able to indulge in certain foods does not mean that you cannot also enjoy eating healthily. Remember that eating healthy benefits everyone, not just diabetics.

You can start with managing portion sizes and learning about which foods raise blood sugar levels. Use this knowledge to guide you in determining how much of a food you can eat in a day. Consuming more vegetables, whole grains, and plant-based fats and proteins should be your top priority.

Shifting to a vegetarian or vegan diet has been proven to be favorable for people already diagnosed with type 2 diabetes. Going meatless has helped lower cholesterol and blood pressure, maintain a healthy weight, and support kidney health. Thankfully, there are various meat substitutes from soybean and wheat proteins like tofu, tempeh, and seitan to make the transition easier.

Experiment with diabetic-friendly dishes through vegan cookbooks and make it your goal to prepare your meals. Cooking your food at home is not only a healthier option, but it also saves you money. It is easier to control the portion sizes and avoid unhealthy condiments with high salt and sugar content, preservatives, as well as chemical additives.

Try out ethnic restaurants and cuisines like Thai, Korean, Mediterranean, Mexican, and South Indian to immerse yourself in the myriad of vegan food choices and discover new foods to add to your favorites. Another tip is to consider your favorite unhealthy foods and find a vegan counterpart for it.

Creating meal plans and meal preps provides convenience and are conducive to keeping track of your carbohydrate and calorie intake. It is best to consult a healthcare professional or registered dietician to help you form a meal plan since nutritional needs vary from person to person.

Read about the glycemic load, glycemic index, and learn how to count calories. There are mobile apps and online counseling groups that can guide you, especially when you are just beginning to incorporate these changes into your lifestyle.

Chapter 2: Breakfast and Brunch Recipes

Cucumber & Quark Toast

Preparation Time: 5 minutes; Cooking Time: 0 minutes; Serving: 1

Ingredients:
- 1 whole wheat bread
- 2 tablespoons cucumber, diced
- 2 tablespoons quark
- 1 tablespoon cilantro leaves, chopped
- Salt to taste

Method:
1. Toast the bread in the oven.
2. Top with the cucumber and quark.
3. Sprinkle with the cilantro and salt.
4. Serve immediately.

Nutritional Value:
- Calories 141
- Total Fat 5.1 g
- Saturated Fat 2.2 g
- Cholesterol 20 mg
- Total Carbohydrate 13.8 g
- Dietary Fiber 2 g
- Protein 7.6 g
- Total Sugars 2 g

Baked Banana Oatmeal

Preparation Time: 15 minutes; Cooking Time: 25 minutes; Servings: 12

Ingredients:
- Cooking spray
- 3 cups rolled oats
- 1 ½ cups nonfat milk
- ¾ cup mashed bananas
- ⅓ cup brown sugar
- 2 eggs, beaten
- 1 teaspoon baking powder
- 1 teaspoon ground cinnamon
- 1 teaspoon vanilla extract
- ½ teaspoon salt
- ½ cup pecans, toasted and chopped

Method:
1. Preheat your oven to 375 degrees F.
2. Spray your muffin pan with oil.
3. Combine all the ingredients in a bowl. Mix well.
4. Pour the mixture into the muffin cups.
5. Bake for 25 minutes.
6. Let cool before serving.

Nutritional Value:
- Calories 176
- Total Fat 6.2 g
- Saturated Fat 1.2 g
- Cholesterol 33 mg
- Sodium 166 mg
- Total Carbohydrate 26.4 g
- Dietary Fiber 3.1 g
- Protein 5.2 g

Toasted Bread with Goat Cheese & Beet Slices

Preparation Time: 5 minutes; Cooking Time: 0 minutes; Serving: 1

Ingredients:
- 2 tablespoons goat cheese
- 1 slice whole-wheat bread, toasted
- 1 beet, cooked and sliced
- 1 teaspoon freshly squeezed lemon zest

Method:
1. Spread goat cheese on the bread.
2. Top with the beet slices.
3. Sprinkle the lemon zest on top and serve.

Nutritional Value:
- Calories 137
- Total Fat 4.2 g
- Saturated Fat 2.3 g
- Cholesterol 7 mg
- Sodium 288 mg
- Total Carbohydrate 18.1 g
- Dietary Fiber 4 g
- Protein 7.2 g

Oatmeal with Pears & Ginger

Preparation Time: 5 minutes; Cooking Time: 10 minutes; Serving: 1
Ingredients:
- ¼ cup rolled oats
- ⅛ teaspoon ground ginger
- ¼ cup pear, sliced
- ⅛ teaspoon ground cinnamon

Method:
1. Follow the instructions in cooking the oats.
2. Add the ginger.
3. Transfer to a serving bowl.
4. Arrange the pear slices on top.
5. Sprinkle the ground cinnamon on top and serve.

Nutritional Value:
- Calories 108
- Total Fat 2 g
- Saturated Fat 0 g
- Cholesterol 0 mg
- Sodium 5 mg
- Total Carbohydrate 21 g
- Dietary Fiber 3 g
- Protein 3 g

Fruit Bread

Preparation Time: 30 minutes; Cooking Time: 50 minutes; Servings: 12
Ingredients:
- Cooking spray
- 1 cup all-purpose flour

Pinch salt
- 1 ½ teaspoons baking powder
- 1 egg, beaten
- ¼ teaspoon pumpkin pie spice
- ¼ cup whole-wheat flour
- ½ cup granulated sugar
- 2 tablespoons vegetable oil
- ½ cup applesauce
- ½ cup dried apricots, chopped

Method:
1. Preheat your oven to 350 degrees F.
2. Spray your loaf pan with oil.
3. Combine all the ingredients in a bowl except the dried apricots.
4. Pour into the pan.
5. Sprinkle the apricots on top.
6. Bake in the oven for 50 minutes.
7. Let cool before slicing and serving.

Nutritional Value:
- Calories 128
- Total Fat 3.1 g
- Saturated Fat 0.6 g
- Cholesterol 18 mg
- Sodium 135 mg
- Total Carbohydrate 24 g
- Dietary Fiber 1.4 g
- Protein 2.2 g

Cucumber Yogurt

Preparation Time: 5 minutes; Cooking Time: 0 minutes; Serving: 1
Ingredients:
- 1 cup reduced-fat plain yogurt
- ¼ teaspoon lemon juice

- ¼ teaspoon lemon zest
- ½ cup cucumber, sliced into cubes
- Fresh mint, chopped
- Salt to taste

Method:
1. Put your yogurt in a bowl.
2. Stir in the lemon juice, lemon zest and cucumber.
3. Top with the mint and season with salt.

Nutritional Value:
- Calories 164
- Total Fat 3.9 g
- Saturated Fat 2.5 g
- Cholesterol 15 mg
- Sodium 319 mg
- Total Carbohydrate 19.1 g
- Dietary Fiber 0.6 g
- Protein 13.3 g

Mexican Scrambled Eggs

Preparation Time: 15 minutes; Cooking Time: 15 minutes; Servings: 4

Ingredients:
- 1 onion, chopped
- 1 cup red bell pepper strips
- 1 jalapeño chili pepper, chopped
- 2 links chicken sausages, cooked and sliced
- 8 eggs, beaten
- ¼ cup fresh cheese, crumbled
- 4 corn tortillas, toasted in the oven and sliced into small pieces
- Salt to taste
- Cilantro, sliced

Method:
1. In a pan over medium low heat, cook the onion, bell pepper, jalapeño and sausages for 5 to 6 minutes.
2. Stir in the eggs, cheese and tortillas pieces.
3. Season with the salt.
4. Cook until firm.
5. Garnish with cilantro before serving.

Nutritional Value:
- Calories 227
- Total Fat 4.8 g
- Saturated Fat 1.2 g
- Cholesterol 33 mg
- Sodium 558 mg
- Total Carbohydrate 21.8 g
- Dietary Fiber 2.8 g
- Protein 23.8 g

Breakfast Fruit Medley

Preparation Time: 15 minutes; Cooking Time: 0 minutes; Servings: 12

Ingredients:
- 2 cups melon, sliced into cubes
- 2 cups strawberries, sliced
- 2 cups grapes, sliced in half
- 2 cups peaches, sliced into cubes
- 1 tablespoon honey
- 3 tablespoons lime juice
- 3 teaspoons lime zest
- ½ teaspoon ground ginger
- ⅓ cup coconut flakes, toasted

Method:
1. Combine all the fruits in a serving bowl.
2. Toss to combine.
3. Stir in the honey and lime juice.
4. Add the lime zest and ginger. Mix.
5. Top with the coconut flakes.

Nutritional Value:
- Calories 65
- Total Fat 1.3 g

- Saturated Fat 1.1 g
- Cholesterol 0 mg
- Sodium 20 mg
- Total Carbohydrate 13.9 g
- Dietary Fiber 1.6 g
- Protein 1 g

Whole Grain Pancakes

Preparation Time: 15 minutes; Cooking Time: 10 minutes; Servings: 16
Ingredients:
- ½ cup rolled oats
- ½ cup yellow cornmeal
- 1 ½ cups all-purpose flour

Pinch salt
- 1 egg, beaten
- ¼ cup nonfat yogurt
- 1 ¾ cups nonfat milk
- 2 ½ teaspoons baking powder
- 3 tablespoons brown sugar
- 3 tablespoons vegetable oil
- Cooking spray

Method:
1. Process the roll oats in your blender until ground.
2. Transfer to a bowl.
3. Stir in the rest of the ingredients.
4. Mix well.
5. Spray your pan with oil.
6. Place it over medium low heat.
7. Pour a few tablespoons of the batter into the pan.
8. Flip once the surface bubbles.
9. Cook for 1 to 2 minutes.

Nutritional Value:
- Calories 220
- Total Fat 6 g
- Saturated Fat 1 g
- Cholesterol 2 mg
- Sodium 265 mg
- Total Carbohydrate 34.9 g
- Dietary Fiber 1.7 g
- Protein 6.5 g

French Toast with Banana

Preparation Time: 10 minutes; Cooking Time: 10 minutes; Servings: 4
Ingredients:
- Cooking spray
- 2 eggs, beaten
- ½ teaspoon vanilla
- ⅛ teaspoon ground cinnamon
- ½ cup nonfat milk
- 4 French bread slices
- 1 banana, sliced thinly

Method:
1. Preheat your oven to 500 degrees F.
2. Cover your baking pan with foil
3. Spray it with oil.
4. In a bowl, mix the eggs, vanilla, cinnamon and milk.
5. Create a hole in the bread slice and fill with bananas.
6. Dip the bread in the mixture.
7. Transfer to the baking pan.
8. Bake for 10 minutes.

Nutritional Value:
- Calories 210
- Total Fat 4.2 g
- Saturated Fat 1.2 g
- Cholesterol 107 mg
- Sodium 352 mg
- Total Carbohydrate 33.8 g

- Dietary Fiber 2.1 g
- Protein 8.8 g

Pear Salad

Preparation Time: 10 minutes; Cooking Time: 0 minutes; Servings: 4
Ingredients:
- 2 pears, sliced into cubes
- 2 tablespoons lemon juice
- ¼ cup pecans, toasted and chopped
- ¼ cup nonfat plain Greek yogurt
- 1 tablespoon agave nectar

Method:
1. Toss the pears in lemon juice.
2. Transfer to serving bowls.
3. Sprinkle the pecans on top.
4. Serve with a mixture of agave nectar and yogurt.

Nutritional Value:
- Calories 140
- Total Fat 7 g
- Saturated Fat 0.8 g
- Cholesterol 1 mg
- Sodium 7 mg
- Total Carbohydrate 19.7 g
- Dietary Fiber 3.5 g
- Protein 2.6 g

Scrambled Eggs with Spinach

Preparation Time: 10 minutes; Cooking Time: 10 minutes; Serving: 1
Ingredients:
- 1 teaspoon vegetable oil
- 1 ½ cups baby spinach
- 2 eggs, beaten
- Salt and pepper to taste
- 1 slice whole-wheat bread, toasted

Method:
1. Pour the oil into a pan over medium heat.
2. Cook the spinach for 1 minute.
3. Transfer to a plate.
4. Add the eggs to the pan.
5. Stir in the cooked spinach into the egg and season with salt and pepper.
6. Serve with bread.

Nutritional Value:
- Calories 296
- Total Fat 15.7 g
- Saturated Fat 3.7 g
- Cholesterol 372 mg
- Sodium 394 mg
- Total Carbohydrate 20.9 g
- Dietary Fiber 7 g
- Protein 17.8 g

Classic Oatmeal

Preparation Time: 10 minutes; Cooking Time: 5 minutes; Serving: 1
Ingredients:
- ½ cup rolled oats
- 1 cup nonfat milk
- Pinch salt
- Almond milk
- Ground cinnamon

Method:
1. Fill a saucepan with milk.
2. Bring to a boil over medium heat.
3. Add the oats.
4. Reduce heat.
5. Cook for 5 minutes.

6. Transfer to a bowl. Let cool.
7. Stir in the salt.
8. Drizzle the almond milk on top.
9. Sprinkle with the cinnamon and serve.

Nutritional Value:
- Calories 150
- Total Fat 3 g
- Saturated Fat 0.5 g
- Cholesterol 0 mg
- Sodium 152 mg
- Total Carbohydrate 27 g
- Dietary Fiber 4 g
- Protein 5 g

Oatmeal with Blueberries

Preparation Time: 5 minutes; Cooking Time: 5 minutes; Serving: 1

Ingredients:
- ¼ cup steel-cut oats
- 1 cup nonfat milk
- 2 teaspoons honey
- 1 cup blueberries, sliced

Method:
1. Follow the instructions for cooking the oats in nonfat milk.
2. Drizzle with the honey.
3. Top with the blueberries and serve.

Nutritional Value:
- Calories 150
- Total Fat 2.5 g
- Saturated Fat 0.5 g
- Cholesterol 0 mg
- Sodium 152 mg
- Total Carbohydrate 27 g
- Dietary Fiber 4 g
- Protein 5 g

Banana Choco Chip Muffins

Preparation Time: 15 minutes; Cooking Time: 15 minutes; Servings: 24

Ingredients:
- Cooking spray
- 1 ½ cups rolled oats
- 1 teaspoon baking powder
- ¼ teaspoon baking soda
- ¼ teaspoon salt
- 2 bananas, mashed
- 2 eggs, beaten
- 1 teaspoon vanilla extract
- 3 tablespoons vegetable oil
- ½ cup dark chocolate chips
- ⅓ cup packed brown sugar

Method:
1. Preheat your oven to 350 degrees F.
2. Spray your muffin pan with oil.
3. Blend the oats in the food processor until ground.
4. Transfer to a bowl.
5. Stir in the rest of the ingredients.
6. Pour the mixture into the muffin cups.
7. Bake for 15 minutes.
8. Let cool before serving.

Nutritional Value:
- Calories 78
- Total Fat 3.6 g
- Saturated Fat 0.9 g
- Cholesterol 16 mg
- Sodium 65 mg
- Total Carbohydrate 10.9 g
- Dietary Fiber 1 g
- Protein 10.9 g

Oatmeal Pancake with Fruits

Preparation Time: 10 minutes; Cooking Time: 10 minutes; Servings: 8
Ingredients:
- ½ cup fresh blueberries
- 3 bananas, sliced
- 2 teaspoons lemon juice
- ¼ cup maple syrup
- ¼ teaspoon ground cinnamon
- 1 cup flour
- ½ cup rolled oats
- 1 ½ teaspoons baking powder
- ½ teaspoon baking soda
- Pinch salt
- 1 cup nonfat milk
- 1 egg, beaten
- 1 tablespoon vegetable oil
- 1 tablespoon no-sugar maple syrup
- 1 teaspoon vanilla

Method:
1. In a bowl, combine the blueberries, bananas, lemon juice, maple syrup and ground cinnamon. Set aside.
2. Prepare the pancake batter by mixing the rest of the ingredients in another bowl.
3. Pour tablespoons of the batter into a pan over medium heat.
4. Cook for 2 to 3 minutes per side.
5. Serve with the fruit mix.

Nutritional Value:
- Calories 159
- Total Fat 2.6 g
- Saturated Fat 0.4 g
- Cholesterol 1 mg
- Sodium 246 mg
- Total Carbohydrate 30.7 g
- Dietary Fiber 2.3 g
- Protein 4.6 g

Baked Oatmeal with Cinnamon & Pears

Preparation Time: 30 minutes; Cooking Time: 50 minutes; Servings: 6
Ingredients:
- Cooking spray
- 2 cups rolled oats
- 2 teaspoons ground cinnamon
- ½ cup walnuts, chopped
- ¼ teaspoon ground nutmeg
- 1 teaspoon baking powder
- 2 cups almond milk
- ⅛ teaspoon ground cloves
- ¼ cup maple syrup
- 1 cup low-fat plain Greek yogurt
- 2 tablespoons olive oil
- 2 cups pears, sliced into cubes
- 1 teaspoon vanilla extract
- Pinch salt

Method:
1. Preheat your oven to 375 degrees F.
2. Spray your baking pan with oil.
3. Mix all the ingredients in a bowl.
4. Pour the mixture into a baking pan.
5. Bake for 50 minutes.

Nutritional Value:
- Calories 311
- Total Fat 14.8 g
- Saturated Fat 2.1 g
- Cholesterol 4 mg
- Sodium 449 mg
- Total Carbohydrate 37.8 g
- Dietary Fiber 5.1 g
- Protein 9.3 g

Sweet Potato Hash Browns

Preparation Time: 15 minutes; Cooking Time: 10 minutes; Servings: 4
Ingredients:

- 3 tablespoons olive oil, divided
- 5 cups sweet potato, shredded
- 1 clove garlic, grated
- ¼ cup shallot, chopped
- Salt and pepper to taste

Method:
1. Add 1 tablespoon olive oil to a bowl.
2. Stir in the rest of the ingredients.
3. Form patties from the mixture.
4. Pour the remaining oil into a pan over medium heat.
5. Cook the patties for 5 minutes per side or until golden.

Nutritional Value:
- Calories 103
- Total Fat 7.1 g
- Saturated Fat 1 g
- Cholesterol 20 mg
- Sodium 208 mg
- Total Carbohydrate 9.3 g
- Dietary Fiber 1.4 g
- Protein 1 g

Waffle with Avocado & Salsa

Preparation Time: 15 minutes; Cooking Time: 5 minutes; Serving: 1

Ingredients:
- 1 whole-wheat waffle
- 1 egg, fried sunny side up
- ¼ cup avocado, sliced into cubes
- 1 tablespoon salsa

Method:
1. Follow the packaging directions in toasting the waffle.
2. Top the waffle with the fried egg and avocado.
3. Serve with salsa.

Nutritional Value:
- Calories 207
- Total Fat 12 g
- Saturated Fat 2 g
- Cholesterol 186 mg
- Sodium 279 mg
- Total Carbohydrate 17 g
- Dietary Fiber 6 g
- Protein 9 g

Cauliflower Hash

Preparation Time: 15 minutes; Cooking Time: 15 minutes; Servings: 4

Ingredients:
- 4 teaspoons olive oil, divided
- 2 cloves garlic, minced
- 1 onion, chopped
- 8 ounces turkey sausage
- 16 ounces cauliflower rice
- Salt and pepper to taste
- 3 tablespoons water
- 8 eggs, scrambled

Method:
1. Pour half of the oil into a pan over medium heat.
2. Cook the garlic and onion for 2 minutes.
3. Stir in the sausage. Cook for 4 minutes.
4. Place the mixture on a plate.
5. Cook the cauliflower rice in the same pan for 2 minutes.
6. Season with the salt and pepper.
7. Add water and simmer for 3 minutes.
8. Put the sausage mixture in the pan.
9. Stir and cook for 2 minutes.
10. Transfer to a plate.
11. Add the remaining oil to the pan.
12. Cook the eggs until firm.

13. Serve the hash with the eggs.

Nutritional Value:
- Calories 317
- Total Fat 18.8 g
- Saturated Fat 4.9 g
- Cholesterol 415 mg
- Sodium 654 mg
- Total Carbohydrate 7.8 g
- Dietary Fiber 2.7 g
- Protein 25.9 g

Egg Peppers with Avocado Salsa

Preparation Time: 15 minutes; Cooking Time: 10 minutes; Servings: 4

Ingredients:

Salsa
- 1 avocado, sliced into cubes
- ½ cup onion, diced
- 2 tomatoes, chopped
- ½ cup cilantro, chopped
- 1 jalapeño pepper, minced
- 1 teaspoon lime juice
- Salt and pepper to taste

Eggs
- 2 red bell peppers, sliced into rings
- 2 teaspoons olive oil, divided
- 8 eggs
- Salt and pepper to taste

Method:
1. Mix the salsa ingredients in a bowl. Set aside.
2. Pour half of the olive oil into a pan over medium heat.
3. Add the bell pepper rings and crack an egg into each ring.
4. Season with salt and pepper.
5. Serve the egg peppers with the avocado salsa.

Nutritional Value:
- Calories 135
- Total Fat 4 g
- Saturated Fat 2 g
- Cholesterol 0 mg
- Sodium 125 mg
- Total Carbohydrate 5 g
- Dietary Fiber 1 g
- Protein 12 g

Baked French Toast

Preparation Time: 15 minutes; Cooking Time: 30 minutes; Servings: 8

Ingredients:
- Cooking spray
- 6 cups whole wheat bread, sliced into cubes
- 1 ½ cups nonfat milk
- 3 eggs, beaten
- ¾ cup canned pumpkin
- ¼ cup brown sugar
- 1 teaspoon ground cinnamon
- ¼ teaspoon ground nutmeg
- 1 cup walnuts, toasted and chopped

Method:
1. Spray your baking pan with oil.
2. Spread the bread slices in the pan.
3. In a bowl, mix the rest of the ingredients except the walnuts.
4. Pour the mixture into the pan over the bread.
5. Sprinkle the walnuts on top.
6. Refrigerate for 2 hours.
7. Bake in the oven at 350 degrees F for 30 minutes.

Nutritional Value:
- Calories 257
- Total Fat 10 g
- Saturated Fat 1 g
- Cholesterol 1 mg
- Sodium 230 mg
- Total Carbohydrate 31 g

- Dietary Fiber 5 g
- Protein 12 g

Banana Pancake

Preparation Time: 10 minutes; Cooking Time: 10 minutes; Servings: 2
Ingredients:
- 1 banana, sliced
- 2 eggs
- Cooking spray

Method:
1. Add the banana slices and eggs in a blender.
2. Process until smooth.
3. Spray your pan with oil.
4. Pour the batter into the pan. Place it over medium heat.
5. Cook for 3 to 5 minutes per side.

Nutritional Value:
- Calories 124
- Total Fat 4.9 g
- Saturated Fat 1.6 g
- Cholesterol 186 mg
- Sodium 280 mg
- Total Carbohydrate 13.8 g
- Dietary Fiber 1.5 g
- Protein 6.9 g

Breakfast Cereal

Preparation Time: 15 minutes; Cooking Time: 30 minutes; Servings: 3
Ingredients:
- ½ cup whole-grain farro, soaked in water overnight
- 1 cup almond milk
- ¼ teaspoon vanilla extract
- Pinch ground cinnamon
- Pinch salt
- 1 tablespoon pure maple syrup
- ½ cup fresh blueberries
- ¼ teaspoon lemon zest
- ¼ cup almonds, toasted and chopped

Method:
1. Drain the farro.
2. In a pan over medium heat, add the milk, vanilla, cinnamon and salt.
3. Bring to a boil.
4. Add the farro.
5. Reduce heat and simmer for 20 minutes.
6. Stir in the rest of the ingredients and serve.

Nutritional Value:
- Calories 226
- Total Fat 6.8 g
- Saturated Fat 0.5 g
- Cholesterol 0 mg
- Sodium 235 mg
- Total Carbohydrate 32.9 g
- Dietary Fiber 4.4 g
- Protein 7.7 g

Cinnamon Overnight Oatmeal

Preparation Time: 1 day and 15 minutes; Cooking Time: 0 minutes; Servings: 6
Ingredients:
- 3 cups almond milk
- 3 cups rolled oats
- 1 ¼ teaspoons ground cinnamon
- 2 ½ teaspoons vanilla extract
- 8 teaspoons brown sugar
- Pinch salt

Method:
1. Mix all the ingredients in glass jars with lids.
2. Seal the jars and refrigerate overnight before serving the next day for breakfast.

Nutritional Value:

- Calories 197
- Total Fat 4.3 g
- Saturated Fat 0.5 g
- Cholesterol 0 mg
- Sodium 318 mg
- Total Carbohydrate 34.7 g
- Dietary Fiber 4.8 g
- Protein 5.5 g

Vegan Crepe

Preparation Time: 15 minutes; Cooking Time: 10 minutes; Servings: 8
Ingredients:
- ¾ cup all-purpose flour
- ¾ cup whole-wheat flour
- 1 ¾ cups almond milk
- 3 tablespoons water
- 1 tablespoon flaxseed meal
- ½ teaspoon salt
- ½ teaspoon sugar

Method:
1. Add all the ingredients in a blender.
2. Pulse until smooth.
3. Refrigerate for 10 minutes.
4. Heat a pan over medium low heat.
5. Pour ¼ cup of the mixture into the pan.
6. Swirl to spread the batter.
7. Cook for 2 minutes.
8. Flip and cook for another 2 minutes.

Nutritional Value:
- Calories 93
- Total Fat 1.1 g
- Saturated Fat 0.1 g
- Cholesterol 0 mg
- Sodium 183 mg
- Total Carbohydrate 18 g
- Dietary Fiber 2 g
- Protein 3.1 g

Yogurt with Vanilla & Dried Apples

Preparation Time: 5 minutes; Cooking Time: 0 minutes; Serving: 1
Ingredients:
- 1 teaspoon vanilla extract
- 5 oz. Greek yogurt
- 2 tablespoons dried apples, chopped

Method:
1. Stir the vanilla extract into the yogurt.
2. Top with the dried apples and serve.

Nutritional Value:
- Calories 150
- Total Fat 0.3 g
- Saturated Fat 0.2 g
- Cholesterol 4 mg
- Sodium 50 mg
- Total Carbohydrate 24.9 g
- Dietary Fiber 1.9 g
- Protein 12.8 g

Cereal Mix

Preparation Time: X minutes; Cooking Time: X minutes; Servings: 14
Ingredients:
- ½ cup almonds, sliced
- 1 cup rolled oats
- 1 cup barley
- 1 cup bulgur
- 1 cup dried cranberries
- ⅓ cup white sugar
- 1 tablespoon ground cinnamon
- Salt to taste

Method:
1. Arrange the almonds in a baking pan.

2. Bake in the oven at 350 degrees F. for 10 minutes.
3. Transfer the almonds to a bowl.
4. Stir in the rest of the ingredients.
5. Serve or store in a jar with lid.

Nutritional Value:
- Calories 158
- Total Fat 2.4 g
- Saturated Fat 0.2 g
- Cholesterol 0 mg
- Sodium 44 mg
- Total Carbohydrate 119 g
- Dietary Fiber 4.7 g
- Protein 3.8 g

Oatmeal Pancake with Sauteed Apples

Preparation Time: 15 minutes; Cooking Time: 10 minutes; Servings: 8

Ingredients:

Sautéed Apples
- 2 teaspoons oil
- 2 apples, sliced into cubes
- ¼ teaspoon apple pie spice

Oatmeal Pancakes
- ½ cup rolled oats
- ¾ cup white whole-wheat flour
- 1 ½ teaspoons brown sugar
- 1 ½ teaspoons baking powder
- ¼ teaspoon apple pie spice
- Pinch salt
- 1 cup nonfat milk
- 1 egg, beaten
- 2 tablespoons oil
- 1 cup no-sugar maple syrup

Method:
1. Pour the oil into a pan over medium heat.
2. Add the apples and season with apple pie spice.
3. Cook until golden. Set aside.
4. Add the oats to a blender.
5. Pulse until ground.
6. Transfer to a bowl.
7. Stir in the rest of the ingredients except the syrup.
8. Pour the batter into a pan over medium heat.
9. Cook for 2 minutes per side.
10. Serve with the syrup and apples.

Nutritional Value:
- Calories 175
- Total Fat 5.3 g
- Saturated Fat 0.5 g
- Cholesterol 1 mg
- Sodium 169 mg
- Total Carbohydrate 29.6 g
- Dietary Fiber 3.1 g
- Protein 5.3 g

Cheesecake Toast with Kiwi & Strawberry

Preparation Time: 15 minutes; Cooking Time: 0 minutes; Servings: 1

Ingredients:
- 1 tablespoon cream cheese
- 2 tablespoons nonfat Greek yogurt
- 1 slice whole-wheat bread, toasted
- 1 cup strawberry, sliced
- 1 kiwi, sliced

Method:
1. Mix the cream cheese and yogurt in a bowl.
2. Spread this mixture on top of the bread.
3. Top with the slices of strawberry and kiwi.

Nutritional Value:

- Calories 187
- Total Fat 6.3 g
- Saturated Fat 3.2 g
- Cholesterol 16 mg
- Sodium 202 mg
- Total Carbohydrate 24.7 g
- Dietary Fiber 3.4 g
- Protein 8.9 g

Italian Breakfast Sandwich

Preparation Time: 10 minutes; Cooking Time: 5 minutes; Servings: 4

Ingredients:
- Cooking spray
- 4 eggs, beaten
- Salt to taste
- ¼ teaspoon Italian seasoning, crushed
- 4 whole-wheat muffins, sliced and toasted
- 2 tablespoons basil pesto
- ¼ cup red bell pepper, sliced into strips
- 4 ounces chicken breast, cooked and shredded

Method:
1. Spray your pan with oil.
2. In a bowl, mix the eggs, salt and Italian seasoning.
3. Cook the eggs in the pan over medium heat.
4. Cook for 3 to 4 minutes.
5. Transfer to a plate.
6. Spread the muffins with pesto.
7. Top with the eggs, red bell pepper and chicken breast.

Nutritional Value:
- Calories 243
- Total Fat 4.8 g
- Saturated Fat 1 g
- Cholesterol 26 mg
- Sodium 588 mg
- Total Carbohydrate 29.5 g
- Dietary Fiber 4.9 g
- Protein 21.5 g

Toasted Bread with Peaches & Pistachios

Preparation Time: 10 minutes; Cooking Time: 0 minutes; Serving: 1

Ingredients:
- 1 teaspoon honey
- 1 tablespoon low fat ricotta cheese
- ⅛ teaspoon cinnamon
- 1 slice whole-wheat bread, toasted
- ½ peach, pitted and sliced
- 1 tablespoon pistachios, chopped

Method:
1. Mix the honey, cheese and cinnamon.
2. Spread this mixture on top of the bread.
3. Top with the slices of peaches.
4. Sprinkle top with the pistachios.

Nutritional Value:
- Calories 193
- Total Fat 6 g
- Saturated Fat 1.4 g
- Cholesterol 5 mg
- Sodium 157 mg
- Total Carbohydrate 29 g
- Dietary Fiber 3.9 g
- Protein 8.2 g

Avocado Toast with Eggs

Preparation Time: 5 minutes; Cooking Time: 0 minutes; Serving: 1

Ingredients:
- ¼ avocado, mashed
- Garlic powder to taste
- Pepper to taste
- 1 slice whole-wheat bread, toasted

- 1 egg, fried
- 1 tablespoon scallion, chopped

Method:
1. Season the avocado with the garlic powder and pepper.
2. Mix well.
3. Spread the mixture on the bread.
4. Top with the egg.
5. Sprinkle the scallions on top.

Nutritional Value:
- Calories 271
- Total Fat 17.7 g
- Saturated Fat 3.5 g
- Cholesterol 186 mg
- Sodium 216 mg
- Total Carbohydrate 18.1 g
- Dietary Fiber 5.4 g
- Protein 11.5 g

Breakfast Casserole

Preparation Time: 20 minutes; Cooking Time: 1 hour minutes; Servings: 6

Ingredients:
- 2 teaspoons olive oil
- 1 onion, chopped
- 1 red bell pepper, chopped
- 1 cup mushrooms, sliced
- 8 oz. bread, sliced into cubes
- 6 ounces turkey sauce, sliced thinly
- 2 ounces cheddar cheese, shredded
- 8 eggs, beaten
- 2 cups nonfat milk
- 1 teaspoon dried oregano, crushed

Method:
1. In a pan over medium heat, cook the onion, red bell pepper and mushrooms for 5 minutes.
2. Spray your baking pan with oil.
3. Spread the bread cubes in the pan.
4. Top with the mushroom mixture, sausages and cheese.
5. In a bowl, mix the eggs, milk and dried oregano.
6. Pour mixture on top of the cheese.
7. Bake in the oven at 350 degrees F for 50 minutes.
8. Let cool before slicing and serving.

Nutritional Value:
- Calories 285
- Total Fat 11.5 g
- Saturated Fat 3.2 g
- Cholesterol 168 mg
- Sodium 533 mg
- Total Carbohydrate 25 g
- Dietary Fiber 5.2 g
- Protein 21.8 g

Spiced Oatmeal

Preparation Time: 15 minutes; Cooking Time: 30 minutes; Servings: 10

Ingredients:
- 1 ½ cups steel-cut oats
- 3 cups water
- 1 teaspoon ground cinnamon
- Pinch salt
- ½ teaspoon ground allspice
- ½ teaspoon ground ginger
- 1 ½ cups nonfat milk
- ½ cup brown sugar
- 1 cup carrots, shredded
- ½ cup dried apricots, chopped
- 1 cup pecans toasted and chopped

Method:
1. Preheat your oven to 350 degrees F.
2. Spread the oats in a baking pan.
3. Bake for 10 minutes.

4. In a pan over medium heat, add the oats and the rest of the ingredients except the carrots, apricots and pecans.
5. Bring to a boil and then simmer for 20 minutes.
6. Add the carrots and apricots.
7. Stir and turn off the heat.
8. Transfer to serving bowls.
9. Sprinkle pecans on top.

Nutritional Value:
- Calories 231
- Total Fat 9.4 g
- Saturated Fat 1 g
- Cholesterol 1 mg
- Sodium 146 mg
- Total Carbohydrate 34.6 g
- Dietary Fiber 4.3 g
- Protein 6.1 g

Honey & Apple Pancakes

Preparation Time: 10 minutes; Cooking Time: 6 minutes; Servings: 8

Ingredients:
- 1 ¼ cups all-purpose flour
- 2 teaspoons baking powder
- ⅛ teaspoon baking soda
- ¼ teaspoon apple pie spice
- Pinch salt
- 1 egg, beaten
- ¾ cup apple juice
- 2 tablespoons honey
- 1 tablespoon vegetable oil
- Cooking spray

Method:
1. Combine the flour, baking powder, baking soda, apple pie spice and salt.
2. Mix well.
3. Stir in the rest of the ingredients.
4. Spray a pan with oil.
5. Place the pan over medium heat.
6. Pour ¼ cup batter into the pan.
7. Cook for 3 minutes per side.

Nutritional Value:
- Calories 122
- Total Fat 2.5 g
- Saturated Fat 0.4 g
- Cholesterol 26 mg
- Sodium 163 mg
- Total Carbohydrate 22.1 g
- Dietary Fiber 0.6 g
- Protein 2.8 g

Breakfast Pizza Bread

Preparation Time: 10 minutes; Cooking Time: 0 minutes; Serving: 1

Ingredients:
- 2 tablespoons pizza sauce
- 1 slice whole-grain bread, toasted
- 2 slices low-fat provolone cheese
- 1 tablespoon green bell pepper, sliced into strips
- ¼ cup tomatoes, chopped
- 1 tablespoon fresh basil, chopped

Method:
1. Spread the pizza sauce on the toasted bread.
2. Sprinkle the cheese on top.
3. Top with the bell pepper and tomatoes.
4. Toast in the oven until the cheese has melted.
5. Garnish with chopped basil.

Nutritional Value:
- Calories 295
- Total Fat 8.5 g

- Saturated Fat 4 g
- Cholesterol 21 mg
- Sodium 502 mg
- Total Carbohydrate 42 g
- Dietary Fiber 8 g
- Protein 17.5 g

Breakfast Cookie with Yogurt

Preparation Time: 5 minutes; Cooking Time: 0 minutes; Serving: 1
Ingredients:
- 1 oatmeal cookie
- 5 ounces vanilla flavored Greek yogurt
- 1 cup raspberry, sliced into cubes

Method:
1. Serve the oatmeal cookie with the yogurt and raspberries.

Nutritional Value:
- Calories 274
- Total Fat 1.5 g
- Saturated Fat 0 g
- Cholesterol 0 mg
- Sodium 141 mg
- Total Carbohydrate 45 g
- Dietary Fiber 10 g
- Protein 18 g

Toasted Bread with Jam

Preparation Time: 5 minutes; Cooking Time: 0 minutes; Servings: 2
Ingredients:
- 2 slices whole wheat bread
- 1 tablespoons reduced-sugar raspberry jam
- 4 ounces cottage cheese
- 4 ounces pineapple chunks

Method:
1. Toast the bread slices in the oven.
2. Spread the bread slices with the jam.
3. Serve with the cheese and pineapple.

Nutritional Value:
- Calories 265
- Total Fat 3.5 g
- Saturated Fat 1.5 g
- Cholesterol 15 mg
- Sodium 590 mg
- Total Carbohydrate 45 g
- Dietary Fiber 5 g
- Protein 17 g

Trail Mix Cereal

Preparation Time: 10 minutes; Cooking Time: 0 minutes; Serving: 1
Ingredients:
- ½ cup cereal, cooked
- 2 tablespoons mixed dried fruits, chopped
- 2 tablespoons mixed nuts, toasted
- 2 teaspoons flaxseed

Method:
1. Combine all the ingredients and serve in a bowl.

Nutritional Value:
- Calories 227
- Total Fat 11 g
- Saturated Fat 1.4 g
- Cholesterol 0 mg
- Sodium 16 mg
- Total Carbohydrate 28.5 g
- Dietary Fiber 3.6 g
- Protein 6.3 g

Turkey Breakfast Strata

Preparation Time: 15 minutes; Cooking Time: 1 hour and minutes; Servings: 6
Ingredients:

- ¼ cup onion, sliced thinly
- 1 red bell pepper, chopped
- 1 cup asparagus, sliced into pieces
- 1 teaspoon vegetable oil
- 4 cups whole-wheat bread cubes
- 2 cups turkey, cooked and shredded
- ½ cup reduced-fat cottage cheese
- 3 teaspoons dried mixed herbs (sage, rosemary and thyme)
- Salt to taste
- 3 eggs, beaten
- 1 cup almond milk

Method:
1. In a pan over medium heat, cook the onion, bell pepper and asparagus in oil for 5 minutes.
2. Grease your baking pan.
3. Spread the bread cubes in the pan.
4. Top with the asparagus mixture, turkey and cheese.
5. Season with the herbs and salt.
6. Mix the egg and milk in a bowl.
7. Pour the mixture on top of the cheese.
8. Bake in the oven at 325 degrees F for 1 hour.
9. Let cool before slicing and serving.

Nutritional Value:
- Calories 228
- Total Fat 4.8 g
- Saturated Fat 1.3 g
- Cholesterol 39 mg
- Sodium 394 mg
- Total Carbohydrate 20.2 g
- Dietary Fiber 4.7 g
- Protein 26.2 g

Zucchini & Cheese Frittata

Preparation Time: 15 minutes; Cooking Time: 15 minutes; Servings: 4

Ingredients:
- 4 eggs, beaten
- 2 tablespoons parsley, chopped
- Salt and pepper to taste
- 2 teaspoons olive oil
- 4 green onions, chopped
- 12 ounces zucchini, sliced
- 1 cup shredded cheddar cheese

Method:
1. Preheat your oven to 450 degrees F.
2. In a bowl, mix the eggs, parsley, salt and pepper.
3. In a pan over medium heat, cook the green onion and zucchini for 5 minutes.
4. Add the egg mixture to the pan.
5. Cook until the edges have firmed.
6. Turn off the heat.
7. Top with the cheese.
8. Transfer the pan to the oven.
9. Bake in the oven until the cheese has turned golden.

Nutritional Value:
- Calories 115
- Total Fat 5.5 g
- Saturated Fat 2.4 g
- Cholesterol 10 mg
- Sodium 321 mg
- Total Carbohydrate 5.7 g
- Dietary Fiber 1.4 g
- Protein 10.9 g

Yogurt & Granola Sundae

Preparation Time: 10 minutes; Cooking Time: 12 minutes; Servings: 6

Ingredients:
- Cooking spray
- ¼ cup almond butter

- 1 ½ cups rolled oats
- 3 tablespoons honey, divided
- ½ teaspoon ground cinnamon
- 1 egg white
- Pinch salt
- 1 ½ cups reduced-fat plain Greek yogurt
- 6 strawberries, chopped

Method:
1. Preheat your oven to 350 degrees F.
2. Spray your muffin pan with oil.
3. In a bowl, combine the almond butter, oats, half of honey, cinnamon, egg white and salt.
4. Press the mixture into the muffin cups.
5. Bake for 12 minutes.
6. While waiting, mix the honey and yogurt.
7. Put a scoop of the yogurt mixture into the baked cups.
8. Top with the strawberries.

Nutritional Value:
- Calories 241
- Total Fat 9.7 g
- Saturated Fat 2.4 g
- Cholesterol 6 mg
- Sodium 150 mg
- Total Carbohydrate 30.3 g
- Dietary Fiber 3.8 g
- Protein 11.3 g

Cantaloupe Breakfast Smoothie in a Bowl

Preparation Time: 40 minutes; Cooking Time: 0 minutes; Servings: 2

Ingredients:
- ¾ cup carrot juice
- 4 cups cantaloupe, sliced into cubes
- Pinch of salt
- Frozen melon balls
- Fresh basil

Method:
1. Add the carrot juice and cantaloupe cubes to a blender. Sprinkle with salt.
2. Process until smooth.
3. Transfer to a bowl.
4. Chill in the refrigerator for at least 30 minutes.
5. Top with the frozen melon balls and basil before serving.

Nutritional Value:
- Calories 135
- Total Fat 0.6 g
- Saturated Fat 0.2 g
- Cholesterol 0 mg
- Sodium 180 mg
- Total Carbohydrate 31.7 g
- Dietary Fiber 3.1 g
- Protein 3.4 g

Oat Bran Pancake

Preparation Time: 15 minutes; Cooking Time: 5 minutes; Servings: 4

Ingredients:
- ⅓ cup oat bran
- ⅔ cup all-purpose flour
- 2 teaspoons baking powder
- 1 tablespoon packed brown sugar
- Pinch salt
- 1 cup nonfat milk
- 1 tablespoon vegetable oil
- 2 egg whites, beaten
- Cooking spray
- 1 teaspoon orange zest

Method:
1. Mix all the ingredients except the orange zest in a bowl.
2. Spray your pan with oil.
3. Place the pan over medium heat.
4. Pour ¼ cup batter into the pan.

5. Cook for 2 minutes per side.
6. Sprinkle with the orange zest.

Nutritional Value:
- Calories 180
- Total Fat 4 g
- Saturated Fat 1 g
- Cholesterol 1 mg
- Sodium 299 mg
- Total Carbohydrate 32 g
- Dietary Fiber 2 g
- Protein 7 g

Egg & Veggie Muffin

Preparation Time: 20 minutes; Cooking Time: 30 minutes; Servings: 6

Ingredients:
- Cooking spray
- ⅓ cup bulgur
- ⅔ cup water
- ¾ cup zucchini, chopped
- ¼ cup onion, chopped
- 1 tablespoon olive oil
- ½ cup low-fat feta cheese, crumbled
- 1 tomato, chopped
- 8 eggs, beaten
- 2 teaspoons fresh rosemary, chopped
- Pepper to taste

Method:
1. Preheat your oven to 350 degrees F.
2. Spray your muffin pan with oil.
3. In a pan over medium heat, mix the bulgur and water.
4. Bring to a boil.
5. Reduce heat and simmer for 15 minutes.
6. Drain the bulgur.
7. In a pan over medium heat, pour the oil and cook the onion and zucchini for 10 minutes.
8. Turn off the heat.
9. Stir in the bulgur, cheese and tomato.
10. Pour the mixture into the muffin cups.
11. In a bowl, mix the eggs, rosemary and pepper.
12. Pour into the muffin cups.
13. Bake for 15 minutes.
14. Let cool before serving.

Nutritional Value:
- Calories 117
- Total Fat 4.2 g
- Saturated Fat 1.3 g
- Cholesterol 3 mg
- Sodium 294 mg
- Total Carbohydrate 9.5 g
- Dietary Fiber 2 g
- Protein 11.3 g

Cheesy Spinach Strata

Preparation Time: 15 minutes; Cooking Time: 30 minutes; Servings: 6

Ingredients:
- Cooking spray
- 4 cups whole grain bread, sliced into cubes
- 1 lb. asparagus, sliced into small pieces and steamed
- 1 cup onion, chopped and cooked
- 2 cups baby spinach, steamed
- 1 cup nonfat milk
- 6 eggs, beaten
- Salt and pepper to taste
- 2 tomatoes, sliced thinly
- ½ cup low-fat feta cheese
- ¼ cup fresh basil, chopped

Method:
1. Spray your pan with oil.

2. Spread the bread cubes in a baking pan.
3. Spread the onion and asparagus in the pan.
4. In a bowl, mix the milk and eggs.
5. Season with salt and pepper.
6. Pour mixture into the baking pan.
7. Top with the tomatoes, cheese and fresh basil.
8. Bake in the oven at 325 degrees F for 30 minutes.
9. Let cool before serving.

Nutritional Value:
- Calories 247
- Total Fat 9 g
- Saturated Fat 3 g
- Cholesterol 216 mg
- Sodium 419 mg
- Total Carbohydrate 27 g
- Dietary Fiber 7 g
- Protein 18 g

Chapter 3: Main Course Recipes

Veggies & Grains with Turmeric

Preparation Time: 10 minutes; Cooking Time: 5 minutes; Servings: 4
Ingredients:
- 16 ounces cooked quinoa
- 1 tablespoon oil
- 1 pack frozen veggie mix, thawed
- 1 can chickpeas, rinsed and drained
- ½ cup turmeric dressing

Method:
1. Transfer the quinoa to a bowl. Set aside.
2. Pour the oil into a pan over medium heat.
3. Stir fry the veggie mix for 3 to 4 minutes or until tender.
4. Put the veggie mix on top of the quinoa.
5. Sprinkle with the chickpeas and turmeric dressing.
6. Serve immediately.

Nutritional Value:
- Calories 306
- Total Fat 7.4 g
- Saturated Fat 0.4 g
- Cholesterol 10 mg
- Sodium 148 mg
- Total Carbohydrate 47.7 g
- Dietary Fiber 10 g
- Protein 11.9 g

Artichoke with Shredded Chicken

Preparation Time: 10 minutes; Cooking Time: 0 minutes; Servings: 4
Ingredients:
- 12 artichokes, trimmed and shaved
- 2 tablespoons olive oil
- 2 tablespoons fresh mint leaves, chopped
- Salt and pepper to taste
- 2 cups chicken breast, cooked and shredded

Method:
1. Toss the artichokes in the oil and mint.
2. Season with salt and pepper.
3. Serve the artichokes topped with the shredded chicken.

Nutritional Value:
- Calories 243
- Total Fat 14.4 g
- Saturated Fat 2 g
- Cholesterol 68 mg
- Sodium 237 mg
- Total Carbohydrate 18.3 g
- Dietary Fiber 9.4 g
- Protein 14.3 g

Asian Chicken With Cabbage

Preparation Time: 10 minutes; Cooking Time: 0 minutes; Servings: 4
Ingredients:
- 9 ounces coleslaw mix
- 12 chicken strips, seasoned and cooked
- ½ cup sesame dressing
- ½ cup almonds, chopped

Method:
1. Add the coleslaw mix to a bowl.
2. Top with the chicken strips.
3. Pour the sesame dressing on top.
4. Sprinkle with the almonds and serve.

Nutritional Value:

- Calories 330
- Total Fat 21.6 g
- Saturated Fat 3.9 g
- Cholesterol 55 mg
- Sodium 493 mg
- Total Carbohydrate 13.6 g
- Dietary Fiber 2.3 g
- Protein 22.7 g

Roasted Chicken & Veggies with Hummus

Preparation Time: 15 minutes; Cooking Time: 25 minutes; Servings: 4

Ingredients:
- 2 cloves garlic, thinly sliced
- 2 cups cauliflower florets
- 1 tablespoon olive oil
- Salt to taste
- 1 teaspoon dried oregano
- 1 cup zucchini, diced
- ½ cup red bell pepper strips
- 1 cup shredded roasted chicken
- 1 cup hummus

Method:
1. Preheat your oven to 425 degrees F.
2. Spread the garlic and cauliflower in a baking pan.
3. Drizzle the olive oil on top.
4. Season with the salt and oregano.
5. Roast for 12 minutes.
6. Stir in the zucchini and bell pepper.
7. Roast for 10 more minutes.
8. Serve the roasted veggies with the shredded chicken and hummus.

Nutritional Value:
- Calories 360
- Total Fat 19 g
- Saturated Fat 2.8 g
- Cholesterol 20 mg
- Sodium 415 mg
- Total Carbohydrate 39.5 g
- Dietary Fiber 12.1 g
- Protein 12.3 g

Corned Beef & Cabbage

Preparation Time: 30 minutes; Cooking Time: 50 minutes; Servings: 8

Ingredients:
- 2 ½ pounds beef brisket, trimmed
- 2 tablespoons ground pickling spice
- Salt to taste
- 2 tablespoons olive oil
- 2 cups reduced-sodium beef broth
- 1 onion, chopped
- 2 lb. cabbage, sliced into wedges and steamed
- 2 lb. carrots, sliced and steamed

Method:
1. Coat the beef brisket with the pickling spice and salt.
2. Pour the oil into a pan.
3. Cook the beef until brown on all sides.
4. Transfer the beef to a pressure cooker.
5. Pour in the broth.
6. Add the onion.
7. Seal the pot.
8. Cook on high pressure for 40 minutes.
9. Release the pressure naturally.
10. Shred the beef.
11. Serve the beef with the steamed veggies.

Nutritional Value:
- Calories 295
- Total Fat 10.1 g

- Saturated Fat 2.9 g
- Cholesterol 89 mg
- Sodium 418 mg
- Total Carbohydrate 19.2 g
- Dietary Fiber 6.2 g
- Protein 32 g

Sweet & Spicy Flank Steak

Preparation Time: 20 minutes; Cooking Time: 30 minutes; Servings: 4
Ingredients:
- 1 tablespoon brown sugar
- 1 tablespoon chili powder
- Salt and pepper to taste
- 1 lb. flank steak, trimmed
- 1 tablespoon sesame oil
- 1 scallion, minced

Method:
1. Preheat your broiler and set it to high.
2. Line your baking pan with foil.
3. Mix the brown sugar, chili powder, salt and pepper.
4. Coat the steak with this mixture.
5. Transfer to the pan.
6. Drizzle with the oil.
7. Broil the steak for 15 to 30 minutes.
8. Sprinkle scallions on top and serve.

Nutritional Value:
- Calories 263
- Total Fat 12.8 g
- Saturated Fat 3.9 g
- Cholesterol 68 mg
- Sodium 441 mg
- Total Carbohydrate 11.2 g
- Dietary Fiber 2.7 g
- Protein 24.6 g

Chicken with Broccoli

Preparation Time: 20 minutes; Cooking Time: 35 minutes; Servings: 2
Ingredients:
- 1 cup onion, chopped
- 3 cups broccoli florets
- 1 tablespoon olive oil
- Salt and pepper to taste
- 3 teaspoons whole-grain mustard
- 1/2 tsp. dried rosemary
- 8 ounces chicken breast fillet
- 2 teaspoons canola oil
- 1 teaspoon butter

Method:
1. Preheat your oven to 350 degrees F.
2. Toss the onion and broccoli in oil.
3. Season with salt and pepper.
4. In another bowl, mix the mustard and rosemary.
5. Season the chicken with the pepper.
6. Pour the oil into a pan over medium heat.
7. Cook the chicken for 3 minutes per side.
8. Brush the chicken with the mustard sauce.
9. Spread the broccoli on top.
10. Transfer the pan to the oven.
11. Roast for 15 minutes.
12. Top with the butter and serve.

Nutritional Value:
- Calories 338
- Total Fat 17 g
- Saturated Fat 3 g
- Cholesterol 88 mg
- Sodium 370 mg
- Total Carbohydrate 16 g

- Dietary Fiber 4 g
- Protein 28 g

Chicken Stew

Preparation Time: 10 minutes; Cooking Time: 40 minutes; Servings: 4

Ingredients:
- 1 tablespoon Moroccan spice blend
- 2 tablespoons all-purpose flour
- 1 lb. chicken breast fillet, sliced into cubes
- 1 tablespoon olive oil
- 15 oz. canned diced tomatoes
- Salt and pepper to taste

Method:
1. Combine the spice blend and flour in a bowl.
2. Coat the chicken with this mixture.
3. Pour the oil into a pan over medium heat.
4. Cook the chicken for 3 minutes per side.
5. Stir in the rest of the ingredients.
6. Bring to a boil.
7. Reduce heat and simmer for 30 minutes.

Nutritional Value:
- Calories 225
- Total Fat 10 g
- Saturated Fat 2 g
- Cholesterol 63 mg
- Sodium 388 mg
- Total Carbohydrate 9 g
- Dietary Fiber 2 g
- Protein 24 g

Baked Chicken with Tomato & Basil

Preparation Time: 20 minutes; Cooking Time: 20 minutes; Servings: 4

Ingredients:
- 1 lb. chicken fillets, skin removed
- Salt and pepper to taste
- ¼ cup all-purpose flour
- 1 egg, beaten
- ½ cup whole-wheat breadcrumbs
- ¼ cup Parmesan cheese, grated
- 2 cups cherry tomatoes, sliced in half
- ¼ cup basil leaves, slivered
- 1 tablespoon olive oil

Method:
1. Season chicken with salt and pepper.
2. Dredge the chicken with flour.
3. Dip it in egg and then coat with a mixture of breadcrumbs and Parmesan cheese.
4. Preheat your oven to 425 degrees F.
5. Bake the chicken for 20 minutes.
6. Toss the tomatoes and basil in oil.
7. Top the chicken with this mixture and serve.

Nutritional Value:
- Calories 290
- Total Fat 9.5 g
- Saturated Fat 2.3 g
- Cholesterol 134 mg
- Sodium 249 mg
- Total Carbohydrate 18.4 g
- Dietary Fiber 2.5 g
- Protein 31.8 g

Chicken Thighs with Orange & Fennel

Preparation Time: 20 minutes; Cooking Time: 1 hour; Servings: 4

Ingredients:
- 4 chicken thighs
- Salt and pepper to taste
- 1 tablespoon olive oil
- 1 cup onion, chopped

- 4 cloves garlic, minced
- Pinch red pepper flakes
- 4 teaspoons fennel seeds, crushed
- 2 teaspoons orange zest
- ½ cup orange juice
- 15 oz. canned diced tomatoes
- 1 bay leaf
- 2 tablespoons olives, chopped

Method:
1. Sprinkle both sides of chicken with salt and pepper.
2. Pour oil into a pan over medium heat.
3. Cook the chicken for 3 to 4 minutes per side.
4. Transfer to a paper towel lined plate.
5. Cook the onion in the pan for 3 minutes.
6. Stir in the garlic, red pepper flakes and fennel.
7. Cook for 30 seconds, stirring.
8. Pour in the orange juice and simmer for 1 minute.
9. Add the tomatoes and chicken.
10. Add the rest of the ingredients.
11. Reduce heat and simmer for 40 minutes.

Nutritional Value:
- Calories 311
- Total Fat 15 g
- Saturated Fat 3 g
- Cholesterol 151 mg
- Sodium 425 mg
- Total Carbohydrate 14 g
- Dietary Fiber 3 g
- Protein 30 g

Balsamic Beef & Mushrooms

Preparation Time: 15 minutes; Cooking Time: 20 minutes; Servings: 4

Ingredients:
- 4 tablespoons olive oil
- Salt and pepper to taste
- 2 teaspoon dried marjoram
- ½ lb. mushrooms, sliced
- ½ lb. thin beef strips
- 2 tablespoons balsamic vinegar
- ¼ cup Parmesan cheese, grated

Method:
1. Preheat your oven to 450 degrees F.
2. Mix the oil, salt, pepper and marjoram in a bowl.
3. Divide into 2 bowls.
4. Toss the beef in the first bowl, and the mushrooms in the second bowl.
5. Put the beef on one side of a baking pan and the mushrooms on the other side.
6. Roast in the oven for 12 minutes.
7. Drizzle with the balsamic vinegar and sprinkle with the Parmesan cheese.
8. Roast for another 5 minutes and serve.

Nutritional Value:
- Calories 114
- Total Fat 8.5 g
- Saturated Fat 1.9 g
- Cholesterol 4 mg
- Sodium 238 mg
- Total Carbohydrate 5.5 g
- Dietary Fiber 1.3 g
- Protein 5.5 g

Chicken with Kale & Sweet Potato

Preparation Time: 10 minutes; Cooking Time: 20 minutes; Servings: 4

Ingredients:
- 2 sweet potatoes, cubed
- 1 ½ teaspoons olive oil
- Salt and pepper to taste
- ½ cup peanut dressing
- 2 cups chicken breast, cooked and shredded

- 6 cups kale, chopped
- ¼ cup peanuts, chopped

Method:
1. Preheat your oven to 425 degrees F.
2. Line your baking pan with foil.
3. Coat the sweet potatoes in oil.
4. Season with salt and pepper.
5. Spread these in a baking pan.
6. Roast in the oven for 20 minutes.
7. Transfer to serving plates.
8. Put the chicken and kale on the side.
9. Drizzle with the dressing and sprinkle with the peanuts.

Nutritional Value:
- Calories 393
- Total Fat 15.4 g
- Saturated Fat 2.7 g
- Cholesterol 60 mg
- Sodium 566 mg
- Total Carbohydrate 31.9 g
- Dietary Fiber 5.9 g
- Protein 30.4 g

Bacon & Green Beans

Preparation Time: 15 minutes; Cooking Time: 15 minutes; Servings: 8

Ingredients:
- 2 slices bacon, minced
- 24 oz. green beans, trimmed
- 1 shallot, minced
- ½ teaspoon smoked paprika
- Salt and pepper to taste
- 2 teaspoons red wine vinegar
- 1 teaspoon lemon juice

Method:
1. Preheat your oven to 450 degrees F.
2. Roast the bacon in the oven for 5 minutes.
3. Take the pan out of the oven. Stir in the rest of the ingredients.
4. Roast for another 10 minutes.

Nutritional Value:
- Calories 49
- Total Fat 1.2 g
- Saturated Fat 0.4 g
- Cholesterol 0.4 mg
- Sodium 192 mg
- Total Carbohydrate 8.1 g
- Dietary Fiber 3 g
- Protein 2.9 g

Fried Chicken with Collard Greens

Preparation Time: 15 minutes; Cooking Time: 20 minutes; Servings: 4

Ingredients:
- 6 tablespoons vegetable oil, divided
- 1 lb. collars, chopped
- ½ cup water
- 1 tablespoon cider vinegar
- Salt to taste
- ½ teaspoon smoked paprika
- 4 chicken breast fillets
- ½ teaspoon onion powder
- ½ teaspoon garlic powder
- ¼ teaspoon cayenne pepper
- 1 cup nonfat buttermilk
- 1 cup whole-wheat panko

Method:
1. Pour 1 tablespoon into a pot over medium heat.
2. Add water and collards.
3. Cook for 8 minutes.
4. Turn off the heat.
5. Stir in the vinegar and season with salt and paprika.

6. Dip the chicken in buttermilk.
7. Season it with the onion powder, garlic powder and cayenne pepper.
8. Dredge with panko breadcrumbs.
9. Fry in the remaining oil until golden on both sides.
10. Serve with the collard greens.

Nutritional Value:
- Calories 366
- Total Fat 26.9 g
- Saturated Fat 3 g
- Cholesterol 1 mg
- Sodium 518 mg
- Total Carbohydrate 20 g
- Dietary Fiber 7 g
- Protein 16.5 g

Oven Fried Chicken

Preparation Time: 15 minutes; Cooking Time: 15 minutes; Servings: 4

Ingredients:
- 2 cups fat-free buttermilk
- Salt to taste
- 4 chicken thigh fillets
- ¾ cup panko breadcrumbs
- ½ teaspoon onion powder
- ½ teaspoon garlic powder
- ¼ teaspoon cayenne pepper
- ½ teaspoon smoked paprika
- 1 tablespoon cornstarch
- Pepper to taste
- 3 tablespoons cooking oil

Method:
1. Pour the buttermilk in a bowl.
2. Toss the chicken and season with salt.
3. Marinate for 2 hours in the refrigerator, covered.
4. Preheat your oven to 475 degrees F.
5. Mix the rest of the ingredients except the cooking oil in a plate.
6. Dredge the chicken in this mixture.
7. In a pan over medium high heat, pour the oil and brown the chicken.
8. Transfer to a baking pan.
9. Bake in the oven for 15 minutes.

Nutritional Value:
- Calories 389
- Total Fat 19.9 g
- Saturated Fat 3.4 g
- Cholesterol 88 mg
- Sodium 643 mg
- Total Carbohydrate 20.4 g
- Dietary Fiber 0.6 g
- Protein 30.1 g

Sausage Pasta with Kale

Preparation Time: 15 minutes; Cooking Time: 15 minutes; Servings: 2

Ingredients:
- 1 tablespoon olive oil
- 2 links turkey sausage, removed from casing and crumbled
- 1 onion, chopped
- 1 red bell pepper, chopped
- 2 cloves garlic, minced
- 4 cups kale, chopped
- 2 cups cooked whole-wheat penne pasta
- 2 tablespoons Parmesan cheese, grated

Method:
1. Pour the oil into a pan over medium high heat.
2. Cook the sausage for 3 minutes.
3. Drain on a plate with paper towel.
4. Cook the onion and bell pepper in the pan for 5 minutes.
5. Stir in the sausage, garlic, kale and pasta.

6. Cook for 3 minutes.
   7. Top with the Parmesan cheese.

Nutritional Value:
- Calories 463
- Total Fat 19.1 g
- Saturated Fat 4.7 g
- Cholesterol 82 mg
- Sodium 531 mg
- Total Carbohydrate 46.3 g
- Dietary Fiber 7.7 g
- Protein 30 g

Kung Pao Chicken

Preparation Time: 15 minutes; Cooking Time: 20 minutes; Servings: 4

Ingredients:
- 2 teaspoons cornstarch
- 1 teaspoon dry sherry
- 2 teaspoons low-sodium soy sauce
- 1 lb. chicken breast fillet, sliced into cubes
- 2 teaspoons balsamic vinegar
- 2 tablespoons chicken broth
- 2 teaspoons chili garlic sauce
- 1 teaspoon soy sauce
- 2 tablespoons vegetable oil
- 2 teaspoons toasted sesame oil
- 3 slices ginger, crushed
- 1 red bell pepper, chopped
- Salt to taste
- Peanuts, chopped

Method:
1. Mix the cornstarch, dry sherry and soy sauce.
2. Toss the chicken in this mixture.
3. Mix the vinegar, broth, chili garlic sauce, and remaining soy sauce in another bowl.
4. Add the vegetable oil and sesame oil to the pan.
5. Cook the ginger for 10 seconds.
6. Add the chicken and stir fry for 1 minute.
7. Add the rest of the ingredients.
8. Pour in the reserved sauce.
9. Cook for 2 minutes and serve.

Nutritional Value:
- Calories 264
- Total Fat 14.4 g
- Saturated Fat 2.5 g
- Cholesterol 63 mg
- Sodium 459 mg
- Total Carbohydrate 7.4 g
- Dietary Fiber 1.6 g
- Protein 25.2 g

Beef Stir Fry with Bok Choy

Preparation Time: 10 minutes; Cooking Time: 5 minutes; Servings: 4

Ingredients:
- 1 teaspoon toasted sesame oil
- 1 ½ teaspoons low-sodium soy sauce
- 1 tablespoon ginger, minced
- 1 teaspoon cornstarch
- 12 ounces flank steak, sliced into strips
- 1 tablespoon vegetable oil
- 1 lb. bok choy, sliced and steamed
- 2 tablespoons reduced-sodium oyster sauce

Method:
1. Mix the sesame oil, soy sauce, ginger and cornstarch in a bowl.
2. Dip the beef into the mixture.
3. Pour the oil into a pan over medium heat.
4. Cook the beef for 2 to 3 minutes.
5. Stir in the bok choy and oyster sauce.

6. Cook for 2 minutes and serve.

Nutritional Value:
- Calories 247
- Total Fat 12.8 g
- Saturated Fat 4 g
- Cholesterol 69 mg
- Sodium 569 mg
- Total Carbohydrate 6.3 g
- Dietary Fiber 1.1 g
- Protein 25.5 g

Beef Picadillo

Preparation Time: 15 minutes; Cooking Time: 20 minutes; Servings: 4

Ingredients:
- 2 teaspoons olive oil
- 1 clove garlic, crushed and minced
- 1 shallot, chopped
- 1 red bell pepper, chopped
- 1 lb. lean ground beef
- 1 teaspoon capers, rinsed and drained
- 1 cup chopped tomatoes
- Salt and pepper to taste
- 1 teaspoon ground cumin

Method:
1. Pour the oil into a pan over medium heat.
2. Cook the garlic, shallot and bell pepper for 2 minutes.
3. Stir in the beef.
4. Cook for 3 minutes.
5. Add the rest of the ingredients.
6. Simmer for 12 minutes.

Nutritional Value:
- Calories 339
- Total Fat 14.6 g
- Saturated Fat 4.1 g
- Cholesterol 55 mg
- Sodium 48 mg
- Total Carbohydrate 7 g
- Dietary Fiber 3.3 g
- Protein 19.3 g

Turkey Burger

Preparation Time: 15 minutes; Cooking Time: 10 minutes; Servings: 2

Ingredients:
- 2 teaspoons vegetable oil
- 2 sweet onion slices
- 2 tomato slices
- 4 lettuce leaves
- Salad or cauliflower rice

Burger patty
- 8 oz. lean ground turkey
- 2 teaspoons Worcestershire sauce
- ¼ cup cheddar cheese, shredded
- Salt and pepper to taste
- ½ teaspoon garlic powder

Method:
1. Combine all the ingredients for the burger patty.
2. Form patties from the mixture.
3. Pour the oil into a pan over medium heat.
4. Cook the patties for 2 to 3 minutes per side.
5. Top the turkey burgers with the onion and tomatoes.
6. Wrap with the lettuce leaves.

Nutritional Value:
- Calories 463
- Total Fat 23.1 g
- Saturated Fat 6.3 g
- Cholesterol 58 mg
- Sodium 690 mg
- Total Carbohydrate 33.5 g
- Dietary Fiber 7.9 g
- Protein 35.4 g

Pork Carnitas

Preparation Time: 30 minutes; Cooking Time: 12 hours; Servings: 6

Ingredients:
- 1 pork shoulder roast, sliced into cubes
- Salt and pepper to taste
- 2 teaspoons cumin seeds
- 2 teaspoons peppercorns
- 3 bay leaves
- 1 teaspoon dried oregano
- 4 cloves garlic, minced
- 28 oz. low-sodium chicken stock
- 2 teaspoons lime zest
- 2 tablespoons lime juice
- 12 corn tortillas
- 2 scallions, chopped
- Salsa
- Sour cream

Method:
1. Season the pork with salt and pepper.
2. Add this to a slow cooker.
3. On a cheesecloth, add the cumin, peppercorns, bay leaves, oregano and garlic.
4. Tie the corners to make a small spice bag.
5. Add this to the pot.
6. Pour in the broth.
7. Cover the pot and cook on low for 12 hours.
8. Take the meat out and shred.
9. Coat with the lime juice and lime zest.
10. Serve with the tortillas, scallions, sour cream and salsa.

Nutritional Value:
- Calories 318
- Total Fat 10 g
- Saturated Fat 3 g
- Cholesterol 90 mg
- Sodium 377 mg
- Total Carbohydrate 24 g
- Dietary Fiber 4 g
- Protein 32 g

Sweet Pot Roast

Preparation Time: 30 minutes; Cooking Time: 10 hours and 5 minutes; Servings: 8

Ingredients:
- 3 lb. beef chuck pot roast, fat trimmed
- 2 teaspoons garlic pepper seasoning
- ½ cup water
- 1 tablespoon chipotle peppers in adobo sauce, chopped
- 7 oz. dried fruit mix
- 1 tablespoon cold water mixed with 2 teaspoons cornstarch

Method:
1. Season the pot roast with the garlic pepper seasoning.
2. Add to a slow cooker.
3. Pour in the water.
4. Add the chipotle peppers in adobo sauce and dried fruits.
5. Cover the pot.
6. Cook on low for 10 hours.
7. Take 5 tablespoons of the cooking liquid and transfer to a pan over low heat.
8. Stir in the cornstarch mixture.
9. Simmer for 3 minutes.
10. Slice the pot roast.
11. Pour the sauce on top of the pot roast slices and serve.

Nutritional Value:

- Calories 338
- Total Fat 6.7 g
- Saturated Fat 2.5 g
- Cholesterol 94 mg
- Sodium 436 mg
- Total Carbohydrate 36.1 g
- Dietary Fiber 2.4 g
- Protein 34 g

Cinnamon Pork Tenderloin

Preparation Time: 30 minutes; Cooking Time: 2 hours and 15 minutes; Servings: 4

Ingredients:

Seasoning blend
- ¼ teaspoon ground allspice
- ½ teaspoon ground cinnamon
- Salt and pepper to taste

Pork
- 1 lb. pork tenderloin
- 2 teaspoons vegetable oil, divided
- 1 onion, chopped
- ¼ cup orange juice
- ½ teaspoon orange zest
- 2 tablespoons low-sodium soy sauce
- 2 teaspoons cornstarch
- 2 teaspoons granulated sugar

Method:
1. Mix the spice blend ingredients.
2. Coat the pork tenderloin with this mixture.
3. Pour half of oil into a pan over medium heat.
4. Cook the pork for 4 minutes per side.
5. Add the pork to the slow cooker.
6. Add the remaining oil to the pan.
7. Cook the onion for 4 minutes.
8. Add the onion to the slow cooker.
9. Pour in the orange juice and add orange zest.
10. Cover the pot.
11. Cook on low for 2 hours.
12. Put the pork on a cutting board and slice.
13. Mix the rest of the ingredients.
14. Simmer mixture in a pan for 15 minutes.
15. Pour the sauce over the pork slices and serve.

Nutritional Value:
- Calories 340
- Total Fat 10 g
- Saturated Fat 1.8 g
- Cholesterol 71 mg
- Sodium 408 mg
- Total Carbohydrate 32.5 g
- Dietary Fiber 3.8 g
- Protein 29.5 g

Italian Pork

Preparation Time: 15 minutes; Cooking Time: 8 hours; Servings: 4

Ingredients:
- 1 teaspoon fennel seeds, crushed
- ½ teaspoon dried oregano, crushed
- ½ teaspoon garlic powder
- ½ teaspoon paprika
- Salt and pepper to taste
- 1 pork shoulder roast
- 1 cup reduced-sodium chicken broth

Method:
1. Combine all the spices in a bowl.
2. Season the pork with this mixture.
3. Place in a slow cooker.
4. Pour in the broth.

5. Cover the pot.
6. Cook on low for 8 hours.
7. Slice the pork and drizzle with the cooking liquid.

Nutritional Value:
- Calories 341
- Total Fat 10 g
- Saturated Fat 3.6 g
- Cholesterol 110 mg
- Sodium 490 mg
- Total Carbohydrate 23.8 g
- Dietary Fiber 3.8 g
- Protein 36.3 g

Barbecue Brisket

Preparation Time: 15 minutes; Cooking Time: 10 hours; Servings: 10

Ingredients:
- 3 lb. beef brisket
- 2 onions, sliced into rings
- 1 clove garlic, minced
- 2 tablespoons brown sugar
- ¼ cup chili sauce
- 12 oz. beer
- ½ teaspoon dried thyme, crushed
- 1 bay leaf
- Salt and pepper to taste
- 2 tablespoons cornstarch mixed with 2 tablespoons cold water

Method:
1. Combine all the ingredients except cornstarch mixture in the slow cooker.
2. Mix well.
3. Cover the pot.
4. Cook on low for 10 hours.
5. Take the beef out of the pot and slice.
6. Pour the cooking liquid into a pan.
7. Stir in the cornstarch mixture.
8. Pour the sauce over the meat and serve.

Nutritional Value:
- Calories 182
- Total Fat 5.6 g
- Saturated Fat 1.8 g
- Cholesterol 57 mg
- Sodium 217 mg
- Total Carbohydrate 8.9 g
- Dietary Fiber 0.8 g
- Protein 20.2 g

Rosemary Turkey Roast

Preparation Time: 15 minutes; Cooking Time: 9 hours and 15 minutes; Servings: 8

Ingredients:
- ¼ teaspoon dried thyme, crushed
- 1 teaspoon dried rosemary, crushed
- ¼ teaspoon garlic powder
- Salt and pepper to taste
- 1 turkey breast, skinned
- 1 tablespoon vegetable oil
- 1 onion, sliced
- 8 carrots, sliced
- 1 lb. potatoes, sliced in half
- ¼ cup low-sodium chicken broth
- ¼ cup all-purpose flour

Method:
1. Mix the thyme, rosemary, garlic powder, salt and pepper in a bowl.
2. Coat the turkey with the spice mixture.
3. Cook in a pan over medium heat for 3 to 5 minutes per side.
4. Transfer the turkey to the slow cooker.
5. Stir in the rest of the ingredients except the flour.
6. Cover the pot and cook on low for 9 hours.
7. Transfer turkey to a cutting board.

8. Shred with a fork.
9. Add the flour to the cooking liquid.
10. Simmer until thickened.
11. Serve the turkey with the veggies and sauce.

Nutritional Value:
- Calories 256
- Total Fat 2.7 g
- Saturated Fat 0.5 g
- Cholesterol 76 mg
- Sodium 272 mg
- Total Carbohydrate 23.4 g
- Dietary Fiber 3.7 g
- Protein 33.5 g

Balsamic Chicken with Herbs

Preparation Time: 20 minutes; Cooking Time: 4 hours and 30 minutes; Servings: 6

Ingredients:
- 1 onion, sliced into wedges
- 1 tablespoon tapioca, crushed
- 6 chicken breast fillet, skin removed
- Salt and pepper to taste
- 1 teaspoon dried thyme
- 1 teaspoon dried rosemary
- 2 tablespoons low-sodium chicken broth
- ¼ cup balsamic vinegar
- 1 red bell pepper, sliced into strips
- 9 oz. green beans

Method:
1. Add the onion to a slow cooker.
2. Sprinkle tapioca on top of the onion.
3. Place the chicken on top.
4. Season with the herbs, salt and pepper.
5. Pour the chicken broth and vinegar over the ingredients.
6. Cover the pot and cook for 4 hours on high.
7. Stir in the veggies.
8. Cook for another 30 minutes.
9. Pour the cooking liquid over the chicken and veggies and serve.

Nutritional Value:
- Calories 234
- Total Fat 2.2 g
- Saturated Fat 0.6 g
- Cholesterol 100 mg
- Sodium 308 mg
- Total Carbohydrate 9.9 g
- Dietary Fiber 1.9 g
- Protein 40.9 g

Italian Meatballs

Preparation Time: 10 minutes; Cooking Time: 4 hours; Servings: 12

Ingredients:
- 2 red bell peppers, sliced into strips
- 12 oz. frozen meatballs
- Red pepper flakes
- 1 cup low-sodium Italian pasta sauce
- Fresh basil, chopped

Method:
1. Put the bell pepper and meatballs in the slow cooker.
2. Season with the red pepper flakes.
3. Pour in the pasta sauce.
4. Cover the pot and cook on low for 4 hours.
5. Garnish with basil and serve.

Nutritional Value:
- Calories 68
- Total Fat 3.8 g
- Saturated Fat 1 g
- Cholesterol 30 mg

- Sodium 182 mg
- Total Carbohydrate 2.8 g
- Dietary Fiber 0.2 g
- Protein 5.8 g

Mustard Pepper Steak

Preparation Time: 15 minutes; Cooking Time: 8 hours and 15 minutes; Servings: 6

Ingredients:
- 2 lb. beef sirloin steak, sliced into strips
- Pepper to taste
- 1 tablespoon cooking oil
- 1 onion, sliced
- 2 cups baby carrots, peeled
- 2 tablespoons Dijon mustard
- 10 oz. cream of celery soup (low fat and low sodium)

Method:
1. Season beef with pepper.
2. Pour the oil into a pan over medium heat.
3. Brown the beef.
4. Transfer to a slow cooker.
5. Add the rest of the ingredients.
6. Mix well.
7. Cover the pot and cook on low for 8 hours.

Nutritional Value:
- Calories 275
- Total Fat 9.4 g
- Saturated Fat 3 g
- Cholesterol 65 mg
- Sodium 410 mg
- Total Carbohydrate 9.9 g
- Dietary Fiber 1.5 g
- Protein 34.4 g

Italian Chicken

Preparation Time: 30 minutes; Cooking Time: 6 hours and 15 minutes; Servings: 6

Ingredients:
- 12 chicken drumsticks, skin removed
- Salt and pepper to taste
- 2 tablespoons flour
- 1 tablespoon olive oil
- 1 onion, chopped
- 6 cloves garlic, crushed and minced
- 1 cup celery, chopped
- 1 cup carrots, chopped
- 1 teaspoon dried thyme
- 8 oz. canned tomato sauce
- 2 tablespoons quick-cooking tapioca
- ¾ cup low-sodium chicken broth
- 1 tablespoon lemon juice
- 1 teaspoon lemon zest

Method:
1. Season chicken with salt and pepper.
2. Coat with flour.
3. Pour oil into a pan over medium heat.
4. Cook chicken until brown on all sides.
5. Transfer to a slow cooker.
6. Stir in the rest of the ingredients.
7. Cover the pot.
8. Cook on low for 6 hours.

Nutritional Value:
- Calories 346
- Total Fat 7.1 g
- Saturated Fat 1.4 g
- Cholesterol 98 mg
- Sodium 522 mg
- Total Carbohydrate 33.1 g
- Dietary Fiber 3.9 g
- Protein 32.8 g

Lettuce Wraps

Preparation Time: 15 minutes; Cooking Time: 10 hours; Servings: 12
Ingredients:
- 1 beef chuck pot roast, fat trimmed
- ½ cup green onions, chopped
- 1 tablespoon fresh ginger, chopped
- 1 cup celery, chopped
- ¼ cup low-sodium soy sauce
- ¼ cup rice vinegar
- 2 tablespoons hoisin sauce
- ½ teaspoon chili oil
- Salt and pepper to taste
- 2 tablespoons cornstarch mixed with 2 tablespoons cold water
- 24 lettuce leaves

Method:
1. Mix all the ingredients except cornstarch mixture and lettuce leaves in a slow cooker.
2. Cover and cook on low for 10 hours.
3. Uncover the pot and stir in the cornstarch mixture.
4. Cook for 15 minutes.
5. Shred the meat using a fork.
6. Put it back to the pot and stir.
7. Top the lettuce leaves with the beef mixture.
8. Roll it up and serve.

Nutritional Value:
- Calories 169
- Total Fat 4.5 g
- Saturated Fat 1.4 g
- Cholesterol 67 mg
- Sodium 472 mg
- Total Carbohydrate 5.1 g
- Dietary Fiber 0.3 g
- Protein 25 g

Beef & Veggie Soup

Preparation Time: 15 minutes; Cooking Time: 10 hours and 15 minutes; Servings: 4
Ingredients:
- 1 tablespoon cooking oil
- 1 lb. beef chuck roast, sliced into cubes
- 30 oz. canned diced tomatoes
- 1 cup water
- 3 carrots, sliced
- 2 potatoes, sliced
- 1 onion, chopped
- Salt to taste
- ½ teaspoon dried thyme

Method:
1. Pour the oil into a pan over medium heat.
2. Brown the beef on all sides.
3. Transfer to a slow cooker along with the rest of the ingredients.
4. Cover the pot.
5. Cook on low for 10 hours.

Nutritional Value:
- Calories 314
- Total Fat 8.5 g
- Saturated Fat 2.2 g
- Cholesterol 50 mg
- Sodium 517 mg
- Total Carbohydrate 30.3 g
- Dietary Fiber 7.4 g
- Protein 29.8 g

Beef Brisket with Wine

Preparation Time: 15 minutes; Cooking Time: 10 hours; Servings: 6
Ingredients:
- 1 beef brisket, fat trimmed
- 1 onion, chopped
- 6 carrots, sliced
- ¼ cup tomato paste

- 1 cup dry red wine
- 2 teaspoons Worcestershire sauce
- 4 teaspoons quick-cooking tapioca
- ½ teaspoon garlic powder
- 1 teaspoon chili powder
- Salt to taste

Method:
1. Add the beef to your slow cooker.
2. Stir in the rest of the ingredients.
3. Cover the pot.
4. Cook on low for 10 hours.
5. Serve the beef with the veggies and sauce.

Nutritional Value:
- Calories 338
- Total Fat 9.1 g
- Saturated Fat 2.6 g
- Cholesterol 75 mg
- Sodium 495 mg
- Total Carbohydrate 30.7 g
- Dietary Fiber 3.9 g
- Protein 28.4 g

Barbecue Beef Sandwich

Preparation Time: 20 minutes; Cooking Time: 2 hours; Servings: 8

Ingredients:
- 2 lb. beef brisket
- 1 onion, sliced
- 1 teaspoon chili powder
- ½ teaspoon garlic powder
- 1 tablespoon vinegar
- ⅓ cup ketchup
- ⅓ cup chili sauce
- ¼ teaspoon celery seeds
- 2 tablespoons brown sugar
- ¼ teaspoon dry mustard
- 1 tablespoon Worcestershire sauce
- Pepper to taste
- 2 tablespoons cold water mixed with 1 tablespoon all-purpose flour
- 8 whole-wheat burger buns

Method:
1. Add all the ingredients except flour mixture and buns to a pot over medium heat.
2. Mix well.
3. Bring to a boil.
4. Reduce heat to low and cook for 2 hours.
5. Transfer brisket to a cutting board and shred.
6. Pour the cooking liquid into a pan.
7. Stir in the flour mixture.
8. Simmer until thickened.
9. Add the shredded beef to the sauce.
10. Stuff the beef mixture into the burger buns and serve.

Nutritional Value:
- Calories 301
- Total Fat 7.8 g
- Saturated Fat 2.1 g
- Cholesterol 68 mg
- Sodium 430 mg
- Total Carbohydrate 27.8 g
- Dietary Fiber 2.8 g
- Protein 28.1 g

Beef Stew

Preparation Time: 15 minutes; Cooking Time: 10 hours; Servings: 8

Ingredients:
- 2 lb. pot roast, fat removed
- 1 tablespoon vegetable oil
- 2 cups mushrooms, sliced
- 4 carrots, sliced
- 1 lb. potatoes, sliced
- 2 parsnips, sliced
- 2 celery stalks, chopped
- 1 onion, sliced

- 3 cloves garlic, minced
- 2 teaspoons dried rosemary
- 4 cups reduced-sodium beef broth
- 1 clove garlic, minced
- 2 teaspoons fresh thyme, chopped
- ¾ cup sour cream

Method:
1. In a pan over medium heat, cook meat until brown.
2. Transfer to a slow cooker.
3. Stir in the rest of the ingredients except thyme and sour cream.
4. Cover the pot and cook on low for 10 hours.
5. Top with the thyme and sour cream before serving.

Nutritional Value:
- Calories 289
- Total Fat 8.7 g
- Saturated Fat 3.1 g
- Cholesterol 80 mg
- Sodium 342 mg
- Total Carbohydrate 20.6 g
- Dietary Fiber 3.2 g
- Protein 29.7 g

Mediterranean Beef

Preparation Time: 20 minutes; Cooking Time: 10 hours; Servings: 8
Ingredients:
- 1 beef brisket, fat removed
- 3 teaspoons dried Italian seasoning
- 2 medium fennel bulbs, sliced
- ½ cup reduced-sodium beef broth
- 14 oz. canned diced tomatoes with herbs
- 1 teaspoon lemon zest
- ½ cup olives, pitted
- Salt and pepper to taste
- ¼ cup cold water mixed with 2 tablespoons flour

Method:
1. Season the meat with the Italian seasoning.
2. Add to a slow cooker.
3. Sprinkle fennel bulbs on top.
4. Stir in the rest of the ingredients except the flour mixture.
5. Cover the pot.
6. Cook on low for 10 hours.
7. Transfer the meat to a cutting board. Slice.
8. In a pan over medium heat, simmer the cooking liquid and flour mixture until thickened.
9. Serve the meat with the veggies and sauce.

Nutritional Value:
- Calories 254
- Total Fat 34.8 g
- Saturated Fat 2.9 g
- Cholesterol 103 mg
- Sodium 337 mg
- Total Carbohydrate 10.2 g
- Dietary Fiber 5.3 g
- Protein 34.8 g

Shredded Beef Sandwich

Preparation Time: 20 minutes; Cooking Time: 1 hour and 15 minutes; Servings: 6
Ingredients:
- 1 tablespoon instant coffee granules
- 1 lb. beef chuck roast, fat removed
- Cooking spray
- 4 cups reduced-sodium beef broth
- 3 onions, chopped
- 4 cloves garlic, crushed and minced
- 1 red bell pepper, sliced into strips
- 1 green bell pepper, sliced into strips
- 2 bay leaves
- 2 tablespoons cider vinegar
- ½ cup red wine
- 1 tablespoon Worcestershire sauce
- Salt to taste
- 6 slices cheese

- 6 slices Italian bread

Method:
1. Sprinkle all sides of the roast with the coffee granules.
2. Spray your pan with oil.
3. Brown the meat on all sides.
4. Add the beef to the pressure cooker.
5. Pour in the broth.
6. Seal the pot and cook on high for 30 minutes.
7. Release pressure naturally.
8. Transfer the beef to a cutting board.
9. Shred and transfer to a pot over medium heat.
10. Stir in the rest of the ingredients.
11. Bring to a boil.
12. Reduce heat and simmer for 30 minutes.
13. Preheat your broiler.
14. Add the cheese to the bread slices.
15. Broil until cheese has melted.
16. Put the beef on top of the cheese.

Nutritional Value:
- Calories 273
- Total Fat 7.7 g
- Saturated Fat 3.6 g
- Cholesterol 41 mg
- Sodium 441 mg
- Total Carbohydrate 26.2 g
- Dietary Fiber 4.2 g
- Protein 20.7 g

Garlic Chicken with Thyme

Preparation Time: 15 minutes; Cooking Time: 50 minutes; Servings: 6

Ingredients:
- 6 cloves garlic, minced
- 1 teaspoon dried thyme
- 3 lb. chicken breast fillets
- 1 tablespoon balsamic vinegar
- ¼ cup orange juice

Method:
1. Season the chicken with the thyme and garlic.
2. Add to a pot.
3. Stir in the vinegar and orange juice.
4. Cover the pot.
5. Bring to a boil.
6. Reduce heat and simmer for 40 minutes.

Nutritional Value:
- Calories 134
- Total Fat 1.3 g
- Saturated Fat 0.3 g
- Cholesterol 64 mg
- Sodium 58 mg
- Total Carbohydrate 2.3 g
- Dietary Fiber 0.1 g
- Protein 25.7 g

Moroccan-Style Pot Roast

Preparation Time: 30 minutes; Cooking Time: 1 hour and 20 minutes; Servings: 6

Ingredients:

Spice Mixture
- 2 teaspoons pumpkin pie spice
- 1 teaspoon ground cumin
- Salt and pepper to taste

Beef

- 1 tablespoon olive oil
- 1 beef chuck roast, fat removed and sliced into cubes
- 2 onions, sliced into wedges
- 2 red bell peppers, sliced
- 3 cups parsnips, sliced
- 1 lb. carrots, sliced
- 3 tablespoons tapioca, crushed
- 1 cup low-sodium beef broth
- ½ teaspoon dry mustard
- 2 tablespoons tomato paste

Method:
1. In a bowl, mix the ingredients for the spice mixture.
2. Sprinkle this on all sides of beef.
3. Cook the beef in oil in a pan over medium heat for 8 minutes.
4. Add the beef to a pot over medium heat.
5. Stir in the rest of the ingredients.
6. Bring to a boil.
7. Simmer for 1 hour.

Nutritional Value:
- Calories 414
- Total Fat 8.8 g
- Saturated Fat 3.1 g
- Cholesterol 37.4 mg
- Sodium 473 mg
- Total Carbohydrate 37.4 g
- Dietary Fiber 8.6 g
- Protein 45.6 g

Pork Pot Roast

Preparation Time: 30 minutes; Cooking Time: 10 hours and 20 minutes; Servings: 6

Ingredients:
- 1 tablespoon cooking oil
- 1 pork shoulder roast, fat removed
- 3 tablespoons Dijon mustard
- ½ teaspoon dried rosemary
- 1 teaspoon dried thyme
- Salt and pepper to taste
- 12 potatoes, sliced
- 3 parsnips, sliced
- 3 carrots, sliced
- 1 onion, sliced
- 1 cup chicken broth
- 3 tablespoons quick-cooking tapioca

Method:
1. Add the oil to a pan over medium heat.
2. Brown the pork on all sides.
3. Transfer to a plate.
4. Brush with the mustard and season with the salt, pepper, rosemary and thyme.
5. Place in the slow cooker.
6. Add the rest of the ingredients to the pot.
7. Cover the pot.
8. Cook on low for 10 hours.
9. Slice the pork and serve with the sauce and veggies.

Nutritional Value:
- Calories 364
- Total Fat 11.4 g
- Saturated Fat 3.5 g
- Cholesterol 98 mg
- Sodium 453 mg
- Total Carbohydrate 29.4 g
- Dietary Fiber 5 g
- Protein 32.6 g

Garlic Beef & Broccoli

Preparation Time: 15 minutes; Cooking Time: 35 minutes; Servings: 4

Ingredients:

Marinade
- 3 cloves garlic, minced
- 1 tablespoon toasted sesame oil

- 2 tablespoons lemon juice
- 2 tablespoons low-sodium soy sauce
- Red pepper flakes
- 1 teaspoon ground ginger

Beef & Broccoli
- 1 lb. beef sirloin steak, fat removed and sliced into strips
- 4 cups broccoli florets, steamed
- 1 onion, sliced
- Pepper to taste

Method:
1. Combine the marinade ingredients.
2. Marinate the beef in this mixture for 30 minutes.
3. In a pan over medium heat, cook the onion for 1 minute.
4. Add the broccoli florets and season with pepper.
5. Stir in the beef.
6. Cook for 3 minutes.

Nutritional Value:
- Calories 357
- Total Fat 9.7 g
- Saturated Fat 2.5 g
- Cholesterol 59 mg
- Sodium 336 mg
- Total Carbohydrate 39.2 g
- Dietary Fiber X g
- Protein X g

Chicken Kebabs

Preparation Time: 1 hour and 30 minute; Cooking Time: 20 minutes; Servings: 4

Ingredients:
- 1 onion, chopped
- 2 teaspoons ginger, grated
- 1 tablespoon orange juice
- 1 teaspoon orange zest
- 2 tablespoons mustard
- Salt and pepper to taste
- 1 ½ lb. chicken breast fillet, sliced into 2 inch pieces

Method:
1. Add all the ingredients except the chicken in a large bowl.
2. Mix well.
3. Stir in the chicken.
4. Cover with foil and marinate in the refrigerator for 1 hour.
5. Preheat your grill.
6. Thread chicken cubes onto skewers.
7. Grill for 7 to 8 minutes per side.

Nutritional Value:
- Calories 452
- Total Fat 15.8 g
- Saturated Fat 2 g
- Cholesterol 94 mg
- Sodium 1226 mg
- Total Carbohydrate 36.9 g
- Dietary Fiber 6.4 g
- Protein 40.8 g

Grilled Beef & Veggies

Preparation Time: 1 hour; Cooking Time: 10 minutes; Servings: 4

Ingredients:

Marinade
- ¾ cup olive oil
- 2 cloves garlic, minced
- ¾ cup balsamic vinegar
- 2 tablespoons mustard
- 1 tablespoon dried rosemary
- 1 tablespoon dried oregano
- Salt and pepper to taste

Kebab

- 1 lb. steak, sliced into chunks
- 2 red bell peppers, sliced into 16 pieces
- 16 cherry tomatoes
- 16 large button mushrooms

Method:
1. Combine the marinade ingredients in a bowl.
2. Mix well.
3. Transfer half of the mixture to another bowl and reserve.
4. Add the beef to the first bowl and marinate for 30 minutes.
5. Thread the beef and veggies onto skewers.
6. Grill for 5 minutes per side, brushing the kebabs with the reserved marinade.

Nutritional Value:
- Calories 237
- Total Fat 10.1 g
- Saturated Fat 2.4 g
- Cholesterol 59 mg
- Sodium 95 mg
- Total Carbohydrate 11.7 g
- Dietary Fiber 3.4 g
- Protein 24.8 g

Pork & Rice Noodles

Preparation Time: 20 minutes; Cooking Time: 10 minutes; Servings: 4

Ingredients:
- 1 tablespoon chili-garlic sauce
- 1 tablespoon fish sauce
- 4 teaspoons honey
- 2 tablespoons olive oil
- 1 lb. pork tenderloin, sliced into strips
- 1 tablespoon garlic, minced
- 1 tablespoon ginger, minced
- 6 scallions, chopped
- Pepper to taste
- 4 cups cooked rice noodles
- Bean sprouts
- Shredded carrots
- Fresh mint leaves

Method:
1. Mix the chili garlic sauce, fish sauce and honey in a bowl. Set aside.
2. Pour oil into a pan over medium heat.
3. Cook the pork with the garlic, ginger and scallions for 3 to 5 minutes.
4. Season with pepper and stir.
5. Pour in the chili garlic sauce into the pan.
6. Reduce heat and cook for 2 to 3 minutes.
7. Add noodles to the pan and stir.
8. Turn off the heat.
9. Transfer to a bowl.
10. Top with the rest of the ingredients.

Nutritional Value:
- Calories 375
- Total Fat 13 g
- Saturated Fat 2.6 g
- Cholesterol 57 mg
- Sodium 495 mg
- Total Carbohydrate 38.2 g
- Dietary Fiber 3.8 g
- Protein 24.9 g

Chicken with Peanut Sauce

Preparation Time: 30 minutes; Cooking Time: 15 minutes; Servings: 4

Ingredients:
- 2 tablespoons low-sodium soy sauce
- ¼ cup natural creamy peanut butter
- 2 tablespoons honey
- 2 teaspoons toasted sesame oil
- 2 tablespoons water
- 2 teaspoons olive oil
- 2 teaspoons garlic, minced
- 1 tablespoon ginger, minced

- 3 scallions, chopped
- 1 lb. chicken fillet, sliced into strips
- Cooked brown rice

Method:
1. Mix soy sauce, peanut butter, honey, sesame oil and water in a bowl.
2. Pour olive oil into a pan over medium heat.
3. Cook the garlic, ginger and scallions for 2 minutes, stirring.
4. Stir in the chicken and cook for 4 minutes.
5. Pour in the peanut butter mixture.
6. Cook for 3 to 5 minutes.
7. Serve the chicken with peanut sauce with the brown rice.

Nutritional Value:
- Calories 521
- Total Fat 26 g
- Saturated Fat 2.6 g
- Cholesterol 54 mg
- Sodium 485 mg
- Total Carbohydrate 43.8 g
- Dietary Fiber 11.1 g
- Protein 34 g

Chicken With Jerk Sauce

Preparation Time: 3 hours and 15 minutes; Cooking Time: 15 minutes; Servings: 4

Ingredients:

Jerk Sauce
- 2 cloves garlic, chopped
- 2 scallions, chopped
- 2 jalapeño peppers, chopped
- 1 ½ teaspoons ginger, minced
- 2 tablespoons lime juice
- 2 tablespoons brown sugar
- 1 tablespoon olive oil
- 1 tablespoon white vinegar
- 1 tablespoon reduced-sodium soy sauce
- 1 tablespoon fresh thyme, chopped
- ½ teaspoon ground nutmeg
- 1 teaspoon ground allspice
- Salt to taste

Chicken
- 4 chicken thighs

Method:
1. Combine all the jerk sauce ingredients in a bowl.
2. Transfer to a blender.
3. Pulse until smooth.
4. Reserve 6 tablespoons and refrigerate.
5. Add the chicken to the remaining mixture.
6. Cover and marinate in the refrigerator for 3 hours.
7. Preheat your grill.
8. Grill the chicken for 7 minutes per side.
9. Serve with the reserved sauce.

Nutritional Value:
- Calories 258
- Total Fat 13.1 g
- Saturated Fat 3 g
- Cholesterol 86 mg
- Sodium 365 mg
- Total Carbohydrate 9.9 g
- Dietary Fiber 0.7 g
- Protein 24.7 g

Grilled Pork Tenderloin

Preparation Time: 15 minutes; Cooking Time: 20 minutes; Servings: 4

Ingredients:
- 1 tablespoon olive oil
- 2 cloves garlic, minced
- ½ teaspoon ground cumin
- ¾ teaspoon chili powder

- Salt and pepper to taste
- 1 lb. pork tenderloin, fat removed
- Salsa

Method:
1. Pour oil into a bowl.
2. Stir in the garlic, cumin, chili powder, salt and pepper. Mix well.
3. Add the pork tenderloin.
4. Preheat your grill.
5. Grill the pork for 7 to 8 minutes per side.
6. Slice the pork on a cutting board and serve with salsa.

Nutritional Value:
- Calories 219
- Total Fat 9.5 g
- Saturated Fat 1.8 g
- Cholesterol 74 mg
- Sodium 512 mg
- Total Carbohydrate 8 g
- Dietary Fiber 1.5 g
- Protein 24.7 g

Chicken with Tomatoes & Capers

Preparation Time: 20 minutes; Cooking Time: 15 minutes; Servings: 4

Ingredients:

Sauce
- 1 ½ teaspoons olive oil
- 2 cloves garlic, minced
- 2 cups tomatoes, chopped
- ½ cup dry white wine
- 2 tablespoons capers, rinsed and drained
- Salt and pepper to taste
- 2 teaspoons butter, sliced into cubes
- 2 tablespoons fresh basil leaves, chopped

Chicken
- 1 lb. chicken breast fillet
- 1 tablespoon olive oil
- Salt and pepper to taste

Method:
1. Preheat your grill.
2. Prepare the sauce by adding the oil into a pan over medium heat.
3. Cook the garlic for 1 minute.
4. Stir in the rest of the ingredients for the sauce.
5. Cook for 3 minutes.
6. Coat the chicken with oil and season with salt and pepper.
7. Grill for 5 minutes per side.
8. Top with the sauce and serve.

Nutritional Value:
- Calories 232
- Total Fat 9.9 g
- Saturated Fat 2.7 g
- Cholesterol 68 mg
- Sodium 398 mg
- Total Carbohydrate 6.1 g
- Dietary Fiber 1.6 g
- Protein 24.2 g

Sweet & Sour Pork Tenderloin

Preparation Time: 15 minutes; Cooking Time: 30 minutes; Servings: 4

Ingredients:
- 1 tablespoon olive oil
- 1 onion, diced
- Salt to taste
- 2 teaspoons ginger, grated
- 1 clove garlic, minced
- 3 tablespoons honey
- 1 tablespoon rice vinegar
- ½ teaspoon garlic, minced

- 1 tablespoon brown sugar
- 1 lb. pork tenderloin, fat removed

Method:
1. Preheat your grill.
2. Pour oil into a pan over medium heat.
3. Cook onion for 3 minutes.
4. Sprinkle with salt.
5. Stir in ginger and garlic. Cook for 1 minute.
6. Add honey and vinegar. Simmer for 6 minutes.
7. Turn off heat and set aside.
8. In a bowl, mix the garlic, sugar and salt.
9. Season the pork with this mixture.
10. Grill the pork for 9 minutes per side.
11. Pour the sauce over the pork and serve.

Nutritional Value:
- Calories 239
- Total Fat 6.1 g
- Saturated Fat 1.3 g
- Cholesterol 74 mg
- Sodium 330 mg
- Total Carbohydrate 12.5 g
- Dietary Fiber 1.5 g
- Protein 24.7 g

Sweet & Spicy Sirloin

Preparation Time: 30 minutes; Cooking Time: 15 minutes; Servings: 4

Ingredients:

Rub
- 1 tablespoon instant coffee granules
- ¼ teaspoon ground cinnamon
- Salt and pepper to taste

Beef
- 1 lb. beef sirloin steak, fat removed
- 1 cup corn kernels
- 2 teaspoons vegetable oil
- 1 ½ teaspoons sugar
- ⅓ cup balsamic vinegar
- ⅓ cup dry red wine
- 4 cups arugula
- 1 poblano chili pepper, sliced thinly
- 16 cherry tomatoes, sliced in half
- ¼ cup onion, sliced thinly

Method:
1. Mix the rub ingredients.
2. Sprinkle mixture on both sides of the steak.
3. Marinate for 15 minutes.
4. While waiting, cook corn for 2 minutes.
5. Transfer to a plate.
6. Pour oil into a pan over medium heat.
7. Cook the beef for 10 minutes.
8. Transfer to a cutting board and slice.
9. Add the sugar, wine and vinegar to the pan.
10. Bring to a boil.
11. Reduce until sauce is reduced.
12. Serve the beef with the corn and the rest of the ingredients.
13. Pour the sauce on top.

Nutritional Value:
- Calories 283
- Total Fat 7.6 g
- Saturated Fat 2 g
- Cholesterol 48 mg
- Sodium 154 mg
- Total Carbohydrate 21.5 g
- Dietary Fiber 2.4 g
- Protein 28.3 g

Turkey Kebab

Preparation Time: 4 hours and 20 minutes; **Cooking Time:** 15 minutes; **Servings:** 4

Ingredients:
- 1 tablespoon olive oil
- ⅓ cup pineapple juice
- 1 tablespoon lemon zest
- 1 tablespoon brown sugar
- 12 oz. turkey breast fillet, sliced into chunks
- 1 onion, sliced into wedges
- 1 orange, sliced into chunks
- 2 cups pineapple chunks

Method:
1. Combine the olive oil, pineapple juice, lemon zest and brown sugar in a bowl.
2. Stir in the turkey chunks.
3. Cover and marinate in the refrigerator for 4 hours.
4. After 4 hours, transfer the marinade in a pan over medium heat.
5. Bring to a boil and then simmer until thickened.
6. Thread turkey onto skewers with the rest of the ingredients.
7. Grill the kebabs for 5 to 6 minutes per side, brushing with the warmed sauce.

Nutritional Value:
- Calories 235
- Total Fat 6 g
- Saturated Fat 1 g
- Cholesterol 37 mg
- Sodium 37 mg
- Total Carbohydrate 24 g
- Dietary Fiber 2 g
- Protein 17 g

Chicken with Mango Chutney

Preparation Time: 20 minutes; **Cooking Time:** 6 hours; **Servings:** 4

Ingredients:
- 3 lb. chicken drumsticks
- 1 onion, sliced into wedges
- ½ cup low-sodium barbecue sauce
- ¼ cup mango chutney
- ½ teaspoon curry powder
- Pepper to taste
- 1 mango, chopped

Method:
1. Combine all the ingredients except chopped mango in a slow cooker.
2. Mix well.
3. Cover the pot.
4. Cook on low for 6 hours.
5. Serve the chicken with mango chutney topped with the fresh mango cubes.

Nutritional Value:
- Calories 433
- Total Fat 8.2 g
- Saturated Fat 2.1 g
- Cholesterol 155 mg
- Sodium 419 mg
- Total Carbohydrate 47.6 g
- Dietary Fiber 3.4 g
- Protein 41.7 g

Smoky Paprika Pork

Preparation Time: 15 minutes; **Cooking Time:** 10 minutes; **Servings:** 4

Ingredients:
- 3 pork chops, fat removed
- Cooking spray
- 2 teaspoons smoked paprika
- Salt and pepper to taste
- 8 scallions, chopped
- Sour cream
- Grape tomatoes, sliced in half

Method:

1. Spray both sides of the pork chop with oil.
2. Sprinkle with paprika, salt and pepper.
3. Spray your grill pan with oil.
4. Place over medium heat.
5. Cook the pork for 4 to 5 minutes per side.
6. Transfer to a plate.
7. Sprinkle pork chops with the scallions and serve with sour cream and tomatoes.

Nutritional Value:
- Calories 311
- Total Fat 10 g
- Saturated Fat 4 g
- Cholesterol 55 mg
- Sodium 383 mg
- Total Carbohydrate 33 g
- Dietary Fiber 6 g
- Protein 24 g

Pot Roast with Mashed Potatoes

Preparation Time: 20 minutes; Cooking Time: 10 hours and 15 minutes; Servings: 8

Ingredients:
- 3 lb. beef chuck pot roast, fat trimmed and sliced into cubes
- Garlic salt to taste
- Pepper to taste
- ½ cup water
- ½ cup beef stock
- 1 tablespoon cold water mixed with 2 teaspoons cornstarch
- 4 cups mashed potatoes, cooked

Method:
1. Add the pot roast to a slow cooker.
2. Season with garlic salt and pepper.
3. Pour in water and beef stock.
4. Cover the pot.
5. Cook on low for 10 hours.
6. Transfer the pork to a cutting board.
7. Slice into strips.
8. Transfer to a serving plate.
9. Take 6 tablespoons of the cooking liquid.
10. Add to a pan over medium heat.
11. Stir in the cornstarch mixture.
12. Simmer until sauce has thickened.
13. Pour the gravy over the pork and serve with the mashed potatoes.

Nutritional Value:
- Calories 338
- Total Fat 6.7 g
- Saturated Fat 2.5 g
- Cholesterol 94 mg
- Sodium 436 mg
- Total Carbohydrate 36.1 g
- Dietary Fiber 2.4 g
- Protein 34 g

Lemon Chicken

Preparation Time: 15 minutes; Cooking Time: 30 minutes; Servings: 4

Ingredients:
- 2 tablespoons olive oil
- 1 lb. chicken fillet, skin removed
- Salt and pepper to taste
- 1 lb. potatoes, sliced
- 4 cloves garlic, minced
- 1 lemon, sliced
- 1 tablespoon fresh tarragon, chopped
- ½ cup reduced-sodium chicken broth
- 6 cups baby kale

Method:

1. Preheat your oven to 400 degrees F.
2. Pour the oil into a pan over medium heat.
3. Season chicken with salt and pepper.
4. Cook for 3 minutes per side.
5. Transfer to a plate.
6. Add the potatoes and cook for 3 minutes.
7. Stir in the rest of the ingredients except the kale.
8. Put the chicken back to the pan.
9. Place inside the oven.
10. Roast for 15 minutes.
11. Add kale and roast for another 5 minutes.
12. Serve warm.

Nutritional Value:
- Calories 374
- Total Fat 19.3 g
- Saturated Fat 3.9 g
- Cholesterol 76 mg
- Sodium 378 mg
- Total Carbohydrate 25.6 g
- Dietary Fiber 2.9 g
- Protein 24.7 g

Pork Tenderloin with Blackberry Sauce

Preparation Time: 15 minutes; Cooking Time: 15 minutes; Servings: 6

Ingredients:
- 1 lb. pork tenderloin, sliced into strips
- 2 tablespoons olive oil, divided
- Salt and pepper to taste
- 2 cloves garlic, minced
- 2 shallots, chopped
- ¼ cup reduced-sodium chicken broth
- 1 cup blackberry preserves
- 1 tablespoon butter
- 1 teaspoon honey

Method:
1. Coat the pork with olive oil and season with salt and pepper.
2. Cook in a pan over medium heat for 10 minutes per side.
3. Transfer the pork to a plate.
4. Add the garlic and shallots to the pan.
5. Stir in the rest of the ingredients.
6. Bring to a boil.
7. Reduce heat.
8. Simmer for 5 minutes.
9. Pour the sauce over the pork and serve.

Nutritional Value:
- Calories 272
- Total Fat 8.3 g
- Saturated Fat 2.3 g
- Cholesterol 70 mg
- Sodium 115 mg
- Total Carbohydrate 30.7 g
- Dietary Fiber 0.5 g
- Protein 18 g

Pork Chops with Grape Sauce

Preparation Time: 20 minutes; Cooking Time: 25 minutes; Servings: 4

Ingredients:
- 1 tablespoon olive oil
- 4 pork chops
- 1 onion, sliced thinly
- 1 clove garlic, minced
- ½ cup low-sodium chicken broth
- 1 cup apple cider
- 1 tablespoon cornstarch
- 1 tablespoon balsamic vinegar
- 1 teaspoon honey
- 1 cup grapes, sliced in half

Method:
1. Pour oil into a pan over medium heat.
2. Cook the pork chops for 5 minutes per side.
3. Transfer to a plate.
4. Cook the onion and garlic in the pan for 2 minutes.
5. Pour in the broth and apple cider.
6. Put the pork chops back to the pan.
7. Bring to a boil and then simmer for 4 minutes.
8. In a bowl, mix the remaining ingredients.
9. Add to the pan.
10. Cook for 5 minutes.
11. Serve warm.

Nutritional Value:
- Calories 188
- Total Fat 4 g
- Saturated Fat 1 g
- Cholesterol 47 mg
- Sodium 117 mg
- Total Carbohydrate 18 g
- Dietary Fiber 1 g
- Protein 19 g

Roasted Pork & Apples

Preparation Time: 20 minutes; Cooking Time: 20 minutes; Servings: 4

Ingredients:
- 1 lb. pork tenderloin
- Salt and pepper to taste
- 1 teaspoon fresh sage, chopped
- 1 tablespoon vegetable oil
- 1 onion, sliced into wedges
- 3 apples, sliced into wedges
- ⅔ cup apple cider

Method:
1. Season the pork with salt, pepper and sage.
2. Pour oil into a pan over medium heat.
3. Brown the pork on all sides.
4. Transfer to a baking pan.
5. Sprinkle onion around the pork.
6. Roast at 425 degrees F for 10 minutes.
7. Add the apples and roast for another 10 minutes.
8. Boil the apple cider in a pan.
9. Pour over the meat and serve.

Nutritional Value:
- Calories 239
- Total Fat 6.1 g
- Saturated Fat 1.1 g
- Cholesterol 74 mg
- Sodium 209 mg
- Total Carbohydrate 22 g
- Dietary Fiber 3 g
- Protein 24.3 g

Lime Pork Piccata

Preparation Time: 15 minutes; Cooking Time: 25 minutes; Servings: 2

Ingredients:
- 8 oz. pork tenderloin, fat removed and sliced
- 3 tablespoons lime juice
- 2 teaspoons vegetable oil
- 1 teaspoon butter
- 4 oz. kale leaves, chopped
- 2 tablespoons shallot, minced
- 2 teaspoons honey

Method:
1. Toss pork in lime juice.

2. Marinate for 15 minutes.
3. Pour oil into a pan over medium heat.
4. Cook the pork for 3 minutes per side.
5. Transfer to a plate.
6. Add butter to the pan.
7. Stir in the rest of the ingredients except honey.
8. Serve the pork with the kale mixture and drizzle with honey.

Nutritional Value:
- Calories 329
- Total Fat 9.5 g
- Saturated Fat 2.4 g
- Cholesterol 79 mg
- Sodium 354 mg
- Total Carbohydrate 33.7 g
- Dietary Fiber 1.6 g
- Protein 28.8 g

Philly Chicken Sandwich

Preparation Time: 15 minutes; Cooking Time: 20 minutes; Servings: 6

Ingredients:
- 1 tablespoon olive oil
- 1 lb. chicken breast fillet, sliced into strips
- 2 cups onion, sliced thinly
- 2 cloves garlic, minced
- 1 cup red bell pepper, sliced into strips
- Pepper to taste
- 1 teaspoon dried Italian seasoning
- 6 slices low-fat Provolone cheese
- 6 slices whole-grain bread

Method:
1. Preheat your broiler.
2. Pour the oil into a pan over medium heat.
3. Cook the chicken for 5 minutes per side.
4. Reduce heat and stir in the rest of the ingredients except cheese and bread.
5. Cook while stirring for 5 minutes.
6. Add the mixture on top of the bread and top with the cheese slice.
7. Broil until cheese has melted.

Nutritional Value:
- Calories 321
- Total Fat 9.8 g
- Saturated Fat 3.3 g
- Cholesterol 71 mg
- Sodium 435 mg
- Total Carbohydrate 20 g
- Dietary Fiber 4.6 g
- Protein 31.3 g

Lamb with Apples & Onions

Preparation Time: 20 minutes; Cooking Time: 20 minutes; Servings: 2

Ingredients:
- 8 oz. lamb tenderloin, sliced into strips
- Pepper to taste
- ⅛ teaspoon dried thyme, crushed
- 1 tablespoon olive oil
- 1 onion, sliced thinly
- 8 oz. apples, sliced thinly
- ¼ cup water
- 2 tablespoons cider vinegar
- 1 teaspoon honey
- Salt to taste

Method:
1. Season the lamb with pepper and thyme.
2. Add the oil to the pan.
3. Cook the lamb for 3 to 4 minutes per side.
4. Transfer to a plate.
5. Add the onion to the pan.
6. Cook for 4 minutes.

7. Stir in the rest of the ingredients.
8. Bring to a boil then simmer for 5 minutes.
9. Put the lamb back to the pan.
10. Cook for 2 minutes.

Nutritional Value:
- Calories 219
- Total Fat 2.4 g
- Saturated Fat 0.8 g
- Cholesterol 73 mg
- Sodium 344 mg
- Total Carbohydrate 24.5 g
- Dietary Fiber 3.8 g
- Protein 24.7 g

Steak Rice Bowl

Preparation Time: 15 minutes; Cooking Time: 20 minutes; Servings: 6

Ingredients:
- 1 tablespoon olive oil
- ¼ cup onion, chopped
- 1 lb. sirloin steak, sliced into strips
- ½ cup low-sodium beef stock
- 15 oz. canned diced tomatoes
- Pepper to taste
- 1 teaspoon dried thyme
- 6 cups brown rice, cooked

Method:
1. Add the oil to a pan over medium heat.
2. Cook the onion and beef for 5 minutes.
3. Add the rest of the ingredients except the rice to the pan.
4. Bring to a boil.
5. Reduce heat and simmer for 10 minutes.
6. Serve the beef mixture with the cooked brown rice.

Nutritional Value:
- Calories 266
- Total Fat 6.9 g
- Saturated Fat 1.7 g
- Cholesterol 57 mg
- Sodium 250 mg
- Total Carbohydrate 24.9 g
- Dietary Fiber 2.4 g
- Protein 24.4 g

Fruit Glazed Meatballs

Preparation Time: 30 minutes; Cooking Time: 40 minutes; Servings: 6

Ingredients:

Meatballs
- 1 lb. lean ground pork loin
- 1 clove garlic, minced
- 2 teaspoons ginger, grated
- ⅓ cup water chestnuts, chopped
- 1 egg, beaten
- ¼ cup fine dry breadcrumbs
- Salt and pepper to taste

Sauce
- ¼ cup pineapple juice
- 1 tablespoon lemon juice
- 1 red bell pepper, sliced
- ¼ teaspoon ground cardamom
- ½ cup fruit preserve (reduced sugar)

Method:
1. Combine the ingredients for the meatballs.
2. Mix well.
3. Form meatballs from the mixture.
4. Thread meatballs onto skewers.
5. Grill for 15 minutes, turning once or twice.
6. In a pan over medium heat, add the sauce ingredients.
7. Bring to a boil.

8. Reduce heat and simmer for 15 minutes.
9. Add the meatballs to the pan.
10. Simmer for 10 minutes.
11. Serve warm.

Nutritional Value:
- Calories 187
- Total Fat 3.8 g
- Saturated Fat 1.2 g
- Cholesterol 85 mg
- Sodium 268 mg
- Total Carbohydrate 18 g
- Dietary Fiber 0.9 g
- Protein 18.9 g

Zucchini Lasagna with Turkey Sausage

Preparation Time: 20 minutes; Cooking Time: 40 minutes; Servings: 8

Ingredients:
- 8 oz. turkey sausage, removed from casing and crumbled
- 10 oz. spinach
- 28 oz. tomato sauce
- 8 lasagna noodles
- 1 cup mozzarella cheese, divided
- 1 cup ricotta cheese, divided
- 3 zucchini, sliced into long strips
- ½ cup Parmesan cheese, grated

Method:
1. Preheat your oven to 375 degrees F.
2. Spray your baking pan with oil.
3. Cook the sausage in a pan over medium heat for 3 minutes.
4. Transfer to a plate.
5. Cook the spinach in the pan for 3 minutes.
6. Transfer to a strainer.
7. Let cool and then chop.
8. Spread tomato sauce on the baking pan.
9. Top with the lasagna noodles.
10. Add tomato sauce on top.
11. Sprinkle with half of the mozzarella and ricotta.
12. Add a layer of zucchini and spinach.
13. Sprinkle with the sausage and Parmesan cheese on top.
14. Repeat the layers.
15. Bake in the oven for 30 minutes.

Nutritional Value:
- Calories 262
- Total Fat 9.6 g
- Saturated Fat 4.6 g
- Cholesterol 47 mg
- Sodium 442 mg
- Total Carbohydrate 27.3 g
- Dietary Fiber 3.8 g
- Protein 19 g

Spicy Pork Tenderloin

Preparation Time: 10 minutes; Cooking Time: 20 minutes; Servings: 4

Ingredients:
- 1 ½ teaspoons onion powder
- 1 ½ teaspoons garlic powder
- 1 ½ teaspoons sweet paprika
- 1 ½ teaspoons smoked paprika
- 1 ½ teaspoons chili powder
- Salt and pepper to taste
- 1 lb. pork tenderloin, fat removed and sliced into strips
- 2 tablespoons olive oil

Method:
1. Preheat your oven to 450 degrees F.

2. Cover your baking pan with foil.
3. Mix all the spices with the salt and pepper in a bowl.
4. Toss the pork in the mixture.
5. Pour the oil into a pan over medium heat.
6. Cook the pork for 5 minutes, stirring frequently.
7. Transfer the pork to a baking pan.
8. Roast the pork for 15 minutes.
9. Let rest before serving.

Nutritional Value:
- Calories 493
- Total Fat 32.6 g
- Saturated Fat 5.4 g
- Cholesterol 92 mg
- Sodium 298 mg
- Total Carbohydrate 19.3 g
- Dietary Fiber 5.7 g
- Protein 34.1 g

Persian Chicken with Rice

Preparation Time: 15 minutes; Cooking Time: 50 minutes; Servings: 8

Ingredients:
- Cooking spray
- 2 tablespoons olive oil, divided
- 8 chicken thigh fillets, skin removed
- 2 onions, sliced thinly
- Salt to taste
- 3 cloves garlic, minced
- 2 teaspoons ground turmeric
- 1 teaspoon paprika
- 3 cups cabbage, shredded
- ¼ cup lemon juice
- 4 cups cooked rice

Method:
1. Preheat your oven to 375 degrees F.
2. Spray your baking pan with oil.
3. Pour half of the oil into a pan over medium heat.
4. Cook the chicken for 3 minutes per side.
5. Transfer to a plate.
6. Add the remaining oil to the pan.
7. Cook the onion for 10 minutes, sprinkling it with salt.
8. Stir in the spices and garlic.
9. Add the cabbage, lemon juice and rice to the pan.
10. Stir-fry for 5 minutes.
11. Spread the rice in the baking pan, topped with the chicken.
12. Bake in the oven for 30 minutes.

Nutritional Value:
- Calories 274
- Total Fat 9.7 g
- Saturated Fat 2.2 g
- Cholesterol 50 mg
- Sodium 194 mg
- Total Carbohydrate 29.4 g
- Dietary Fiber 3.3 g
- Protein 17 g

Eggplant with Lamb

Preparation Time: 30 minutes; Cooking Time: 1 hour minutes; Servings: 6

Ingredients:
- Cooking spray
- 6 eggplants, sliced in half lengthwise
- 1 tablespoon olive oil
- 1 onion, diced
- 2 cloves garlic, minced
- 1 red bell pepper, diced
- 1 tablespoon fresh ginger, minced
- 1 lb. lean ground lamb
- 1 tablespoon ground cumin
- 2 teaspoons ground coriander

- 2 teaspoons turmeric
- Salt and pepper to taste
- ¼ teaspoon cayenne pepper
- 2 tablespoons tomato paste

Method:
1. Preheat your oven to 400 degrees F.
2. Spray your baking pan with oil.
3. Score the eggplants.
4. Bake in the oven for 20 minutes. Set aside.
5. Pour the oil into a pan over medium heat.
6. Cook the onion, garlic, bell pepper and ginger for 3 minutes.
7. Add the lamb and cook for 5 minutes.
8. Stir in the rest of the ingredients.
9. Bring to a boil.
10. Reduce heat and simmer for 10 minutes.
11. Stuff the eggplant with the lamb mixture.
12. Place in the baking pan and bake for 10 minutes.

Nutritional Value:
- Calories 292
- Total Fat 11.6 g
- Saturated Fat 4.4 g
- Cholesterol 29 mg
- Sodium 455 mg
- Total Carbohydrate 35.3 g
- Dietary Fiber 10 g
- Protein 14.3 g

Chicken & Sweet Potatoes

Preparation Time: 10 minutes; Cooking Time: 0 minutes; Servings: 1

Ingredients:
- 3 oz. cooked chicken, shredded
- ½ cup sweet potato, cooked and diced
- ¼ apple, sliced
- 3 cups Romaine lettuce, chopped
- ½ ounce low-fat cheddar cheese, sliced into cubes
- 2 tablespoons apple-cider vinaigrette

Method:
1. Combine all the ingredients in a bowl and serve.

Nutritional Value:
- Calories 542
- Total Fat 31.5 g
- Saturated Fat 5.1 g
- Cholesterol 75 mg
- Sodium 384 mg
- Total Carbohydrate 31.8 g
- Dietary Fiber 10 g
- Protein 36.5 g

Chicken & Squash Bake

Preparation Time: 20 minutes; Cooking Time: 35 minutes; Servings: 8

Ingredients:
- Cooking spray
- 1 tablespoon oil
- 1 onion, chopped
- 2 cloves garlic, minced
- 10 oz. mushrooms, sliced
- 1 lb. spaghetti squash, boiled and shredded
- 4 cups broccoli florets
- Pepper to taste
- ½ teaspoon dried thyme
- 20 oz. reduced-sodium cream of mushroom soup
- 1 lb. chicken breast fillet, sliced into cubes
- ½ cup cheddar cheese, shredded

Method:
1. Preheat your oven to 375 degrees F.
2. Spray your baking pan with oil.

3. In a pan over medium heat, cook the onion, garlic and mushrooms for 3 minutes.
4. Stir in the squash and broccoli.
5. Season with pepper and thyme.
6. Add the soup and chicken.
7. Cook for 2 minutes.
8. Transfer to the baking pan
9. Top with cheese.
10. Bake in the oven for 30 minutes.

Nutritional Value:
- Calories 273
- Total Fat 11.5 g
- Saturated Fat 2.6 g
- Cholesterol 71 mg
- Sodium 493 mg
- Total Carbohydrate 18.5 g
- Dietary Fiber 4.6 g
- Protein 25.4 g

Thai Chicken

Preparation Time: 15 minutes; Cooking Time: 15 minutes; Servings: 2

Ingredients:
- 2 chicken breast fillet
- Salt to taste
- 1 teaspoon oil
- 1 teaspoon fresh ginger, grated
- 1 clove garlic, minced
- ¼ cup light coconut milk
- 2 tablespoons fresh cilantro, chopped
- 1 tablespoon peanut butter
- Pepper to taste

Method:
1. Season chicken with salt.
2. Pour oil over medium heat.
3. Cook the chicken for 10 minutes.
4. Add garlic and ginger to the pan.
5. Cook for 30 seconds, stirring.
6. Stir in the rest of the ingredients.
7. Simmer until the sauce has thickened.
8. Serve warm.

Nutritional Value:
- Calories 217
- Total Fat 9.3 g
- Saturated Fat 2.4 g
- Cholesterol 66 mg
- Sodium 266 mg
- Total Carbohydrate 4.1 g
- Dietary Fiber 1 g
- Protein 28.4 g

Cranberry Pork Medallions

Preparation Time: 20 minutes; Cooking Time: 20 minutes; Servings: 4

Ingredients:
- 12 oz. pork tenderloin, fat trimmed
- Salt and pepper to taste
- ¼ cup all-purpose flour
- 2 tablespoons olive oil, divided
- 1 onion, sliced thinly
- 1 tablespoon balsamic vinegar
- ¼ cup low-sodium chicken broth
- ¼ cup dried cranberries

Method:
1. Pound the pork using a meat mallet to flatten.
2. In a bowl, mix the salt, pepper and flour.
3. Dredge the pork in this mixture.
4. Pour half of the oil to a pan over medium heat.
5. Cook the pork for 2 minutes per side.

6. Transfer to a plate.
7. Pour remaining oil to the pan.
8. Cook onion for 4 minutes.
9. Pour in the vinegar and broth.
10. Add cranberries.
11. Simmer for 10 minutes.
12. Top the pork with the cranberry mixture and serve.

Nutritional Value:
- Calories 211
- Total Fat 8.7 g
- Saturated Fat 1.5 g
- Cholesterol 53 mg
- Sodium 116 mg
- Total Carbohydrate 14.7 g
- Dietary Fiber 1 g
- Protein 18.2 g

French Dip Sandwich

Preparation Time: 30 minutes; Cooking Time: 10 hours; Servings: 8

Ingredients:
- 1 beef brisket, fat removed
- 2 onions, sliced into rings
- Pepper to taste
- 1 teaspoon dried rosemary
- 3 cloves garlic, minced and divided
- 2 tablespoons Worcestershire sauce
- ¼ cup water
- 14 oz. reduced-sodium beef broth
- 2 tablespoons scallions, chopped
- 2 tablespoons pepperoncini peppers, roasted and chopped
- 1 teaspoon olive oil
- 1 tablespoon chives, chopped
- ¼ cup Dijon mustard
- ¼ cup low-fat sour cream
- 4 whole-wheat rolls

Method:
1. Add the beef and onions to a slow cooker.
2. Season with pepper, rosemary and garlic.
3. Pour in Worcestershire, water and broth.
4. Cover the pot.
5. Cook on low for 10 hours.
6. Transfer beef to a cutting board and shred.
7. Put the shredded beef back to the pot and mix.
8. In a bowl, mix the remaining ingredients except the rolls.
9. Spread the mixture on the rolls.
10. Stuff with the beef and onion mixture.

Nutritional Value:
- Calories 320
- Total Fat 11.5 g
- Saturated Fat 11.5 g
- Cholesterol 88 mg
- Sodium 382 mg
- Total Carbohydrate 20.1 g
- Dietary Fiber 2.8 g
- Protein 33.2 g

Mustard & Maple Pork

Preparation Time: 20 minutes; Cooking Time: 50 minutes; Servings: 8

Ingredients:
- Salt and pepper to taste
- 1 tablespoon maple syrup
- 2 tablespoons Dijon mustard
- 1 teaspoons orange zest
- 2 teaspoons dried sage, crushed
- 1 pork loin roast, fat removed
- 2 lb. potatoes, sliced
- 16 oz. carrots, sliced
- 1 tablespoon olive oil

Method:

1. Preheat your oven to 325 degrees F.
2. In a bowl, mix the salt, pepper, maple syrup, mustard, orange zest and sage.
3. Put the pork roast in a baking pan.
4. Spread the mixture on top of the pork.
5. Roast for 45 minutes.
6. Cook the carrots and potatoes in olive oil for 3 to 5 minutes.
7. Season with salt and pepper.
8. Spread the veggies around the pork roast and serve.

Nutritional Value:
- Calories 284
- Total Fat 9.3 g
- Saturated Fat 2.8 g
- Cholesterol 62 mg
- Sodium 303 mg
- Total Carbohydrate 21.8 g
- Dietary Fiber 2.8 g
- Protein 27.7 g

Meatball Soup

Preparation Time: 15 minutes; Cooking Time: 40 minutes; Servings: 8

Ingredients:
- 1 lb. lean ground beef
- ¾ cup whole-wheat breadcrumbs
- 4 cloves garlic, minced, divided
- 2 teaspoons rosemary, chopped
- 1 egg, beaten
- Pepper to taste
- 1 tablespoon olive oil
- 1 onion, chopped
- 2 red bell peppers, sliced into strips
- 3 carrots, chopped
- 2 cups low-sodium beef stock
- 15 oz. Great Northern beans, rinsed and drained
- 2 cups water

Method:
1. Combine ground beef, breadcrumbs, 2 cloves minced garlic, 1 teaspoon rosemary, egg and pepper in a bowl.
2. Mix well.
3. Form meatballs from the mixture.
4. Transfer to a baking pan.
5. Bake in the oven at 350 degrees F for 15 minutes.
6. Pour the oil into a soup pot over medium heat.
7. Cook the onion, bell pepper, remaining garlic and carrot for 5 minutes.
8. Stir in the remaining ingredients and remaining rosemary.
9. Bring to a boil.
10. Reduce heat and simmer for 15 minutes.
11. Add meatballs and simmer for 5 minutes before serving.

Nutritional Value:
- Calories 301
- Total Fat 10 g
- Saturated Fat 3 g
- Cholesterol 49 mg
- Sodium 400 mg
- Total Carbohydrate 31 g
- Dietary Fiber 7 g
- Protein 25 g

Italian Beef Pasta

Preparation Time: 20 minutes; Cooking Time: 1 hour and 30 minutes; Servings: 4

Ingredients:
- 1 tablespoon olive oil
- 1 lb. round steak, sliced into strips
- 1 onion, chopped
- 2 cloves garlic, minced
- 2 red bell peppers, chopped
- 2 cups mushrooms, sliced
- ½ cup celery, chopped
- 14 oz. canned diced tomatoes

- ½ teaspoon dried basil
- 4 cups cooked linguine pasta
- 2 tablespoons Parmesan cheese, grated

Method:
1. Cook the steak strips in olive oil in a pan over medium heat.
2. Brown both sides.
3. Add the onion, garlic, red bell pepper, mushrooms and celery.
4. Cook for 3 minutes.
5. Stir in the tomatoes and basil.
6. Simmer for 1 hour and 15 minutes.
7. Serve mixture over pasta and sprinkle Parmesan cheese on top.

Nutritional Value:
- Calories 212
- Total Fat 4 g
- Saturated Fat 1.3 g
- Cholesterol 51 mg
- Sodium 296 mg
- Total Carbohydrate 13.5 g
- Dietary Fiber 2.6 g
- Protein 30.3 g

Chicken Rice Bowls

Preparation Time: 15 minutes; Cooking Time: 15 minutes; Servings: 4

Ingredients:
- 1 lb. chicken breast fillet, sliced into strips
- Salt and pepper to taste
- 3 tablespoons all-purpose flour
- 2 tablespoons olive oil
- 1 cup thin carrot strips
- 2 red bell peppers, sliced into strips
- 4 cups cabbage, sliced thinly
- 4 cups cooked brown rice
- Chopped chives
- 4 tablespoons peanut sauce

Method:
1. Season chicken with salt and pepper.
2. Dredge with flour.
3. Cook in olive oil until brown on all sides.
4. In a bowl, mix the carrots, red bell pepper and cabbage.
5. Divide brown rice into 4 bowls.
6. Top with the chicken and cabbage slaw.
7. Sprinkle chives on top.
8. Drizzle with the peanut sauce and serve.

Nutritional Value:
- Calories 351
- Total Fat 20 g
- Saturated Fat 2.6 g
- Cholesterol 63 mg
- Sodium 498 mg
- Total Carbohydrate 14.4 g
- Dietary Fiber 4.6 g
- Protein 28.1 g

Pork Stew

Preparation Time: 15 minutes; Cooking Time: 8 hours; Servings: 6

Ingredients:
- 2 lb. pork sirloin, fat removed and sliced
- 1 tablespoon vegetable oil
- 1 onion, chopped
- 4 potatoes, cubed
- 8 oz. green chili peppers, chopped
- 15 oz. corn kernels
- 1 teaspoon garlic salt
- ½ teaspoon ancho chili powder
- ½ teaspoon ground cumin
- ¼ teaspoon dried oregano
- Pepper to taste
- 3 cups water

Method:
1. Brown the beef in oil and transfer to a slow cooker.
2. Stir in the rest of the ingredients.
3. Cover the pot and cook on low for 8 hours.
4. Serve warm.

Nutritional Value:
- Calories 180
- Total Fat 4.1 g
- Saturated Fat 1.3 g
- Cholesterol 37 mg
- Sodium 251 mg
- Total Carbohydrate 22.5 g
- Dietary Fiber 3 g
- Protein 15 g

Grilled Curry Burgers

Preparation Time: 20 minutes; Cooking Time: 20 minutes; Servings: 4

Ingredients:
- ½ teaspoon curry powder
- ¼ cup Dijon mustard
- 1 lb. lean ground beef
- ¼ cup scallions, chopped
- ½ cup carrot, shredded
- 2 tablespoons milk
- ¼ cup breadcrumbs
- Salt and pepper to taste
- ¼ teaspoon dried Italian seasoning
- Burger buns

Method:
1. Combine curry powder and mustard in a bowl.
2. In another bowl, mix the rest of the ingredients except burger buns.
3. Form patties from the mixture.
4. Grill the burgers for 7 to 9 minutes per side.
5. Spread the curry mustard on burger buns and top with grilled burger patties.

Nutritional Value:
- Calories 257
- Total Fat 9 g
- Saturated Fat 4 g
- Cholesterol 54 mg
- Sodium 409 mg
- Total Carbohydrate 24 g
- Dietary Fiber 3 g
- Protein 20 g

Pork Burger

Preparation Time: 15 minutes; Cooking Time: 30 minutes; Servings: 4

Ingredients:
- 1 tablespoon Dijon mustard
- 1 teaspoon honey
- 3 tablespoons light mayonnaise
- 12 oz. lean ground pork
- ½ teaspoon paprika
- ¼ teaspoon ground cumin
- ¼ teaspoon garlic powder
- Salt and pepper to taste
- Burger buns, split
- Lettuce leaves

Method:
1. Mix mustard, honey and mayo in a bowl. Set aside.
2. In another bowl, combine the rest of the ingredients except buns and lettuce.
3. Form patties from the mixture.
4. Grill burgers for 10 to 12 minutes per side.
5. Spread honey mixture on the buns.
6. Add the lettuce and burgers and top with the other buns.

Nutritional Value:
- Calories 272
- Total Fat 8 g
- Saturated Fat 1.5 g
- Cholesterol 63 mg
- Sodium 510 mg
- Total Carbohydrate 25.9 g

- Dietary Fiber 3 g
- Protein 23.1 g

Grilled Lamb & Veggies

Preparation Time: 4 hours and 30 minutes; Cooking Time: 20 minutes; Servings: 4

Ingredients:

Spice blend
- 12 whole cloves
- 1 tablespoon cardamom seeds
- 1 tablespoon black peppercorns
- 1 tablespoon cumin seeds
- 1 cinnamon stick

Lamb and veggies
- 1 lb. lean lamb, sliced into cubes
- 1 onion, chopped
- 4 cloves garlic, minced
- 2 teaspoons ginger, grated
- 2 tablespoons lemon juice
- ¼ cup cilantro, chopped
- Salt to taste
- 1 cup onion wedges
- 1 cup eggplant chunks
- 1 cup squash chunks

Method:
1. Add the spice blend ingredients to a pan over medium heat.
2. Cook for 3 minutes, stirring.
3. Crush the cinnamon stick using a mallet.
4. Add the rest to a spice grinder.
5. Grind until powdery.
6. Mix with the powdered cinnamon.
7. Add this mixture to a bowl.
8. Stir in the rest of the ingredients except the veggies.
9. Marinate the lamb cubes in this mixture for 4 hours.
10. Thread the lamb cubes onto skewers alternating with the veggie pieces.
11. Grill for 15 minutes, turning once or twice.

Nutritional Value:
- Calories 232
- Total Fat 4 g
- Saturated Fat 1 g
- Cholesterol 71 mg
- Sodium 226 mg
- Total Carbohydrate 22 g
- Dietary Fiber 5 g
- Protein 27 g

Savory Chicken

Preparation Time: 15 minutes; Cooking Time: 15 minutes; Servings: 4

Ingredients:
- 1 tablespoon olive oil
- 16 oz. chicken breast fillets
- 1 teaspoons herbs de Provence
- Salt and pepper to taste
- Cooked brown rice
- Steamed veggies

Method:
1. Add the olive oil to a pan over medium heat.
2. Season the chicken with herbs, salt and pepper.
3. Cook until brown on both sides.
4. Serve with brown rice and steamed veggies.

Nutritional Value:
- Calories 153
- Total Fat 6.1 g
- Saturated Fat 1.2 g
- Cholesterol 63 mg
- Sodium 346 mg
- Total Carbohydrate 0.1 g
- Dietary Fiber 2 g
- Protein 22.9 g

Jambalaya

Preparation Time: 30 minutes; Cooking Time: 5 hours and 30 minutes; Servings: 6

Ingredients:
- 4 oz. turkey sausage, chopped
- 1 lb. chicken breast, sliced into strips
- ¾ cup onion, chopped
- 4 cloves garlic, minced
- 1 cup green bell pepper, chopped
- 2 celery stalks, chopped
- 28 oz. diced tomatoes
- 3 cups collard greens, chopped
- Red pepper flakes
- 1 teaspoon dried thyme
- 8 oz. shrimp, peeled and deveined
- Cooked brown rice

Method:
1. Add all the ingredients except shrimp and rice to a slow cooker.
2. Mix well.
3. Cover the pot and cook on low for 5 hours.
4. Add the shrimp and cook for another 30 minutes.
5. Serve with rice.

Nutritional Value:
- Calories 292
- Total Fat 5 g
- Saturated Fat 1.1 g
- Cholesterol 108 mg
- Sodium 536 mg
- Total Carbohydrate 31.8 g
- Dietary Fiber 5.3 g
- Protein 29.1 g

Pork Chops with Cider Sauce

Preparation Time: 15 minutes; Cooking Time: 4 hours and 10 minutes; Servings: 4

Ingredients:
- 1 onion, sliced into wedges
- 2 celery, chopped
- 3 cups squash, sliced into cubes
- Cooking spray
- 4 pork chops
- 1 tablespoon chipotle peppers in adobo sauce, chopped
- 1 cup apple cider
- ½ teaspoon dried basil
- ¼ teaspoon garlic powder
- Salt to taste

Method:
1. Add the onion, celery and squash to your slow cooker.
2. Spray your pan with oil.
3. Place it over medium heat.
4. Cook the pork chops until brown on both sides.
5. Transfer on top of the veggies in the slow cooker.
6. In a bowl, mix the remaining ingredients.
7. Pour mixture over the pork chops.
8. Cover the pot.
9. Cook on low for 4 hours.

Nutritional Value:
- Calories 289
- Total Fat 10.3 g
- Saturated Fat 2.3 g
- Cholesterol 55 mg
- Sodium 259 mg
- Total Carbohydrate 27.7 g
- Dietary Fiber 3.7 g
- Protein 21.7 g

Spicy Pot Roast

Preparation Time: 10 minutes; Cooking Time: 8 hours and 15 minutes; Servings: 6

Ingredients:

- 1 teaspoon cayenne pepper
- 1 teaspoon ground cumin
- Salt and pepper to taste
- 1 beef chuck pot roast, fat removed
- 1 tablespoon olive oil
- 1 cup reduced-sodium beef broth
- ½ cup tomato sauce
- Fresh cilantro

Method:
1. Mix cayenne pepper, cumin, salt and pepper in a bowl.
2. Season beef with this mixture.
3. Pour the oil into a pan over medium heat.
4. Cook the beef until brown on all sides.
5. Transfer to a slow cooker.
6. Pour in the broth and tomato sauce.
7. Cover and cook on low for 8 hours.
8. Shred the beef and drizzle with the cooking liquid.
9. Garnish with the cilantro.

Nutritional Value:
- Calories 414
- Total Fat 8.8 g
- Saturated Fat 3.1 g
- Cholesterol 123 mg
- Sodium 473 mg
- Total Carbohydrate 37.4 g
- Dietary Fiber 8.6 g
- Protein 45.6 g

Aromatic Steak Dinner

Preparation Time: 15 minutes; Cooking Time: 10 hours and 15 minutes; Servings: 8

Ingredients:
- 2 lb. beef round steak, sliced
- Salt and pepper to taste
- 1 tablespoon oil
- 1 onion, sliced thinly
- 1 bulb fennel, sliced
- 1 cup carrots, sliced into thin strips
- ½ cup reduced-sodium beef broth
- 15 oz. tomato sauce
- 28 oz. canned crushed tomatoes
- 2 teaspoons dried Italian seasoning
- Red pepper flakes

Method:
1. Season steak with salt and pepper.
2. Brown the steak in oil in a pan over medium heat.
3. Add all the ingredients to a slow cooker.
4. Stir in the beef.
5. Cover the pot.
6. Cook on low for 10 hours.
7. Drizzle with sauce before serving.

Nutritional Value:
- Calories 365
- Total Fat 8.1 g
- Saturated Fat 2.4 g
- Cholesterol 72 mg
- Sodium 535 mg
- Total Carbohydrate 33.4 g
- Dietary Fiber 5.8 g
- Protein 35.6 g

Mexican Chicken & Rice

Preparation Time: 15 minutes; Cooking Time: 5 hours and 10 minutes; Servings: 8

Ingredients:
- 1 onion, chopped
- 3 cloves garlic, minced
- 3 red bell peppers, chopped
- 15 oz. canned tomatoes
- 15 oz. tomato sauce
- 2 cups chicken broth
- 1 tablespoon paprika
- 2 tablespoons chili powder

- ¼ teaspoon ground turmeric
- ½ teaspoon ground cumin
- Salt and pepper to taste
- 2 lb. chicken fillet
- 1 cup peas
- 2 cups cooked brown rice

Method:
1. Combine all the ingredients except rice and peas in the slow cooker.
2. Mix well.
3. Cover the pot.
4. Cook on low for 5 hours.
5. Shred the chicken and put it back to the pot.
6. Stir in the peas and rice.
7. Cook for 10 minutes.

Nutritional Value:
- Calories 299
- Total Fat 5.8 g
- Saturated Fat 0.9 g
- Cholesterol 90 mg
- Sodium 669 mg
- Total Carbohydrate 34.5 g
- Dietary Fiber 5.2 g
- Protein 28.8 g

Beef with Tomato & Wine

Preparation Time: 20 minutes; Cooking Time: 10 hours and 15 minutes; Servings: 6

Ingredients:
- 3 tablespoons olive oil
- 2 lb. beef chuck pot roast, fat trimmed and sliced
- 3 carrots, sliced into cubes
- 2 cups chopped turnips
- ¼ cup red wine
- 15 oz. tomato sauce
- ⅛ teaspoon ground allspice
- Salt and pepper to taste
- 2 cups chopped squash

Method:
1. Pour oil into a pan over medium heat.
2. Cook the beef slices until brown.
3. Transfer to a slow cooker.
4. Stir in the rest of the ingredients.
5. Cover the pot and cook on low for 10 hours.
6. Pour sauce on top of beef and veggies and serve.

Nutritional Value:
- Calories 273
- Total Fat 5.7 g
- Saturated Fat 1.9 g
- Cholesterol 89 mg
- Sodium 575 mg
- Total Carbohydrate 18.6 g
- Dietary Fiber 3.1 g
- Protein 34.2 g

Chicken Teriyaki

Preparation Time: 10 minutes; Cooking Time: 1 hour; Servings: 4

Ingredients:
- 2 tablespoons olive oil
- 4 chicken breast fillets, sliced
- 16 oz. frozen mixed vegetables
- 1 cup low-sodium chicken broth
- 3 tablespoons reduced-sugar orange jam
- 2 tablespoons teriyaki sauce
- 1 teaspoon dry mustard
- ½ teaspoon ground ginger
- Cooked brown rice
- Chopped scallions

Method:
1. Pour oil into a pan over medium heat.
2. Cook the chicken until brown on both sides.

3. Transfer to a plate.
4. Add the veggies and stir fry until tender.
5. Put the chicken back to the pan.
6. Mix the rest of the ingredients except rice and scallions in a bowl.
7. Pour mixture into the pan.
8. Bring to a boil.
9. Simmer for 30 minutes.
10. Serve with rice and garnish with scallions.

Nutritional Value:
- Calories 320
- Total Fat 2.4 g
- Saturated Fat 0.5 g
- Cholesterol 66 mg
- Sodium 432 mg
- Total Carbohydrate 40.7 g
- Dietary Fiber 4.5 g
- Protein 31.6 g

Pork & Rigatoni Stew

Preparation Time: 30 minutes; Cooking Time: 5 hours and 5 minutes; Servings: 6

Ingredients:
- 2 lb. beef chuck pot roast, fat removed and sliced into cubes
- Salt and pepper to taste
- 1 tablespoon olive oil
- 2 cups low-sodium beef broth
- 15 oz. canned stewed tomatoes
- 1 onion, chopped
- ½ cup celery, chopped
- ½ cup carrot, chopped
- ½ cup cranberry juice
- ¼ cup nonfat half-and-half
- 1 tablespoon all-purpose flour
- 6 ounces dried rigatoni pasta, cooked according to package directions
- Parmesan cheese, grated

Method:
1. Season beef with salt and pepper.
2. In a pan over medium heat, cook the beef in oil until brown.
3. Transfer to a slow cooker along with the rest of the ingredients except half and half, flour, pasta and Parmesan cheese.
4. Cover the pot.
5. Cook on low for 5 hours.
6. Put the meat in a cutting board and shred.
7. In a bowl, mix the remaining ingredients.
8. Add mixture to the pot along with the shredded beef.
9. Cook for 5 minutes.

Nutritional Value:
- Calories 401
- Total Fat 9.7 g
- Saturated Fat 3.1 g
- Cholesterol 100 mg
- Sodium 509 mg
- Total Carbohydrate 31.9 g
- Dietary Fiber 3 g
- Protein 40.1 g

Pork Stew with Beer

Preparation Time: 30 minutes; Cooking Time: 8 hours; Servings: 8

Ingredients:
- Cooking spray
- 1 lb. boneless pork shoulder, fat trimmed and sliced
- 2 sweet potatoes, sliced into cubes
- 3 parsnips, sliced
- 2 apples, sliced
- 1 onion, sliced
- 2 cloves garlic, minced
- 3 cups vegetable broth
- 1 tablespoon Dijon mustard

- 1 tablespoon brown sugar
- 1 ½ teaspoons dried thyme
- 12 oz. beer
- Red pepper flakes

Method:
1. Spray your pan with oil.
2. Place it over medium heat.
3. Cook the pork cubes until brown on all sides.
4. Transfer to a slow cooker.
5. Add the rest of the ingredients.
6. Cook on low for 8 hours.

Nutritional Value:
- Calories 209
- Total Fat 3.8 g
- Saturated Fat 1.2 g
- Cholesterol 37 mg
- Sodium 471 mg
- Total Carbohydrate 27.4 g
- Dietary Fiber 5 g
- Protein 13.6 g

Chicken Vera Cruz

Preparation Time: 15 minutes; Cooking Time: 10 hours; Servings: 6

Ingredients:
- 1 onion, sliced into wedges
- 1 tablespoon garlic, chopped
- 6 chicken thigh fillets
- 1 lb. potatoes, sliced
- 1 jalapeño chili pepper, sliced
- 30 oz. canned diced tomatoes
- 2 tablespoons Worcestershire sauce
- ⅛ teaspoon ground cloves
- ¼ teaspoon ground cinnamon
- 1 teaspoon dried oregano, crushed
- ½ cup fresh parsley, chopped

Method:
1. Add all the ingredients except parsley in your slow cooker.
2. Mix well.
3. Cover the pot.
4. Cook on low for 10 hours.
5. Garnish with parsley.
6. Serve warm.

Nutritional Value:
- Calories 228
- Total Fat 4.7 g
- Saturated Fat 1.1 g
- Cholesterol 78 mg
- Sodium 287 mg
- Total Carbohydrate 25.3 g
- Dietary Fiber 5.2 g
- Protein 21.8 g

Beef & Mushroom Stew

Preparation Time: 15 minutes; Cooking Time: 8 hours; Servings: 8

Ingredients:
- 2 tablespoons cooking oil
- 2 lb. steak, sliced into cubes
- 3 tablespoons all-purpose flour
- 6 carrots, sliced
- 2 onions, chopped
- 12 oz. mushrooms, sliced
- 30 oz. canned diced tomatoes
- 2 tablespoons molasses
- ¼ cup cider vinegar
- ¼ teaspoon ground ginger
- ¼ cup raisins
- Salt and pepper to taste

Method:
1. Pour the oil into a pan over medium heat.
2. Dredge the beef cubes in flour.
3. Cook the beef until brown on all sides.

4. Transfer to the slow cooker.
5. Stir in the rest of the ingredients.
6. Cover the pot.
7. Cook on low for 8 hours.

Nutritional Value:
- Calories 263
- Total Fat 8.5 g
- Saturated Fat 2 g
- Cholesterol 67 mg
- Sodium 444 mg
- Total Carbohydrate 20.5 g
- Dietary Fiber 2.6 g
- Protein 26.8 g

Bloody Mary Pork

Preparation Time: 20 minutes; Cooking Time: 10 hours and 20 minutes; Servings: 10

Ingredients:
- 3 lb. beef chuck pot roast, fat trimmed and sliced into cubes
- 1 teaspoon Worcestershire sauce
- ¼ cup water
- 1 cup tomato juice
- 2 cloves garlic, minced
- 2 tablespoons cold water mixed with 4 teaspoons cornstarch
- 1 tablespoon horseradish
- Salt and pepper to taste

Method:
1. Add the beef to the slow cooker.
2. Mix the Worcestershire sauce, water and tomato juice.
3. Pour mixture into the pot.
4. Cover the pot.
5. Cook on low for 10 hours.
6. Pour the cooking liquid into a pan over medium low.
7. Stir in the cornstarch mixture.
8. Simmer for 5 minutes.
9. Stir in the horseradish and season with salt and pepper.
10. Serve meat drizzled with the gravy.

Nutritional Value:
- Calories 176
- Total Fat 5.3 g
- Saturated Fat 1.8 g
- Cholesterol 81 mg
- Sodium 255 mg
- Total Carbohydrate 1.2 g
- Dietary Fiber 0.1 g
- Protein 29.2 g

Asian Pork with Cabbage

Preparation Time: 30 minutes; Cooking Time: 15 minutes; Servings: 4

Ingredients:
- 1 red sweet pepper, roasted
- 1 teaspoon water
- 4 tablespoons pineapple juice
- 1 tablespoon brown sugar
- 2 tablespoons low-sodium soy sauce
- 2 cloves garlic
- 2 teaspoons fresh ginger, grated
- 2 teaspoons rice vinegar
- 1 tablespoon cornstarch
- 4 teaspoons oil
- 12 oz. pork loin, sliced into strips
- 8 oz. canned pineapple chunks
- 4 cups cabbage, shredded

Method:
1. Add the red sweet pepper and water to a blender. Pulse until smooth.
2. Stir in the rest of the ingredients except oil, pork, pineapple and cabbage.
3. Pulse until fully combined.
4. Pour the oil into a pan over medium heat.

5. Cook the pork loin for 3 minutes per side.
6. Add the pineapple and cabbage.
7. Cook for 2 minutes.
8. Pour in the sauce.
9. Bring to a boil and then simmer for 10 minutes.

Nutritional Value:
- Calories 274
- Total Fat 10.7 g
- Saturated Fat 2.4 g
- Cholesterol 47 mg
- Sodium 341 mg
- Total Carbohydrate 23.4 g
- Dietary Fiber 3.6 g
- Protein 21.9 g

Cheesy Chicken

Preparation Time: 15 minutes; Cooking Time: 8 hours and 15 minutes; Servings: 8

Ingredients:
- Cooking spray
- 8 chicken thigh fillets
- 2 sweet peppers, sliced
- ½ teaspoon dried rosemary
- 1 cup spaghetti sauce
- ½ cup Kalamata olives, pitted and chopped
- 4 oz. mozzarella cheese
- ¼ cup fresh basil, chopped
- 2 tablespoons Parmesan cheese, grated

Method:
1. Spray your slow cooker with oil.
2. Place this over medium heat.
3. Cook the chicken for 2 minutes per side.
4. Add the chicken to the slow cooker and stir in the rest of the ingredients except mozzarella, basil and Parmesan cheese.
5. Cover the pot and cook on low for 8 hours.
6. Shred the chicken using a fork.
7. Transfer to a baking pan.
8. Spread the mozzarella, basil and Parmesan cheese on top.
9. Broil for 5 minutes.

Nutritional Value:
- Calories 296
- Total Fat 10.2 g
- Saturated Fat 2.8 g
- Cholesterol 118 mg
- Sodium 584 mg
- Total Carbohydrate 19.7 g
- Dietary Fiber 5.7 g
- Protein 30.5 g

Chicken & Veggie Curry

Preparation Time: 15 minutes; Cooking Time: 7 hours minutes; Servings: 4

Ingredients:
- 4 chicken thighs, skin removed
- 16 oz. frozen veggies
- 10 oz. low-fat cream of chicken soup
- Pepper to taste
- 2 teaspoons curry powder
- 1 tablespoon fresh cilantro, chopped

Method:
1. Add all the ingredients except cilantro to the slow cooker.
2. Mix well.
3. Cover the pot.
4. Cook on low for 7 hours.
5. Garnish with cilantro before serving.

Nutritional Value:
- Calories 299
- Total Fat 8 g

- Saturated Fat 2 g
- Cholesterol 147 mg
- Sodium 486 mg
- Total Carbohydrate 19 g
- Dietary Fiber 2 g
- Protein 35 g

Sausage & Potatoes

Preparation Time: 15 minutes; Cooking Time: 30 minutes; Servings: 6
Ingredients:
- Cooking spray
- 12 oz. chicken sausages
- 1 onion, sliced into wedges
- 1 red bell pepper, sliced into strips
- 1 lb. potatoes, sliced
- Salt and pepper to taste

Method:
1. Spray your pan with oil.
2. Add the sausages and cook until brown.
3. Transfer to a plate.
4. Add the onion and cook for 1 minute.
5. Stir in the red bell pepper and potatoes.
6. Season with salt and pepper.
7. Cook until potatoes are tender.
8. Serve sausages with potato mixture.

Nutritional Value:
- Calories 281
- Total Fat 12 g
- Saturated Fat 4 g
- Cholesterol 262 mg
- Sodium 485 mg
- Total Carbohydrate 23 g
- Dietary Fiber 3 g
- Protein 21 g

Cajun Pork

Preparation Time: 15 minutes; Cooking Time: 6 hours and 15 minutes; Servings: 8
Ingredients:
- 2 lb. pork sirloin roast, fat trimmed and sliced into strips
- Salt and pepper to taste
- Cooking spray
- 1 onion, chopped
- 1 cup celery, chopped
- 14 oz. canned diced tomatoes
- 15 oz. red beans, rinsed and drained
- 1 tablespoons Cajun seasoning (salt-free)
- Chopped cilantro

Method:
1. Season pork with salt and pepper.
2. Coat the pan with oil.
3. Place it over medium heat.
4. Cook the pork until brown on all sides.
5. Add pork to the slow cooker along with all the ingredients except cilantro.
6. Mix well.
7. Cover and cook on low for 6 hours.
8. Garnish with cilantro and serve.

Nutritional Value:
- Calories 306
- Total Fat 4.8 g
- Saturated Fat 1.3 g
- Cholesterol 109 mg
- Sodium 370 mg
- Total Carbohydrate 35 g
- Dietary Fiber 6 g
- Protein 31.9 g

Creamy Beef Pasta

Preparation Time: 10 minutes; Cooking Time: 1 hour and 10 minutes; Servings: 4

Ingredients:
- 1 lb. beef, sliced into thin strips
- 2 cups water
- 2 tablespoons reduced-sodium soy sauce
- 2 cups mushrooms
- 3 cups cream of mushroom soup
- 4 cups cooked whole-wheat pasta
- Herb sprigs

Method:
1. Boil the beef strips in a pot of water.
2. Pour in the soy sauce.
3. Bring to a boil and then simmer for 1 hour.
4. Stir in the mushrooms and mushroom soup.
5. Simmer for 10 minutes.
6. Serve over cooked pasta.
7. Garnish with herb sprigs.

Nutritional Value:
- Calories 221
- Total Fat 2 g
- Saturated Fat 0 g
- Cholesterol 14 mg
- Sodium 222 mg
- Total Carbohydrate 32 g
- Dietary Fiber 4 g
- Protein 24 g

Shawarma Rice

Preparation Time: 20 minutes; Cooking Time: 0 minutes; Servings: 4

Ingredients:
- 4 cups hot cooked brown rice
- 1 cup chopped tomato
- 1 cup chopped white onion
- 1 cup chopped cucumber
- 1 cup cooked beef strips
- Reduced-sodium garlic sauce
- Hot sauce

Method:
1. Add the rice to serving bowls.
2. Top with the beef and veggies.
3. Drizzle with the garlic sauce and hot sauce before serving.

Nutritional Value:
- Calories 332
- Total Fat 12 g
- Saturated Fat 2 g
- Cholesterol 18 mg
- Sodium 241 mg
- Total Carbohydrate 23 g
- Dietary Fiber 2 g
- Protein 20 g

Chapter 4: Fish and Seafood Recipes

Baked Tuna Steak with Mustard Sauce

Preparation Time: 15 minutes; Cooking Time: 15 minutes; Servings: 4
Ingredients:
- 1 teaspoon honey
- ¼ cup mayonnaise
- 2 teaspoons Dijon mustard
- ½ teaspoon ground turmeric
- 1 tablespoon fresh parsley, chopped
- 4 tuna steaks
- Salt and pepper to taste

Method:
1. Preheat your oven to 450 degrees F.
2. In a bowl, mix the honey, mayo, mustard, turmeric and parsley in a bowl.
3. Add the tuna on top of a foil sheet.
4. Spread the honey mixture on top.
5. Season with salt and pepper.
6. Fold the foil sheet and seal.
7. Place it in a baking pan.
8. Bake in the oven for 15 minutes.

Nutritional Value:
- Calories 312
- Total Fat 11.3 g
- Saturated Fat 1.9 g
- Cholesterol 61 mg
- Sodium 512 mg
- Total Carbohydrate 14 g
- Dietary Fiber 1.7 g
- Protein 36.4 g

Miso Glazed Salmon

Preparation Time: 15 minutes; Cooking Time: 15 minutes; Servings: 8
Ingredients:
- 2 tablespoons olive oil
- 2 tablespoons lemon juice
- ¼ cup white miso
- 2 tablespoons maple syrup
- Pinch cayenne pepper
- Pepper to taste
- 2 ½ lb. salmon fillet
- Chopped scallions

Method:
1. Preheat your broiler.
2. In a bowl, mix the olive oil, lemon juice, miso, maple syrup, cayenne, and pepper.
3. Add the fish in a baking pan.
4. Spread the miso sauce on top.
5. Broil the salmon for 15 minutes.
6. Garnish with scallions.

Nutritional Value:
- Calories 405
- Total Fat 17.4 g
- Saturated Fat 2.6 g
- Cholesterol 90 mg
- Sodium 517 mg
- Total Carbohydrate 25.9 g
- Dietary Fiber 3 g
- Protein 35.4 g

Mediterranean Cod

Preparation Time: 15 minutes; Cooking Time: 15 minutes; Servings: 4
Ingredients:
- 2 tablespoons olive oil, divided
- 1 onion, sliced
- 2 cloves garlic, minced
- 3 cups mushrooms
- 1 tomato, diced
- 1 teaspoon dried thyme

- 1 teaspoon dried basil
- 1 tablespoon lemon juice
- Salt and pepper to taste
- 4 cod fillets

Method:
1. Pour half of oil into a pan over medium heat.
2. Cook onion, garlic and mushrooms for 3 minutes.
3. Stir in the tomatoes and herbs.
4. Cook for another 3 minutes.
5. Pour in lemon juice and season with salt and pepper.
6. Transfer to a plate.
7. Season fish with salt and pepper.
8. Add the remaining oil to the pan.
9. Cook the fish for 3 minutes per side.
10. Pour the sauce on top of the fish and serve.

Nutritional Value:
- Calories 214
- Total Fat 11 g
- Saturated Fat 2 g
- Cholesterol 45 mg
- Sodium 598 mg
- Total Carbohydrate 11 g
- Dietary Fiber 3 g
- Protein 18 g

Baked Halibut

Preparation Time: 15 minutes; Cooking Time: 15 minutes; Servings: 4

Ingredients:
- 4 halibut fillets
- 1 tablespoon olive oil
- Salt and pepper to taste
- 2 tablespoons butter
- 2 tablespoons lemon juice
- 2 cloves garlic, minced
- ¼ cup sun-dried tomatoes, chopped
- ¼ cup Kalamata olives, chopped

Method:
1. Coat fish with oil.
2. Season with salt and pepper.
3. Transfer to a baking pan.
4. In a bowl, mix butter, lemon juice and garlic.
5. Brush mixture on top of fish.
6. Bake for 15 minutes.
7. Top with the tomatoes and olives before serving.

Nutritional Value:
- Calories 406
- Total Fat 17.1 g
- Saturated Fat 5.3 g
- Cholesterol 71 mg
- Sodium 560 mg
- Total Carbohydrate 36 g
- Dietary Fiber 7.9 g
- Protein 29.7 g

Turkish Tuna

Preparation Time: 15 minutes; Cooking Time: 12 minutes; Servings: 4

Ingredients:
- 2 tablespoons olive oil
- 4 tuna steaks
- Salt and pepper to taste
- 1 onion, sliced thinly
- ¼ cup fresh dill, chopped
- ¼ cup fresh mint, chopped
- 2 tablespoons parsley, chopped

Method:
1. Pour the oil into a pan over medium heat.
2. Season tuna with salt and pepper.

3. Cook tuna in the pan for 3 to 5 minutes per side.
4. Transfer to a plate.
5. Add onion and herbs to the pan.
6. Cook for 2 minutes.
7. Spread the onion mixture on top of the tuna and serve.

Nutritional Value:
- Calories 405
- Total Fat 16 g
- Saturated Fat 2.4 g
- Cholesterol 44 mg
- Sodium 557 mg
- Total Carbohydrate 43.2 g
- Dietary Fiber 8.2 g
- Protein 35.9 g

Seared Scallops with Lemon

Preparation Time: 15 minutes; Cooking Time: 20 minutes; Servings: 4

Ingredients:
- 2 teaspoons olive oil
- 2 cloves garlic, minced
- 1 lb. scallops, tough parts removed
- 1 tablespoon capers, rinsed, drained and chopped
- 1 cup reduced-sodium chicken broth
- ⅓ cup dry white wine
- 1 tablespoon butter
- Pepper to taste
- 1 tablespoon lemon juice
- Chopped parsley

Method:
1. Add oil to a pan over medium heat.
2. Cook garlic for 1 minute.
3. Add scallops and cook for 4 minutes, stirring.
4. Transfer to a plate.
5. Add the rest of the ingredients to the pan.
6. Bring to a boil and then simmer for 15 minutes.
7. Pour the sauce over the scallops and serve.

Nutritional Value:
- Calories 255
- Total Fat 8.3 g
- Saturated Fat 2.6 g
- Cholesterol 35 mg
- Sodium 590 mg
- Total Carbohydrate 21 g
- Dietary Fiber 5.3 g
- Protein 21.4 g

Greek Salmon

Preparation Time: 20 minutes; Cooking Time: 25 minutes; Servings: 4

Ingredients:
- 4 salmon fillets
- Salt and pepper to taste
- 8 oz. green beans, steamed
- 4 cups cooked quinoa
- 1 tomato, chopped
- ¼ cup olives, sliced
- ¼ cup feta cheese, crumbled
- 3 tablespoons lemon juice
- 2 tablespoons olive oil
- 1 clove garlic, minced
- 2 teaspoons fresh oregano, chopped

Method:
1. Preheat your oven to 400 degrees F.
2. Season fish with salt and pepper.
3. Place in a baking pan.
4. Bake for 25 minutes.
5. Let cool and then flake salmon.
6. Divide the quinoa in serving bowls.

7. Top with the salmon, tomatoes, olives and feta cheese.
8. In a smaller bowl, combine the rest of the ingredients.
9. Drizzle mixture into the bowl and serve.

Nutritional Value:
- Calories 484
- Total Fat 28 g
- Saturated Fat 6 g
- Cholesterol 69 mg
- Sodium 577 mg
- Total Carbohydrate 28 g
- Dietary Fiber 4 g
- Protein 30 g

Spicy Salmon

Preparation Time: 15 minutes; Cooking Time: 40 minutes; Servings: 4

Ingredients:
- 2 tablespoons olive oil, divided
- 1 yellow onion, diced
- 4 cloves garlic, chopped
- 2 tablespoons fresh dill, chopped
- 15 oz. canned tomatoes
- Salt to taste
- ¼ cup lemon juice
- 4 salmon fillets
- Chili powder

Method:
1. Preheat your oven to 425 degrees F.
2. Cover your baking pan with foil.
3. In a pan over medium heat, add half of oil.
4. Cook onion and garlic for 3 minutes.
5. Add dill and tomatoes.
6. Season with salt.
7. Bring to a boil and then simmer for 20 minutes.
8. In a bowl, mix remaining oil and lemon juice.
9. Coat the salmon with this mixture.
10. Sprinkle with chili powder.
11. Roast in the oven for 10 minutes.
12. Serve the salmon with the tomato mixture.

Nutritional Value:
- Calories 311
- Total Fat 15 g
- Saturated Fat 2 g
- Cholesterol 72 mg
- Sodium 397 mg
- Total Carbohydrate 16 g
- Dietary Fiber 5 g
- Protein 29 g

Garlic Salmon

Preparation Time: 10 minutes; Cooking Time: 15 minutes; Servings: 4

Ingredients:
- 2 tablespoons olive oil, divided
- 4 cloves garlic, minced
- ¼ cup Kalamata olives, pitted and sliced
- 2 cups cherry tomatoes, sliced in half
- 1 tablespoon thyme, chopped
- Salt and pepper to taste
- 4 salmon fillets

Method:
1. Preheat your oven to 400 degrees F.
2. In a bowl, combine half of oil, garlic, olives, tomatoes, thyme, salt and pepper.
3. Spread this on one side of a baking pan.
4. Place the salmon on the other side, sprinkling it with salt and pepper.
5. Bake for 15 minutes.

Nutritional Value:

- Calories 276
- Total Fat 15 g
- Saturated Fat 2.2 g
- Cholesterol 66 mg
- Sodium 545 mg
- Total Carbohydrate 4.9 g
- Dietary Fiber 1.1 g
- Protein 29.1 g

Roasted Salmon & Asparagus

Preparation Time: 15 minutes; Cooking Time: 15 minutes; Servings: 4
Ingredients:
- 1 lb. asparagus, trimmed
- 2 tablespoons olive oil, divided
- Salt and pepper to taste
- 4 salmon fillets
- 4 fresh dill sprigs
- 8 lemon slices

Method:
1. Preheat your oven to 425 degrees F.
2. Toss the asparagus in half of the oil.
3. Season with salt and pepper.
4. Brush the salmon with remaining oil and sprinkle with salt and pepper.
5. Place asparagus on one side of the pan and the salmon on the other.
6. Top the salmon with herb sprigs and lemon slices.
7. Roast for 15 minutes.

Nutritional Value:
- Calories 513
- Total Fat 33 g
- Saturated Fat 6 g
- Cholesterol 78 mg
- Sodium 708 mg
- Total Carbohydrate 22 g
- Dietary Fiber 4 g
- Protein 33 g

Baked Fish with Mushrooms

Preparation Time: 15 minutes; Cooking Time: 45 minutes; Servings: 4
Ingredients:
- 1 lb. mushrooms, sliced
- 1 lb. potatoes, sliced into cubes
- 2 tablespoons olive oil, divided
- Salt and pepper to taste
- 2 cloves garlic, sliced
- 4 cod fillet
- 4 tablespoons lemon juice
- 1 teaspoon herbes de Provence

Method:
1. Preheat your oven to 425 degrees F.
2. Coat the mushrooms and potatoes in half of the oil.
3. Transfer to a baking pan.
4. Roast for 30 minutes.
5. Mix the veggies.
6. Add the garlic and stir.
7. Put the fish on top.
8. Mix remaining oil and lemon juice.
9. Pour mixture on top of fish.
10. Season with herbs.
11. Bake for 15 minutes.

Nutritional Value:
- Calories 276
- Total Fat 8.8 g
- Saturated Fat 1.3 g
- Cholesterol 49 mg
- Sodium 219 mg
- Total Carbohydrate 25.3 g
- Dietary Fiber 2.8 g
- Protein 24.4 g

Baked Salmon with Ginger & Veggies

Preparation Time: 15 minutes; Cooking Time: 40 minutes; Servings: 4
Ingredients:
- 1 lb. mushrooms
- 1 sweet potato, sliced into cubes
- 2 tablespoons olive oil, divided
- Salt to taste
- 2 tablespoons low-sodium soy sauce
- 1 tablespoon honey
- 1 teaspoon ginger, grated
- 4 salmon fillets

Method:
1. Preheat your oven to 425 degrees F.
2. Toss the mushrooms and sweet potatoes in half of oil and salt.
3. Spread in a baking pan and roast in the oven for 20 minutes.
4. Mix the soy sauce, honey and ginger in a bowl.
5. Brush both sides of the fish with this mixture.
6. Move the roasted veggies on one side.
7. Place the salmon on the other.
8. Roast for another 20 minutes.

Nutritional Value:
- Calories 555
- Total Fat 29.9 g
- Saturated Fat 5.9 g
- Cholesterol 78 mg
- Sodium 718 mg
- Total Carbohydrate 37.3 g
- Dietary Fiber 7.6 g
- Protein 37.7 g

Swordfish With Tomatoes & Capers

Preparation Time: 10 minutes; Cooking Time: 25 minutes; Servings: 4
Ingredients:
- 4 swordfish steaks
- Salt and pepper to taste
- 1 tablespoon olive oil
- 2 cloves garlic, minced
- 15 oz. canned tomatoes
- ¼ cup green olives, sliced
- 3 tablespoons fresh basil, chopped
- 1 tablespoon capers, rinsed and drained
- Pinch red pepper flakes

Method:
1. Season fish steaks with salt and pepper.
2. Pour oil into a pan over medium heat.
3. Cook the fish for 3 to 4 minutes per side.
4. Transfer to a plate.
5. Add the rest of the ingredients to the pan.
6. Bring to a boil and then simmer for 10 minutes.
7. Pour sauce over the fish and serve.

Nutritional Value:
- Calories 276
- Total Fat 12.1 g
- Saturated Fat 2.3 g
- Cholesterol 65 mg
- Sodium 536 mg
- Total Carbohydrate 18.9 g
- Dietary Fiber 3 g
- Protein 22 g

Barbecue Shrimp

Preparation Time: 15 minutes; Cooking Time: 10 minutes; Servings: 4
Ingredients:
- ½ teaspoon garlic powder
- 1 teaspoon paprika
- ½ teaspoon dried oregano
- ⅛ teaspoon cayenne pepper

- Pepper to taste
- 1 lb. shrimp, peeled and deveined
- 1 tablespoon olive oil
- 2 tablespoons reduced-sodium barbecue sauce
- 3 scallions, chopped

Method:
1. Mix garlic powder, paprika, oregano, cayenne and pepper in a bowl.
2. Coat the shrimp in this mixture.
3. Pour the oil into a pan over medium heat.
4. Cook the shrimp for 3 to 4 minutes.
5. Stir in the barbecue sauce.
6. Garnish with scallions.

Nutritional Value:
- Calories 360
- Total Fat 8.9 g
- Saturated Fat 1.2 g
- Cholesterol 183 mg
- Sodium 554 mg
- Total Carbohydrate 40.6 g
- Dietary Fiber 9.5 g
- Protein 30.1 g

Moroccan Cod

Preparation Time: 15 minutes; Cooking Time: 30 minutes; Servings: 4

Ingredients:
- 4 cod fillets
- 2 tablespoons olive oil, divided
- 1 teaspoon ras el hanout spice mixture
- 2 tablespoons lemon juice
- 2 tablespoons cilantro, chopped
- 2 tablespoons parsley, chopped
- 3 cloves garlic, minced
- 1 teaspoon paprika
- Salt to taste

Method:
1. Preheat your oven to 425 degrees F.
2. Coat the cod fillet with half of oil.
3. Season with the spice mixture.
4. Transfer to a baking pan.
5. Roast for 20 minutes.
6. In a bowl, mix the remaining oil with the rest of the ingredients.
7. Pour mixture over the fish.
8. Roast for another 10 minutes.

Nutritional Value:
- Calories 284
- Total Fat 11.6 g
- Saturated Fat 1.7 g
- Cholesterol 45 mg
- Sodium 610 mg
- Total Carbohydrate 28 g
- Dietary Fiber 4.8 g
- Protein 19 g

Shrimp Boil

Preparation Time: 5 minutes; Cooking Time: 20 minutes; Servings: 4

Ingredients:
- Water
- 3 tablespoons lemon juice
- ¼ cup Old Bay seasoning
- 8 oz. baby potatoes
- 8 oz. shrimp
- 5 oz. chicken sausage, sliced
- 1 leek, sliced
- Melted butter

Method:
1. Fill a pot with water.
2. Add the lemon juice and seasoning.
3. Boil potatoes for 15 minutes.

4. Stir in the rest of the ingredients except the butter.
5. Boil for 5 minutes.
6. Top with the butter and serve.

Nutritional Value:
- Calories 202
- Total Fat 4.8 g
- Saturated Fat 1.3 g
- Cholesterol 109 mg
- Sodium 582 mg
- Total Carbohydrate 22.2 g
- Dietary Fiber 2.4 g
- Protein 19.3 g

Grilled Fish with Peppers

Preparation Time: 15 minutes; Cooking Time: 25 minutes; Servings: 4

Ingredients:
- 4 tablespoons olive oil, divided
- 1 onion, sliced thinly
- 3 cloves garlic, sliced thinly
- 8 cups red and yellow bell peppers, sliced
- 1 teaspoon paprika
- 1 teaspoon fresh oregano, chopped
- 1 teaspoon fresh thyme, chopped
- 2 tablespoons sherry vinegar
- 2 lb. swordfish fillet
- Salt to taste

Method:
1. Pour half of oil into a pan over medium heat.
2. Cook onion and garlic for 3 minutes.
3. Add bell peppers.
4. Season with herbs and spices.
5. Cook while stirring for 5 minutes.
6. Stir in vinegar and cook for 2 minutes.
7. Preheat your grill.
8. Season fish with salt.
9. Grill for 4 to 6 minutes per side.
10. Top with the bell peppers and serve.

Nutritional Value:
- Calories 396
- Total Fat 24.6 g
- Saturated Fat 4.4 g
- Cholesterol 97 mg
- Sodium 462 mg
- Total Carbohydrate 10.9 g
- Dietary Fiber 3.7 g
- Protein 31.2 g

Salmon with Pineapple Salsa

Preparation Time: 10 minutes; Cooking Time: 15 minutes; Servings: 4

Ingredients:
- 2 cups pineapple chunks
- 1 onion, chopped
- 1 red bell pepper, chopped
- 1 teaspoon lime zest
- 3 tablespoons lime juice, divided
- ½ teaspoon chili powder
- 2 tablespoons parsley, chopped
- 4 salmon fillets
- Salt and pepper to taste

Method:
1. Mix the pineapple, onion, bell pepper, half of lime juice, chili powder and parsley.
2. Brush both sides of fish remaining lime juice.
3. Season with salt and pepper.
4. Grill the fish for 6 minutes per side.
5. Top with salsa.

Nutritional Value:

- Calories 257
- Total Fat 12.4 g
- Saturated Fat 2.5 g
- Cholesterol 66 mg
- Sodium 219 mg
- Total Carbohydrate 13.2 g
- Dietary Fiber 1.9 g
- Protein 23.4 g

Fish with Tomato Relish

Preparation Time: 15 minutes; Cooking Time: 30 minutes; Servings: 6
Ingredients:
- 3 tablespoons olive oil, divided
- 1 shallot, minced
- 3 cloves garlic, minced
- 1 teaspoon capers
- 2 stalks celery, sliced
- 1 lb. tomatoes, chopped
- 2 tablespoons white wine
- 1 tablespoon garlic oil
- 1 ½ teaspoons red-wine vinegar
- ½ cup basil leaves
- 2 lb. bass fillet
- 1 tablespoon lemon juice
- Salt and pepper to taste

Method:
1. Add half of oil to a pan over medium heat.
2. Cook the shallot, garlic, capers and celery for 4 minutes, stirring.
3. Add tomatoes, wine, garlic oil and vinegar.
4. Bring to a boil.
5. Simmer for 15 minutes.
6. Drizzle fish with a mixture of lemon juice and remaining oil.
7. Season with salt and pepper.
8. Bake in the oven at 350 degrees F for 30 minutes.
9. Serve with the tomato relish.

Nutritional Value:
- Calories 276
- Total Fat 14.2 g
- Saturated Fat 2.3 g
- Cholesterol 121 mg
- Sodium 209 mg
- Total Carbohydrate 9.4 g
- Dietary Fiber 3.2 g
- Protein 28.6 g

Salmon Burgers

Preparation Time: 20 minutes; Cooking Time: 10 minutes; Servings: 4
Ingredients:
- 20 oz. canned salmon flakes
- ¼ cup panko breadcrumbs
- 2 eggs, beaten
- 2 tablespoons fresh parsley, chopped
- 1 teaspoon lemon zest
- Pepper to taste
- 1 tablespoon olive oil
- ¼ cup mayonnaise
- 4 whole-wheat burger buns

Method:
1. Combine all the ingredients except oil, mayo and buns.
2. Form patties from the mixture.
3. Pour oil into a pan over medium heat.
4. Cook the salmon burgers for 5 minutes per side.
5. Spread mayo on the buns and stuff with the salmon burgers.

Nutritional Value:
- Calories 527
- Total Fat 26 g
- Saturated Fat 5.2 g
- Cholesterol 169 mg
- Sodium 747 mg
- Total Carbohydrate 39.5 g
- Dietary Fiber 4 g
- Protein 33.6 g

Halibut with Eggplant

Preparation Time: 20 minutes; Cooking Time: 20 minutes; Servings: 4
Ingredients:
- 1 tablespoon olive oil
- 1 onion, sliced thinly
- 4 cloves garlic, minced
- 1 red bell pepper, sliced
- 1 eggplant, sliced
- 4 halibut steaks
- Salt and pepper to taste
- 1 teaspoon rosemary, chopped

Method:
1. Add olive oil to a pan over medium heat.
2. Cook the onion, garlic, red bell pepper and eggplant for 10 minutes.
3. Season with salt.
4. Transfer to a plate.
5. Season halibut with salt, pepper and rosemary.
6. Cook the fish for 5 minutes per side.
7. Top with the eggplant mixture and serve.

Nutritional Value:
- Calories 189
- Total Fat 5.2 g
- Saturated Fat 0.8 g
- Cholesterol 56 mg
- Sodium 396 mg
- Total Carbohydrate 12.7 g
- Dietary Fiber 3.8 g
- Protein 23.5 g

Baked Trout

Preparation Time: 20 minutes; Cooking Time: 24 minutes; Servings: 4
Ingredients:
- 4 trout fillets
- ½ teaspoon coriander seeds
- ½ teaspoon cumin seeds
- ½ teaspoon caraway seeds
- 4 teaspoons olive oil
- 1 teaspoon lemon zest
- 1 clove garlic, minced
- Salt and pepper to taste
- ¼ teaspoon ground cinnamon
- ¼ cup pistachios, finely chopped

Method:
1. Preheat your oven to 350 degrees F.
2. Pour oil into a pan over medium heat.
3. Cook seeds for 4 minutes.
4. Add to a spice grinder.
5. Grind the seeds.
6. Place in a bowl and stir in the rest of the ingredients except the fish.
7. Mix well.
8. Dredge the fish with the spice mixture.
9. Bake in the oven for 20 minutes.

Nutritional Value:
- Calories 227
- Total Fat 12.2 g
- Saturated Fat 1.9 g
- Cholesterol 67 mg
- Sodium 283 mg
- Total Carbohydrate 4 g
- Dietary Fiber 1.2 g
- Protein 25.1 g

Lemon Trout

Preparation Time: 20 minutes; Cooking Time: 25 minutes; Servings: 4
Ingredients:
- 4 trout fillets
- Salt and pepper to taste

- ⅓ cup nonfat milk
- ¼ cup whole-wheat flour
- 1 tablespoon olive oil
- 1 tablespoon shallot
- 2 tablespoons low-sodium chicken broth
- 1 tablespoon lemon juice
- 1 tablespoon butter
- 1 tablespoon fresh parsley, chopped

Method:
1. Season fish with salt and pepper.
2. Dip fish in milk.
3. Dredge with flour.
4. Pour oil into a pan over medium heat.
5. Cook fish for 4 to 5 minutes per side.
6. Transfer to a plate.
7. Add the rest of the ingredients to the pan.
8. Cook for 5 minutes, stirring.
9. Reduce heat and simmer for 10 minutes.
10. Pour sauce over the fish and serve.

Nutritional Value:
- Calories 240
- Total Fat 11.8 g
- Saturated Fat 2.9 g
- Cholesterol 71 mg
- Sodium 173 mg
- Total Carbohydrate 7.3 g
- Dietary Fiber 1 g
- Protein 25.5 g

Sesame Tuna

Preparation Time: 20 minutes; Cooking Time: 30 minutes; Servings: 4

Ingredients:
- 2 tablespoons vegetable oil
- 2 tablespoons sesame seeds
- 4 tuna fillets
- ¼ cup tahini
- 3 tablespoons rice vinegar
- 3 tablespoons low-sodium soy sauce
- 2 cloves garlic, minced
- 1 ½ teaspoons fresh ginger, grated
- 1 teaspoon toasted sesame oil

Method:
1. Preheat your oven to 375 degrees F.
2. Brush tuna fillet with oil.
3. Sprinkle both sides with sesame seeds.
4. Place in a baking pan and bake for 20 minutes.
5. Mix the rest of the ingredients in a bowl.
6. Pour into a pan over medium heat.
7. Heat through for 10 minutes.
8. Pour mixture over the fish and serve.

Nutritional Value:
- Calories 534
- Total Fat 19.2 g
- Saturated Fat 2.2 g
- Cholesterol 55 mg
- Sodium 632 mg
- Total Carbohydrate 42 g
- Dietary Fiber 6.5 g
- Protein 46.7 g

Roasted Tilapia

Preparation Time: 15 minutes; Cooking Time: 30 minutes; Servings: 4

Ingredients:
- 2 tablespoons olive oil, divided
- 4 tilapia fillets
- Salt and pepper to taste
- ¼ cup fresh parsley, chopped

- 1 shallot, minced
- 2 teaspoons lemon zest
- 1 ½ tablespoons lemon juice

Method:
1. Preheat your oven to 450 degrees F.
2. Brush fish with half of oil.
3. Season with salt and pepper.
4. Bake in the oven for 20 minutes.
5. Mix the remaining ingredients in a bowl.
6. Pour mixture on top of the fish.
7. Bake for another 10 minutes.

Nutritional Value:
- Calories 262
- Total Fat 15 g
- Saturated Fat 2.2 g
- Cholesterol 71 mg
- Sodium 295 mg
- Total Carbohydrate 3.3 g
- Dietary Fiber 1.2 g
- Protein 30.2 g

Salmon with Pumpkin Pie Spice

Preparation Time: 15 minutes; Cooking Time: 20 minutes; Servings: 4

Ingredients:
- 4 salmon fillets
- ¼ cup maple syrup
- Salt to taste
- ½ teaspoon pumpkin pie spice
- 3 tablespoons pumpkin seeds, chopped
- Cooking spray

Method:
1. Preheat your oven to 425 degrees F.
2. Brush the salmon fillets with maple syrup.
3. Season with salt and pumpkin pie spice.
4. Press pumpkin seeds onto the fish.
5. Spray with oil. Bake in the oven for 20 minutes.

Nutritional Value:
- Calories 359
- Total Fat 14.6 g
- Saturated Fat 2.3 g
- Cholesterol 62 mg
- Sodium 519 mg
- Total Carbohydrate 30.6 g
- Dietary Fiber 4.1 g
- Protein 27.9 g

Salmon with Yogurt

Preparation Time: 5 minutes; Cooking Time: 10 minutes; Servings: 4

Ingredients:
- 4 salmon fillets
- Salt and pepper to taste
- 1 teaspoon garlic powder
- 3 tablespoons olive oil
- 1 cup nonfat Greek yogurt (plain)
- Chopped parsley

Method:
1. Season salmon with salt and pepper.
2. Sprinkle with garlic powder.
3. Add olive oil to the pan over medium heat.
4. Cook salmon for 4 to 5 minutes per side.
5. Serve with yogurt and garnish with parsley.

Nutritional Value:
- Calories 243
- Total Fat 9.6 g
- Saturated Fat 2 g
- Cholesterol 79 mg

- Sodium 293 mg
- Total Carbohydrate 2 g
- Dietary Fiber 0.3 g
- Protein 35 g

Popcorn Shrimp

Preparation Time: 20 minutes; Cooking Time: 30 minutes; Servings: 4
Ingredients:
- Cooking spray
- 1 lb. shrimp, peeled and deveined
- ½ cup all-purpose flour
- 2 eggs, beaten
- 1 ½ cups breadcrumbs
- 1 tablespoon ground cumin
- 1 tablespoon garlic powder
- ½ cup ketchup

Method:
1. Coat the shrimp in flour.
2. Dip in egg and then dredge with breadcrumbs.
3. Sprinkle with cumin and garlic powder.
4. Bake in the oven at 375 degrees F until golden and crispy.
5. Serve with ketchup.

Nutritional Value:
- Calories 297
- Total Fat 3.8 g
- Saturated Fat 0.9 g
- Cholesterol 276 mg
- Sodium 291 mg
- Total Carbohydrate 35.4 g
- Dietary Fiber 1.4 g
- Protein 29.2 g

Cod with Caramelized Onions

Preparation Time: 15 minutes; Cooking Time: 10 minutes; Servings: 8
Ingredients:
- 3 tablespoons olive oil, divided
- 4 cups onions, sliced into rings
- 8 cod fillets
- Salt and pepper to taste
- Pinch garlic powder
- ¼ cup breadcrumbs

Method:
1. Pour 1 tablespoon oil into a pan over medium heat.
2. Cook onions until caramelized.
3. Season cod fillet with salt and pepper.
4. Sprinkle with garlic powder.
5. Dredge with breadcrumbs.
6. Cook in the remaining oil for 4 to 5 minutes per side.
7. Serve with caramelized onions.

Nutritional Value:
- Calories 201
- Total Fat 8.5 g
- Saturated Fat 0.9 g
- Cholesterol 49 mg
- Sodium 210 mg
- Total Carbohydrate 9.4 g
- Dietary Fiber 2 g
- Protein 22 g

Fish with Squash & Peppers

Preparation Time: 15 minutes; Cooking Time: 40 minutes; Servings: 4
Ingredients:
- 4 white fish fillet
- Salt to taste
- ¼ cup all-purpose flour
- 1 tablespoon olive oil
- 2 red bell peppers, sliced
- 1 zucchini, sliced
- 1 cup squash, sliced into cubes

Method:

1. Season fish fillet with salt.
2. Coat with flour.
3. Bake in the oven at 375 degrees F for 30 minutes.
4. Add olive oil to a pan over medium heat.
5. Cook the veggies for 5 minutes.
6. Season with salt.
7. Serve fish with squash mixture.

Nutritional Value:
- Calories 358
- Total Fat 18 g
- Saturated Fat 3 g
- Cholesterol 53 mg
- Sodium 481 mg
- Total Carbohydrate 26 g
- Dietary Fiber 4 g
- Protein 24 g

Fish Curry

Preparation Time: 15 minutes; Cooking Time: 15 minutes; Servings: 4

Ingredients:
- 4 tilapia fillets
- Salt and pepper to taste
- 1 tablespoon olive oil
- 2 cups tomatoes, sliced in half
- 2 cups pea pods
- 1 tablespoon cilantro, chopped
- 1 teaspoon curry powder
- ½ teaspoon garam masala

Method:
1. Preheat your oven to 450 degrees F.
2. Put the fish in a baking pan.
3. Bake for 8 minutes.
4. Pour olive oil into a pan over medium heat.
5. Add tomatoes and pea pods.
6. Add the fish to the pan.
7. Stir in the rest of the ingredients.
8. Reduce heat and simmer for 5 minutes.

Nutritional Value:
- Calories 283
- Total Fat 6.3 g
- Saturated Fat 1.6 g
- Cholesterol 71 mg
- Sodium 231 mg
- Total Carbohydrate 22 g
- Dietary Fiber 7.9 g
- Protein 36.6 g

Fish & Salsa Medley

Preparation Time: 45 minutes; Cooking Time: 15 minutes; Servings: 4

Ingredients:

Salsa
- 1 cup tomato, chopped
- ¼ cup avocado, chopped
- 2 tablespoons cilantro, chopped
- 1 clove garlic, minced
- 1 tablespoon lime juice
- Salt and pepper to taste

Fish
- 4 white fish fillets
- 2 tablespoons lime juice
- ½ teaspoon ground cumin
- Salt and pepper to taste

Method:
1. Combine salsa ingredients in a bowl. Set aside.
2. Brush fish with lime juice.
3. Season with ground cumin, salt and pepper.
4. Marinate for 30 minutes.

5. Grill for 6 minutes per side.
6. Serve fish with salsa.

Nutritional Value:
- Calories 190
- Total Fat 8 g
- Saturated Fat 2 g
- Cholesterol 43 mg
- Sodium 254 mg
- Total Carbohydrate 6 g
- Dietary Fiber 3 g
- Protein 24 g

Shrimp Kebab

Preparation Time: 30 minutes; Cooking Time: 6 minutes; Servings: 6

Ingredients:
- 1 ½ lb. shrimp, peeled and deveined
- ¼ cup olive oil
- ¼ cup lemon juice
- 2 teaspoons lemon zest
- 1 tablespoon fresh parsley, chopped
- 8 tomatoes, sliced
- 2 scallions, chopped

Method:
1. Mix the oil, lemon juice, lemon zest and parsley in a bowl.
2. Reserve half of mixture.
3. Coat the shrimp in the remaining mixture.
4. Marinate for 15 minutes.
5. Thread shrimp onto skewers.
6. Grill for 3 minutes per side.
7. Serve with the reserved sauce.
8. Garnish with scallions.

Nutritional Value:
- Calories 271
- Total Fat 12 g
- Saturated Fat 1.8 g
- Cholesterol 259 mg
- Sodium 255 mg
- Total Carbohydrate 4.2 g
- Dietary Fiber 0.7 g
- Protein 35 g

Salmon with Spring Veggies

Preparation Time: 15 minutes; Cooking Time: 45 minutes; Servings: 2

Ingredients:
- 4 salmon fillets
- 10 oz. asparagus
- 6 baby potatoes, sliced
- 1 teaspoon olive oil
- 2 tablespoons balsamic vinegar
- 1 teaspoon fresh dill, chopped
- Salt and pepper to taste

Method:
1. Place the salmon in a baking pan.
2. Arrange the veggies around the salmon.
3. Combine the remaining ingredients in a bowl.
4. Drizzle over fish and veggies.
5. Bake in the oven at 350 degrees F for 45 minutes.
6. Serve warm.

Nutritional Value:
- Calories 328
- Total Fat 14.8 g
- Saturated Fat 2.9 g
- Cholesterol 67 mg
- Sodium 365 mg
- Total Carbohydrate 23 g
- Dietary Fiber 4.1 g
- Protein 27.5 g

Fish with Blueberry Sauce

Preparation Time: 15 minutes; Cooking Time: 25 minutes; Servings: 4

Ingredients:

Sauce
- 1 teaspoon olive oil
- 1 onion, chopped
- 1 clove garlic, minced
- 2 tablespoons balsamic vinegar
- 2 cups blueberries
- 1 teaspoon ginger, grated
- 1 tablespoon brown sugar
- 1 teaspoon lemon zest

Fish
- Cooking spray
- 4 salmon fillets
- Salt and pepper to taste

Method:
1. Add the oil to a pan over medium heat.
2. Cook the onion and garlic for 3 minutes.
3. Stir in the rest of the sauce ingredients.
4. Simmer for 15 minutes.
5. Spray salmon with oil.
6. Season with salt and pepper.
7. Grill for 3 minutes per side.
8. Pour sauce over the salmon.

Nutritional Value:
- Calories 264
- Total Fat 13.5 g
- Saturated Fat 2.6 g
- Cholesterol 66 mg
- Sodium 143 mg
- Total Carbohydrate 11.5 g
- Dietary Fiber 1.5 g
- Protein 23.1 g

Basil Shrimp

Preparation Time: 15 minutes; Cooking Time: 10 minutes; Servings: 8

Ingredients:
- 16 large shrimp
- 4 cloves garlic, minced
- 1 tablespoon butter
- ¼ cup fresh basil, chopped
- 1 tablespoon balsamic vinegar
- Salt to taste

Method:
1. Preheat your broiler.
2. Arrange the shrimp in a baking pan.
3. Cook the garlic in butter and basil in a pan over medium heat.
4. Stir in vinegar and season with salt.
5. Pour the butter mixture on top of the shrimp.
6. Broil shrimp for 5 minutes.
7. Serve warm.

Nutritional Value:
- Calories 52
- Total Fat 2 g
- Saturated Fat 1 g
- Cholesterol 53 mg
- Sodium 95 mg
- Total Carbohydrate 1 g
- Dietary Fiber 3 g
- Protein 7 g

Tuscan Tuna

Preparation Time: 15 minutes; Cooking Time: 10 minutes; Servings: 4

Ingredients:

- 1 teaspoon olive oil
- 1 teaspoon white wine vinegar
- Salt and pepper to taste
- ½ teaspoon dried Italian seasoning
- 4 tuna steaks
- 1 cloves garlic, minced
- ¼ cup fresh basil, chopped
- 1 cup tomatoes, chopped
- 1 shallot, sliced
- Parmesan cheese, grated

Method:
1. Combine oil, vinegar, salt, pepper and seasoning.
2. Brush tuna with this mixture.
3. In another bowl, combine the rest of the ingredients except Parmesan cheese. Set aside.
4. Grill fish for 4 minutes per side.
5. Serve with tomato salad and sprinkle with Parmesan cheese.

Nutritional Value:
- Calories 255
- Total Fat 10.1 g
- Saturated Fat 2.3 g
- Cholesterol 55 mg
- Sodium 232 mg
- Total Carbohydrate 4.9 g
- Dietary Fiber 1.3 g
- Protein 34.8 g

Grilled Salmon with Herbs

Preparation Time: 10 minutes; Cooking Time: 10 minutes; Servings: 8
Ingredients:
- 2 lb. salmon fillets
- 1 tablespoon olive oil
- 1 tablespoon fresh parsley, chopped
- 1 teaspoon fresh sage
- Salt and pepper to taste

Method:
1. Brush salmon with olive oil.
2. Sprinkle both sides with herbs, salt and pepper.
3. Grill the salmon for 5 minutes per side.

Nutritional Value:
- Calories 256
- Total Fat 15 g
- Saturated Fat 3 g
- Cholesterol 68 mg
- Sodium 176 mg
- Total Carbohydrate 6 g
- Dietary Fiber 1 g
- Protein 23 g

Salmon with Sauteed Kale

Preparation Time: 20 minutes; Cooking Time: 20 minutes; Servings: 2
Ingredients:
- 2 salmon fillets
- Salt and pepper to taste
- ½ teaspoon dried thyme, crushed
- ¼ teaspoon garlic powder
- ½ teaspoon olive oil
- 1 clove garlic, minced
- 1 shallot, chopped
- 6 oz. kale
- ½ teaspoon lemon zest

Method:
1. Season both sides of salmon with salt, pepper, thyme and garlic powder.
2. Grill the fish for 4 to 6 minutes per side. Set aside.
3. Add olive oil to a pan over medium heat.
4. Cook the garlic, shallot, kale and lemon zest until kale has wilted.
5. Serve grilled fish with sautéed kale.

Nutritional Value:
- Calories 357
- Total Fat 21 g
- Saturated Fat 5 g
- Cholesterol 78 mg

- Sodium 340 mg
- Total Carbohydrate 11 g
- Dietary Fiber 2 g
- Protein 32 g

Lemon Shrimp

Preparation Time: 30 minutes; Cooking Time: 15 minutes; Servings: 4

Ingredients:
- 1 lb. shrimp, peeled and deveined
- Salt to taste
- 1 tablespoon lemon juice
- 1 teaspoon lemon zest
- 2 tablespoons olive oil
- 2 cloves garlic, minced

Method:
1. Season shrimp with salt.
2. Coat with lemon juice and lemon zest.
3. Marinate for 15 minutes.
4. Pour oil into a pan over medium heat.
5. Cook garlic until fragrant.
6. Stir in shrimp.
7. Cook for 5 minutes, stirring frequently.

Nutritional Value:
- Calories 290
- Total Fat 8.7 g
- Saturated Fat 1.1 g
- Cholesterol 183 mg
- Sodium 579 mg
- Total Carbohydrate 28.8 g
- Dietary Fiber 2.2 g
- Protein 27 g

Chapter 5: Soup Recipes

Sweet Potato Soup

Preparation Time: 15 minutes; Cooking Time: 25 minutes; Servings: 6

Ingredients:
- 2 tablespoons vegetable oil
- 1 ½ cups yellow onion, diced
- 1 tablespoon ginger, minced
- 1 tablespoon garlic, minced
- 1 lb. sweet potatoes, sliced into cubes
- 1 chili, minced
- 4 teaspoons red curry paste
- 3 cups water
- 1 cup coconut milk
- ¾ cup roasted peanuts
- 15 oz. white beans, rinsed and drained
- 2 tablespoons lime juice
- ¼ cup fresh cilantro, chopped
- Salt and pepper to taste

Method:
1. Pour oil into a pot over medium heat.
2. Cook onion for 4 minutes.
3. Stir in ginger, garlic, sweet potatoes, chili, curry paste and water.
4. Bring to a boil.
5. Simmer for 10 minutes.
6. Transfer to blender.
7. Pulse until smooth.
8. Transfer back to pot.
9. Stir in remaining ingredients.
10. Cook for 5 minutes and serve.

Nutritional Value:
- Calories 354
- Total Fat 19.4 g
- Saturated Fat 4.3 g
- Cholesterol 20 mg
- Sodium 594 mg
- Total Carbohydrate 37.4 g
- Dietary Fiber 8.4 g
- Protein 12.6 g

Turkey & Veggie Soup

Preparation Time: 15 minutes; Cooking Time: 30 minutes; Servings: 8

Ingredients:
- 3 tablespoons olive oil
- 2 cups celery, chopped
- 2 cups leeks, chopped
- 2 cups carrots, chopped
- Salt and pepper to taste
- 4 cups water
- 8 cups low-sodium chicken broth
- 2 oz. Parmesan rind
- 4 cups turkey breast fillet, cooked and shredded
- 4 cups whole-wheat pasta, cooked
- 3 tablespoons parsley, chopped
- 3 tablespoons lemon juice

Method:
1. Pour oil into a pot over medium high heat.
2. Cook celery, leeks and carrots for 8 minutes.
3. Pour in water and broth to the pot.
4. Add Parmesan rind.
5. Bring to a boil.
6. Reduce heat and simmer for 10 minutes.
7. Stir in the rest of the ingredients.
8. Cook for 5 minutes and serve.

Nutritional Value:
- Calories 289
- Total Fat 7 g

- Saturated Fat 1.2 g
- Cholesterol 50 mg
- Sodium 600 mg
- Total Carbohydrate 30.9 g
- Dietary Fiber 4.2 g
- Protein 26.9 g

Mushroom Soup

Preparation Time: 30 minutes; Cooking Time: 4 hours and 30 minutes; Servings: 8

Ingredients:
- 4 cups hot water
- 2 cups dried mushrooms
- 1 tablespoon mushrooms
- 1 tablespoon reduced-sodium soy sauce
- 1 tablespoon cornstarch
- 2 cups water
- Salt and pepper to taste
- 2 tablespoons olive oil
- 2 cups shallots, sliced
- 1 clove garlic, minced
- 1 cup sherry
- 3 lb. mushrooms, sliced
- 1 ½ tablespoons thyme, chopped
- ⅓ cup heavy cream

Method:
1. Soak in mushrooms in hot water for 20 minutes.
2. Drain and set aside.
3. Stir in soy sauce and cornstarch.
4. Add water, salt and pepper.
5. Pour oil into a pan over medium heat.
6. Cook garlic and shallots for 5 minutes.
7. Add sherry and boil for 30 seconds.
8. Transfer to a slow cooker.
9. Add the remaining ingredients.
10. Cook for 4 hours.
11. Transfer to a blender.
12. Blend until smooth.
13. Reheat before serving.

Nutritional Value:
- Calories 101
- Total Fat 5 g
- Saturated Fat 2 g
- Cholesterol 10 mg
- Sodium 173 mg
- Total Carbohydrate 11 g
- Dietary Fiber 2 g
- Protein 5 g

Creamy Tomato Soup

Preparation Time: 5 minutes; Cooking Time: 2 minutes; Serving: 1

Ingredients:
- 1 cup tomato puree
- ¼ cup reduced-sodium chicken broth
- 1 tablespoon low-fat cream cheese

Method:
1. Combine all ingredients in a heatproof bowl.
2. Mix well.
3. Microwave on high for 2 minutes.

Nutritional Value:
- Calories 105
- Total Fat 2.7 g
- Saturated Fat 1.4 g
- Cholesterol 8 mg
- Sodium 245 mg
- Total Carbohydrate 18.3 g
- Dietary Fiber 3.6 g
- Protein 5.1 g

Strawberry Soup with Thyme

Preparation Time: 4 hours and 10 minutes; Cooking Time: 0 minutes; Servings: 4

Ingredients:
- 3 cups fresh strawberries, sliced
- 1 cup nonfat buttermilk
- 2 teaspoons lemon zest
- 1 teaspoon lemon thyme
- 2 tablespoons honey

Method:
1. Mix the strawberries and milk in a blender.
2. Blend in a food processor until smooth.
3. Stir in the rest of the ingredients.
4. Chill for 4 hours.
5. Discard lemon zest and thyme before serving.

Nutritional Value:
- Calories 92
- Total Fat 0.9 g
- Saturated Fat 0.4 g
- Cholesterol 2 mg
- Sodium 66 mg
- Total Carbohydrate 20.1 g
- Dietary Fiber 2.3 g
- Protein 2.8 g

Nacho Soup

Preparation Time: 15 minutes; Cooking Time: 10 minutes; Servings: 2

Ingredients:
- 1 carton reduced-sodium black bean soup
- ¼ teaspoon smoked paprika
- ½ teaspoon lime juice
- 2 tablespoons Mexican cheese, crumbled
- ½ cup tomatoes, chopped
- ½ cup cabbage, shredded
- 2 oz. baked tortilla chips
- ½ medium avocado, sliced into cubes

Method:
1. Add the soup to a saucepan.
2. Season with paprika.
3. Heat for 5 minutes.
4. Pour in lime juice.
5. Heat for another 5 minutes.
6. Transfer the soup to serving bowls.
7. Top with the cheese, tomatoes, cabbage, tortilla chips, and avocado.

Nutritional Value:
- Calories 350
- Total Fat 16.9 g
- Saturated Fat 3.1 g
- Cholesterol 8 mg
- Sodium 291 mg
- Total Carbohydrate 44.1 g
- Dietary Fiber 9.4 g
- Protein 10.1 g

Onion & Mushroom Soup

Preparation Time: 15 minutes; Cooking Time: 40 minutes; Servings: 4

Ingredients:
- 1 tablespoon olive oil
- 4 cups onion, chopped
- 3 leeks, sliced
- 2 teaspoons brown sugar
- 3 cups mushrooms
- 1 cup carrot, chopped
- 14 oz. chicken broth
- 1 ½ cups water

Method:

1. Add olive oil to a pan over medium heat.
2. Cook onion and leeks for 1 minute.
3. Stir in mushrooms and carrot.
4. Cook for 8 to 10 minutes
5. Pour in water and broth.
6. Simmer for 30 minutes.

Nutritional Value:
- Calories 182
- Total Fat 2.7 g
- Saturated Fat 0.4 g
- Cholesterol 0 mg
- Sodium 211 mg
- Total Carbohydrate 13 g
- Dietary Fiber 4 g
- Protein 5 g

Cucumber Soup

Preparation Time: 15 minutes; Cooking Time: 0 minutes; Servings: 4

Ingredients:
- 2 cucumbers, chopped
- 1 cup shallot, chopped
- 2 cloves garlic, crushed
- 1 cup Greek yogurt
- 2 cups milk
- Red pepper flakes
- ¼ cup fresh cilantro leaves
- Pinch lemon-pepper seasoning

Method:
1. Mix all the ingredients in a blender.
2. Pulse until smooth.

Nutritional Value:
- Calories 270
- Total Fat 12.1 g
- Saturated Fat 2.4 g
- Cholesterol 100 mg
- Sodium 346 mg
- Total Carbohydrate 16.8 g
- Dietary Fiber 2.1 g
- Protein 24.6 g

Tomato Soup with Italian Bread

Preparation Time: 20 minutes; Cooking Time: 20 minutes; Servings: 6

Ingredients:
- 4 tablespoons olive oil, divided
- 3 lb. ripe tomatoes, chopped
- 1 cup onion, chopped
- 3 cloves garlic, minced
- ½ cup basil, chopped
- 4 cups reduced-sodium chicken stock
- 2 tablespoons lemon juice
- Salt and pepper to taste
- 4 cups stale Italian bread, sliced

Method:
1. Cook the tomatoes in oil in a pot over medium heat.
2. Transfer to a blender.
3. Pulse until smooth.
4. Put the pureed tomatoes back to the pot.
5. Stir in the rest of the ingredients except the bread.
6. Simmer for 15 minutes.
7. Add the bread before serving.

Nutritional Value:
- Calories 269
- Total Fat 11.3 g
- Saturated Fat 1.7 g
- Cholesterol 20 mg
- Sodium 234 mg
- Total Carbohydrate 36 g
- Dietary Fiber 4.8 g
- Protein 9.4 g

Potato Soup

Preparation Time: 20 minutes; Cooking Time: 20 minutes; Servings: 5

Ingredients:
- 1 tablespoon butter
- 2 slices bacon, chopped
- 1 onion, chopped
- 2 cups reduced-sodium chicken stock
- 2 potatoes, chopped
- ½ cup sour cream
- ½ cup cheddar cheese, shredded
- Salt and pepper to taste
- ¼ cup scallions, chopped

Method:
1. Add butter to a pan over medium heat.
2. Cook bacon for 5 minutes.
3. Drain on a plate lined with paper towel.
4. Cook onion in the bacon drippings for 2 minutes.
5. Transfer to a pressure cooker.
6. Pour in broth and potatoes.
7. Set to high and cook for 10 minutes.
8. Release pressure.
9. Puree contents of the pot in a blender.
10. Transfer to a pot.
11. Stir in the rest of the ingredients.
12. Sprinkle bacon bits on top and serve.

Nutritional Value:
- Calories 87
- Total Fat 4.1 g
- Saturated Fat 2.1 g
- Cholesterol 11 mg
- Sodium 146 mg
- Total Carbohydrate 10 g
- Dietary Fiber 0.8 g
- Protein 3.2 g

Barbecue Meatball Soup

Preparation Time: 30 minutes; Cooking Time: 30 minutes; Servings: 6

Ingredients:

Meatball
- 1 lb. lean ground beef
- ¾ cup breadcrumbs
- 3 cloves garlic, minced
- 1 egg, beaten
- ¼ teaspoon paprika
- Pepper to taste

Soup
- 1 tablespoon vegetable oil
- 1 onion, chopped
- 2 red sweet peppers, sliced into strips
- 2 stalks celery, sliced thinly
- 2 carrots, sliced thinly
- 3 cups water
- ½ cup low-sodium barbecue sauce
- 1 cup reduced-sodium beef broth
- ½ cup blue cheese, crumbled

Method:
1. Preheat your oven to 350 degrees F.
2. Combine meatball ingredients in a bowl.
3. Form meatballs from the mixture.
4. Bake in the oven for 15 minutes.
5. In a soup pot over medium heat, pour oil and cook the onion and veggies.
6. Pour in water, barbecue sauce and broth.
7. Bring to a boil.
8. Reduce heat and simmer for 5 minutes.

9. Add meatballs and cook for another 5 minutes.
10. Top with blue cheese and serve.

Nutritional Value:
- Calories 243
- Total Fat 11.2 g
- Saturated Fat 4.1 g
- Cholesterol 53 mg
- Sodium 540 mg
- Total Carbohydrate 13.6 g
- Dietary Fiber 3.2 g
- Protein 21 g

Squash Soup

Preparation Time: 10 minutes; Cooking Time: 10 minutes; Servings: 4

Ingredients:
- 2 tablespoons butter
- ½ cup onion, chopped
- 12 oz. squash, cubed, boiled and mashed
- 1 teaspoon brown sugar
- 12 oz. nonfat evaporated milk
- 14 oz. low-sodium chicken stock
- ½ teaspoon ground nutmeg
- Salt and pepper to taste

Method:
1. Add butter to a pot over medium heat.
2. Cook onion for 2 minutes.
3. Stir in the rest of the ingredients.
4. Simmer for 5 minutes.
5. Transfer to a blender.
6. Blend until smooth.
7. Reheat before serving.

Nutritional Value:
- Calories 185
- Total Fat 6.4 g
- Saturated Fat 4.2 g
- Cholesterol 15 mg
- Sodium 560 mg
- Total Carbohydrate 25.1 g
- Dietary Fiber 1.9 g
- Protein 8.4 g

Sweet Potato Soup

Preparation Time: 15 minutes; Cooking Time: 30 minutes; Servings: 6

Ingredients:
- 2 teaspoons olive oil
- 1 onion, chopped
- 1 clove garlic, crushed and minced
- 1 leek, chopped
- 28 oz. low-sodium chicken stock
- 1 lb. sweet potatoes, sliced
- ½ cup low-sodium chicken broth
- Salt and pepper to taste
- 1 bay leaf

Method:
1. In a pan over medium heat, pour oil and cook onion, garlic and leek.
2. Cook for 5 minutes.
3. Add the rest of the ingredients.
4. Bring to a boil.
5. Reduce heat and simmer for 20 minutes.
6. Discard bay leaf before serving.

Nutritional Value:
- Calories 142
- Total Fat 4.9 g
- Saturated Fat 0.4 g
- Cholesterol 24 mg
- Sodium 358 mg
- Total Carbohydrate 20 g
- Dietary Fiber 3.2 g
- Protein 3.9 g

Tofu & Veggie Soup

Preparation Time: 4 hours and 30 minutes; Cooking Time: 30 minutes; Servings: 4

Ingredients:
- 12 oz. tofu, sliced into cubes
- 2 tablespoons olive oil
- 1 teaspoon dried Italian seasoning
- Cooking spray
- 14 oz. canned diced tomatoes with herbs
- 2 cups low-sodium chicken broth
- ½ cup asparagus, sliced
- 8 oz. mushrooms, sliced
- ½ cup sweet pepper, roasted
- ¼ cup green olives, sliced
- ¼ cup dried tomatoes, chopped
- ½ cup peas

Method:
1. Coat tofu with oil and season with Italian seasoning.
2. Marinate for 4 hours.
3. Spray pot with oil.
4. Cook tofu until golden.
5. Pour in tomatoes and broth.
6. Bring to a boil.
7. Stir in the rest of the ingredients.
8. Reduce heat and simmer for 5 minutes.
9. Serve warm.

Nutritional Value:
- Calories 259
- Total Fat 14.9 g
- Saturated Fat 1.8 g
- Cholesterol 12 mg
- Sodium 574 mg
- Total Carbohydrate 19 g
- Dietary Fiber 9.8 g
- Protein 15.6 g

Beef & Root Veggie Soup

Preparation Time: 30 minutes; Cooking Time: 1 hour and 50 minutes; Servings: 6

Ingredients:
- 1 lb. beef round steak, sliced into cubes
- 2 tablespoons olive oil
- 1 onion, chopped
- 2 cloves garlic, minced
- 2 stalks celery, sliced
- 1 carrot, sliced
- 28 oz. beef broth
- 1 cup water
- 2 sprigs fresh thyme
- 2 turnips, cubed
- 2 potatoes, cubed
- 1 sweet potato, cubed
- 1 bay leaf

Method:
1. Cook the beef in oil in a pot over medium heat.
2. Transfer to a plate.
3. Cook the onion, garlic, celery and carrot for 3 minutes.
4. Put the beef back to the pot.
5. Bring to a boil and simmer for 1 hour and 15 minutes.
6. Add the rest of the ingredients.
7. Simmer for 30 minutes.
8. Discard bay leaf and herb sprigs before serving.

Nutritional Value:
- Calories 225
- Total Fat 5.1 g
- Saturated Fat 1.2 g
- Cholesterol 30 mg
- Sodium 551 mg
- Total Carbohydrate 25.4 g

- Dietary Fiber 3.7 g
- Protein 19.4 g

Carrot Soup

Preparation Time: 15 minutes; Cooking Time: 1 hour; Servings: 4

Ingredients:
- 1 tablespoon olive oil
- 1 onion, sliced
- 3 cloves garlic, peeled
- 1 ½ lb. carrots, sliced
- 1 cup reduced-sodium chicken broth
- 1 cup water
- 2 cups almond milk
- Salt and pepper to taste

Method:
1. Preheat your oven to 400 degrees F.
2. In a bowl, drizzle oil over onion, garlic and carrots.
3. Spread mixture in a baking pan.
4. Bake for 50 minutes.
5. Transfer to a blender.
6. Stir in the rest of the ingredients.
7. Pulse until smooth.
8. Heat through before serving.

Nutritional Value:
- Calories 138
- Total Fat 5.1 g
- Saturated Fat 0.6 g
- Cholesterol 20 mg
- Sodium 213 mg
- Total Carbohydrate 21 g
- Dietary Fiber 5.9 g
- Protein 3.1 g

Mexican Beef Soup

Preparation Time: 15 minutes; Cooking Time: 1 hour and 40 minutes; Servings: 6

Ingredients:
- 2 teaspoons olive oil
- 1 lb. beef chuck eye steak, sliced into cubes
- 1 onion, chopped
- Salt and pepper to taste
- ½ teaspoon ground cumin
- 1 teaspoon paprika
- 30 oz. canned diced tomatoes
- 14 oz. low-sodium beef stock
- 14 oz. black beans, rinsed and drained
- 1 red sweet pepper, sliced into strips
- ½ cup corn kernels

Method:
1. Add oil to a pan over medium heat.
2. Cook the beef until brown.
3. Stir in onion and season with salt, pepper, cumin and paprika.
4. Cook for 2 more minutes.
5. Pour in broth and tomatoes.
6. Bring to a boil.
7. Simmer for 1 hour and 30 minutes.
8. Shred the beef.
9. Put it back to the pot.
10. Add the rest of the ingredients.
11. Bring to a boil and then simmer for 5 minutes.

Nutritional Value:
- Calories 209
- Total Fat 6 g
- Saturated Fat 2 g
- Cholesterol 37 mg
- Sodium 411 mg
- Total Carbohydrate 23 g
- Dietary Fiber 7 g
- Protein 18 g

Beef & Veggie Soup

Preparation Time: 15 minutes; Cooking Time: 10 hours and 15 minutes; Servings: 4
Ingredients:
- 1 tablespoon oil
- 1 lb. beef chuck roast, sliced
- 28 oz. canned diced tomatoes
- 1 cup water
- 3 carrots, sliced
- 2 potatoes, sliced
- 1 onion, chopped
- Salt to taste

Method:
1. Pour oil into a pot over medium heat.
2. Cook beef until brown.
3. Transfer to a slow cooker.
4. Stir in the rest of the ingredients.
5. Cover the pot and cook on low for 10 hours.

Nutritional Value:
- Calories 314
- Total Fat 8.5 g
- Saturated Fat 2.2 g
- Cholesterol 50 mg
- Sodium 517 mg
- Total Carbohydrate 30.3 g
- Dietary Fiber 7.4 g
- Protein 29.8 g

Roasted Tomato Soup

Preparation Time: 15 minutes; Cooking Time: 30 minutes; Servings: 8
Ingredients:
- 1 tablespoon olive oil
- 1 onion, chopped
- 2 cloves garlic, minced
- 1 stalk celery, sliced
- 1 carrot, chopped
- 2 cups butternut squash, cubed
- 45 oz. low-sodium chicken stock
- 15 oz. roasted diced tomatoes
- Salt and pepper to taste

Method:
1. Add oil to a pot over medium heat.
2. Cook onion, garlic, celery and carrots for 5 minutes.
3. Add the rest of the ingredients.
4. Bring to a boil.
5. Reduce heat and simmer for 20 minutes.

Nutritional Value:
- Calories 92
- Total Fat 2 g
- Saturated Fat 0.3 g
- Cholesterol 10 mg
- Sodium 641 mg
- Total Carbohydrate 16.1 g
- Dietary Fiber 3.8 g
- Protein 5.7 g

Cauliflower Soup

Preparation Time: 10 minutes; Cooking Time: 20 minutes; Serving: 1
Ingredients:
- 2 cups cauliflower florets, cooked
- 1 cup reduced sodium chicken broth
- Salt and pepper to taste
- Pinch garlic powder
- Crispy bacon bits
- Chopped parsley
- Yogurt

Method:
1. Blend cauliflower, broth, salt, pepper and garlic powder in a food processor.
2. Transfer to a pot.

3. Bring to a boil.
4. Reduce heat and simmer for 20 minutes.
5. Top with bacon bits, parsley and yogurt before serving.

Nutritional Value:
- Calories 229
- Total Fat 10.3 g
- Saturated Fat 4.8 g
- Cholesterol 28 mg
- Sodium 348 mg
- Total Carbohydrate 15.4 g
- Dietary Fiber 5.9 g
- Protein 20.6 g

Spinach Soup

Preparation Time: 10 minutes; Cooking Time: 45 minutes; Servings: 6

Ingredients:
- 1 onion, chopped
- 2 cloves garlic, minced
- 15 oz. tomato puree
- 42 oz. vegetable broth
- 1 teaspoon dried basil
- Salt and pepper to taste
- 8 cup spinach leaves

Method:
1. Add all the ingredients except spinach in a pot over medium heat.
2. Stir and bring to a boil.
3. Reduce heat and simmer for 30 minutes.
4. Stir in spinach and simmer for 10 minutes.

Nutritional Value:
- Calories 148
- Total Fat 0.8 g
- Saturated Fat 0.3 g
- Cholesterol 1 mg
- Sodium 451 mg
- Total Carbohydrate 31.1 g
- Dietary Fiber 5 g
- Protein 7.9 g

Salmon Chowder

Preparation Time: 10 minutes; Cooking Time: 15 minutes; Servings: 4

Ingredients:
- 1 tablespoon olive oil
- ¼ cup carrot, chopped
- 2 cups cauliflower florets
- 1 cup salmon fillet, cooked and flaked
- 4 cups low-sodium chicken stock
- 2 tablespoons scallions, chopped
- 2 cups mashed potatoes
- 1 tablespoon mustard
- 2 teaspoons dried tarragon
- Salt and pepper to taste

Method:
1. Pour oil into a pan over medium heat.
2. Cook the celery and carrot for 3 minutes.
3. Add cauliflower, salmon, stock and scallions.
4. Simmer for 5 minutes.
5. Stir in the rest of the ingredients.
6. Simmer for another 5 minutes.

Nutritional Value:
- Calories 178
- Total Fat 5.6 g
- Saturated Fat 1 g
- Cholesterol 27 mg
- Sodium 237 mg
- Total Carbohydrate 16.9 g
- Dietary Fiber 2.3 g
- Protein 17.1 g

Curry Veggie Soup

Preparation Time: 5 minutes; Cooking Time: 10 minutes; Servings: 1

Ingredients:
- 2 cups reduced-sodium chicken stock
- ¼ cup carrot
- ½ cup red bell pepper, chopped
- ½ cup baby spinach
- 1 tablespoon curry paste
- ¼ cup cilantro, chopped

Method:
1. Add all ingredients to a pot over medium heat.
2. Bring to a boil and then simmer for 5 minutes.
3. Serve warm.

Nutritional Value:
- Calories 273
- Total Fat 4.2 g
- Saturated Fat 0.9 g
- Cholesterol 28 mg
- Sodium 465 mg
- Total Carbohydrate 44.9 g
- Dietary Fiber 5.9 g
- Protein 16.2 g

Chilled Melon Soup

Preparation Time: 2 hours and 15 minutes; Cooking Time: 0 minutes; Servings: 4

Ingredients:
- ½ cup cucumber, diced
- 6 cups melon, sliced into cubes
- 6 tablespoons lime juice
- 1 tablespoon scallions, chopped
- 1 cup cold water
- 1 orange zest strip
- ½ cup orange juice
- 1 teaspoon fresh ginger, chopped
- Salt to taste

Method:
1. Blend cucumber, melon and lime juice until smooth.
2. Add the rest of the ingredients.
3. Mix well.
4. Chill for 2 hours and then serve.

Nutritional Value:
- Calories 62
- Total Fat 0.3 g
- Saturated Fat 97 g
- Cholesterol 20 mg
- Sodium 97 mg
- Total Carbohydrate 15 g
- Dietary Fiber 4 g
- Protein 1.3 g

Carrot & Squash Soup

Preparation Time: 15 minutes; Cooking Time: 40 minutes; Servings: 2

Ingredients:
- 1 tablespoon butter
- 1 cup onion, sliced thinly
- 4 carrots, sliced thinly
- 3 cups squash, diced
- 28 oz. low-sodium chicken broth
- ¼ teaspoon ground white pepper
- ¼ teaspoon nutmeg
- ¼ cup light cream

Method:
1. In a pot over medium heat, melt butter and cook onion, carrots and squash.
2. Cook for 10 minutes, stirring.
3. Pour in broth.
4. Bring to a boil.
5. Reduce heat and simmer for 20 minutes.
6. Transfer contents of pot to a blender.
7. Pulse until smooth.
8. Put it back to the pot.
9. Add remaining ingredients.

10. Simmer for 10 minutes and serve.

Nutritional Value:
- Calories 82
- Total Fat 3.3 g
- Saturated Fat 2 g
- Cholesterol 9 mg
- Sodium 364 mg
- Total Carbohydrate 11.5 g
- Dietary Fiber 2.2 g
- Protein 3.1 g

Chilled Cucumber Soup with Lemon

Preparation Time: 15 minutes; Cooking Time: 0 minutes; Servings: 6

Ingredients:
- 4 cucumbers, sliced
- 2 scallions, chopped
- ½ cup fresh mint, chopped
- 2 teaspoons lemon zest
- ¼ cup lemon juice
- 2 cups water
- 1 teaspoon sugar
- Salt and pepper to taste

Method:
1. Add all ingredients to a blender.
2. Pulse until smooth.
3. Chill before serving.

Nutritional Value:
- Calories 38
- Total Fat 0.5 g
- Saturated Fat 0.1 g
- Cholesterol 22 mg
- Sodium 58 mg
- Total Carbohydrate 7.5 g
- Dietary Fiber 2.4 g
- Protein 1.8 g

Tomato & Zucchini Soup

Preparation Time: 50 minutes; Cooking Time: 0 minutes; Servings: 6

Ingredients:
- 1 onion, sliced
- 2 zucchini, sliced
- 3 red bell peppers, broiled
- 1 teaspoon olive oil
- 3 tomatoes, chopped
- 1 clove garlic, peeled
- ½ teaspoon dried oregano
- ¼ cup basil leaves, shredded
- Salt and pepper to taste
- 1 cup water
- 1 tablespoon red-wine vinegar

Method:
1. Add all ingredients to a blender.
2. Pulse until smooth.
3. Chill for 30 minutes before serving.

Nutritional Value:
- Calories 60
- Total Fat 1.3 g
- Saturated Fat 0.2 g
- Cholesterol 20 mg
- Sodium 59 mg
- Total Carbohydrate 11.7 g
- Dietary Fiber 3 g
- Protein 2.3 g

Ginger & Melon Soup

Preparation Time: 45 minutes; Cooking Time: 0 minutes; Servings: 6

Ingredients:
- 1 melon, cubed
- 4 tablespoons crystalized ginger
- 1 teaspoon orange zest
- 1 teaspoon honey
- 1 tablespoon lemon juice
- ¼ cup orange juice
- 1 cup nonfat yogurt

Method:
1. Put all ingredients except lemon juice, orange juice and yogurt in a blender. Pulse until smooth.
2. Stir in remaining ingredients.
3. Chill in the refrigerator for 30 minutes before serving.

Nutritional Value:
- Calories 115
- Total Fat 0.9 g
- Saturated Fat 0.5 g
- Cholesterol 2 mg
- Sodium 51 mg
- Total Carbohydrate 25 g
- Dietary Fiber 1.1 g
- Protein 3.4 g

Strawberry Soup with Rhubarb

Preparation Time: 45 minutes; Cooking Time: 30 minutes; Servings: 4

Ingredients:
- 4 cups rhubarb, sliced
- 3 cups water
- 1 ½ cups strawberries, sliced
- ¼ cup fresh basil leaves
- Salt and pepper to taste

Method:
1. Boil rhubarb in water. Simmer until soft.
2. Transfer to a bowl and refrigerate for 30 minutes.
3. Put the rhubarb in a blender.
4. Stir in the rest of the ingredients.
5. Blend until smooth.
6. Serve chilled.

Nutritional Value:
- Calories 95
- Total Fat 0.5 g
- Saturated Fat 0.1 g
- Cholesterol 20 mg
- Sodium 84 mg
- Total Carbohydrate 23.1 g
- Dietary Fiber 3.5 g
- Protein 1.6 g

Moroccan Chicken Soup

Preparation Time: 20 minutes; Cooking Time: 30 minutes; Servings: 8

Ingredients:
- 2 tablespoons olive oil
- 1 cup onion, chopped
- 2 cloves garlic, minced
- 1 teaspoon ground cumin
- 1 teaspoon ground cinnamon
- ¼ teaspoon cayenne pepper
- 8 cups reduced-sodium chicken broth
- 2 lb. chicken breasts, cooked and shredded
- 3 cups sweet potato, diced
- 2 cups red bell pepper, diced
- Salt and pepper to taste

Method:
1. Pour oil into a pot over medium heat.
2. Cook onion and garlic for 3 minutes.
3. Season with spices.
4. Pour in broth.
5. Bring to a boil.
6. Add chicken, sweet potatoes and red bell pepper.
7. Season with salt and pepper.
8. Simmer until sweet potatoes are tender.

Nutritional Value:
- Calories 281
- Total Fat 7.8 g

- Saturated Fat 1.5 g
- Cholesterol 45 mg
- Sodium 563 mg
- Total Carbohydrate 27.4 g
- Dietary Fiber 5.6 g
- Protein 26 g

Caribbean Pork Soup

Preparation Time: 20 minutes; Cooking Time: 35 minutes; Servings: 4

Ingredients:
- 12 oz. pork tenderloin, sliced into strips
- Salt and pepper to taste
- 2 teaspoons oil, divided
- 1 onion, chopped
- 3 cloves garlic, minced
- 1 bell pepper, chopped
- 2 tablespoons curry powder
- ¼ teaspoon ground cinnamon
- ½ teaspoon ground allspice
- 1 tablespoon fresh thyme, chopped
- 2 cups low-sodium chicken broth
- 1 lb. sweet potatoes, sliced into cubes
- ½ cup tomatoes, chopped
- 1 bay leaf

Method:
1. Sprinkle pork with salt and pepper.
2. Add half of oil to a soup pot.
3. Cook the pork for 6 minutes.
4. Transfer to a plate.
5. Reduce heat and add remaining oil.
6. Cook onion, garlic and bell pepper.
7. Season with herbs and spices.
8. Cook for 1 minute.
9. Add the rest of the ingredients.
10. Bring to a boil and then simmer for 20 minutes.
11. Add pork and discard bay leaf before serving.

Nutritional Value:
- Calories 248
- Total Fat 5 g
- Saturated Fat 1.1 g
- Cholesterol 47 mg
- Sodium 429 mg
- Total Carbohydrate 29.6 g
- Dietary Fiber 6.6 g
- Protein 21.8 g

Creamy Cod Chowder

Preparation Time: 20 minutes; Cooking Time: 40 minutes; Servings: 2

Ingredients:
- 1 slice bacon, diced and cooked crispy
- 1 teaspoon oil
- 1 onion, chopped
- 1 clove garlic, minced
- 1 stalk celery, chopped
- 2 cups potatoes, diced
- 8 oz. cod fillets, sliced into cubes
- 1 cup low-sodium chicken broth
- 1 teaspoon fresh thyme, chopped
- 1 bay leaf
- ¼ cup nonfat milk
- 1 tablespoon water mixed with 2 teaspoons cornstarch
- Pepper to taste

Method:
1. Add oil to a pot over medium heat.
2. Cook onion, garlic and celery for 3 minutes.
3. Stir in the rest of the ingredients except milk, cornstarch mixture and pepper.
4. Bring to a boil and then simmer for 30 minutes.
5. Add the remaining ingredients.
6. Simmer for 1 minute.

7. Sprinkle bacon bits on top.

Nutritional Value:
- Calories 306
- Total Fat 3.8 g
- Saturated Fat 1.6 g
- Cholesterol 67 mg
- Sodium 271 mg
- Total Carbohydrate 39.6 g
- Dietary Fiber 3.1 g
- Protein 29 g

Mexican Style Soup

Preparation Time: 20 minutes; Cooking Time: 1 hour; Servings: 8

Ingredients:
- 1 teaspoon oil
- 1 onion, chopped
- 2 cloves garlic, minced
- 8 oz. lean ground beef
- 3 carrots, sliced
- 8 cups chopped tomatoes
- ½ teaspoon ground cumin
- 1 teaspoon dried oregano
- 1 tablespoon chili powder
- Salt and pepper to taste
- Hot sauce

Method:
1. Add oil to a pot over medium heat.
2. Cook onion, garlic and beef for 3 minutes.
3. Stir in the rest of the ingredients except hot sauce.
4. Bring to a boil.
5. Simmer for 45 minutes.
6. Drizzle with hot sauce before serving.

Nutritional Value:
- Calories 181
- Total Fat 5.1 g
- Saturated Fat 1.3 g
- Cholesterol 18 mg
- Sodium 311 mg
- Total Carbohydrate 25.1 g
- Dietary Fiber 6.7 g
- Protein 11.6 g

Turkey Soup

Preparation Time: 15 minutes; Cooking Time: 15 minutes; Servings: 4

Ingredients:
- 1 tablespoon olive oil
- 1 shallot, chopped
- 2 cups mushrooms, sliced
- ¾ cup celery, chopped
- 1 cup carrots, chopped
- Salt and pepper to taste
- ¼ cup all-purpose flour
- 4 cups low-sodium chicken broth
- 3 cups turkey, cooked and shredded
- ½ cup nonfat sour cream
- Chopped parsley

Method:
1. Add oil to a pot over medium heat.
2. Cook shallots, mushrooms and celery for 5 minutes.
3. Stir in salt, pepper and flour.
4. Cook for another 2 minutes.
5. Pour in broth and bring to a boil.
6. Simmer for 5 minutes.
7. Add the rest of the ingredients.
8. Simmer for 2 minutes and serve.

Nutritional Value:
- Calories 378
- Total Fat 10.6 g
- Saturated Fat 3.7 g
- Cholesterol 80 mg

- Sodium 364 mg
- Total Carbohydrate 28.5 g
- Dietary Fiber 2.7 g
- Protein 36.9 g

Italian Egg-Drop Soup

Preparation Time: 15 minutes; Cooking Time: 15 minutes; Servings: 6

Ingredients:
- 2 cups water
- 6 cups low-sodium chicken broth
- 7 oz. canned chickpeas, rinsed and drained
- Pinch ground nutmeg
- Chopped scallions
- 3 cups arugula, chopped
- 4 eggs, beaten
- 2 tablespoons lemon juice
- Pepper to taste

Method:
1. Add water, broth, chickpeas, nutmeg and scallions in a pot over medium heat.
2. Bring to a boil.
3. Reduce heat and add arugula.
4. Cook for 1 minute.
5. Increase heat and bring to a boil.
6. Turn off heat.
7. Pour in the eggs.
8. Stir.
9. Season with pepper and serve.

Nutritional Value:
- Calories 221
- Total Fat 6.8 g
- Saturated Fat 2.3 g
- Cholesterol 128 mg
- Sodium 235 mg
- Total Carbohydrate 26.8 g
- Dietary Fiber 3.5 g
- Protein 15.9 g

Pesto Chicken Soup

Preparation Time: 20 minutes; Cooking Time: 20 minutes; Servings: 8

Ingredients:
- 2 tablespoons olive oil
- 1 onion, chopped
- 2 cloves garlic, minced
- 1 tablespoon marjoram, chopped
- 1 tablespoon oregano, chopped
- 2 lb. chicken breast, shredded and cooked
- 8 cups reduced-sodium chicken broth
- 2 cups tomatoes, chopped
- ¼ cup pesto
- Salt and pepper to taste

Method:
1. Pour oil into a pot over medium heat.
2. Cook onion and garlic for 3 minutes.
3. Season with herbs.
4. Add chicken and broth.
5. Bring to a boil.
6. Simmer for 10 minutes.
7. Stir in the rest of the ingredients.
8. Simmer for 5 minutes.

Nutritional Value:
- Calories 271
- Total Fat 10.9 g
- Saturated Fat 2.5 g
- Cholesterol 48 mg
- Sodium 806 mg
- Total Carbohydrate 17 g
- Dietary Fiber 4.4 g
- Protein 26.8 g

Seafood Gumbo

Preparation Time: 30 minutes; Cooking Time: 50 minutes; Servings: 8

Ingredients:
- 2 tablespoons oil
- 1 ¼ cups onions, chopped
- 1 clove garlic, minced
- 2 cups green bell peppers, chopped
- 1 cup celery, chopped
- 1 ¼ cups scallions
- 2 cups seafood broth
- 28 oz. canned diced tomatoes
- 2 bay leaves
- 1 tablespoon Worcestershire sauce
- 1 lb. fish fillet, sliced into strips and cooked
- 1 lb. shrimp, peeled, deveined and cooked
- ½ lb. crabmeat, cooked
- 1 teaspoon hot sauce
- Salt to taste

Method:
1. Add oil to a pot over medium heat.
2. Cook onion, garlic, bell pepper and celery for 3 minutes.
3. Stir in the rest of the ingredients.
4. Bring to a boil.
5. Reduce heat and simmer for 45 minutes.

Nutritional Value:
- Calories 243
- Total Fat 10.4 g
- Saturated Fat 1 g
- Cholesterol 104 mg
- Sodium 593 mg
- Total Carbohydrate 17 g
- Dietary Fiber 5.1 g
- Protein 22 g

Garlic Tofu Soup

Preparation Time: 10 minutes; Cooking Time: 30 minutes; Servings: 4

Ingredients:
- 12 oz. tofu, sliced into cubes
- 1 teaspoon garlic powder
- 2 tablespoons olive oil
- 2 cups low-sodium chicken broth
- 15 oz. canned diced tomatoes
- Salt and pepper to taste
- Chopped parsley

Method:
1. Coat the tofu cubes with garlic powder.
2. Cook in olive oil in a pan over medium heat until golden and crispy.
3. Transfer to a pot.
4. Add the broth, tomatoes, salt and pepper.
5. Bring to a boil.
6. Simmer for 20 minutes.
7. Garnish with parsley and serve.

Nutritional Value:
- Calories 259
- Total Fat 14.9 g
- Saturated Fat 1.8 g
- Cholesterol 20 mg
- Sodium 574 mg
- Total Carbohydrate 19.2 g
- Dietary Fiber 9.8 g
- Protein 15.6 g

Turkey Posole

Preparation Time: 20 minutes; Cooking Time: 30 minutes; Servings: 4

Ingredients:
- 2 teaspoons olive oil
- 1 onion, chopped

- 1 red sweet pepper, chopped
- 1 lb. ground turkey
- 1 teaspoon dried oregano, crushed
- 2 teaspoons cocoa powder
- 30 oz. canned diced tomatoes
- ¼ teaspoon ground cinnamon
- ½ teaspoon ground cumin
- Salt to taste
- 8 oz. tomato sauce (unsalted)
- 1 cup water or reduced-sodium chicken broth
- Chopped chives

Method:
1. Pour oil into a pot over medium heat.
2. Cook onion, pepper and turkey until brown.
3. Add the rest of the ingredients.
4. Stir well.
5. Bring to a boil.
6. Reduce heat and simmer for 20 minutes.

Nutritional Value:
- Calories 271
- Total Fat 4.2 g
- Saturated Fat 0.9 g
- Cholesterol 55 mg
- Sodium 590 mg
- Total Carbohydrate 30 g
- Dietary Fiber 9.1 g
- Protein 31 g

Squash Soup with Lentils

Preparation Time: 20 minutes; Cooking Time: 8 hours; Servings: 5

Ingredients:
- 1 onion, chopped
- 2 cloves garlic, minced
- 2 stalks celery, chopped
- 1 cup brown lentils, rinsed and drained
- 2 carrots, chopped
- 2 cups vegetable broth
- 1 lb. butternut squash, sliced into cubes
- 2 cups water
- 1 teaspoon garam masala

Method:
1. Add all ingredients to the slow cooker.
2. Mix well.
3. Cook on low for 8 hours.
4. Serve warm.

Nutritional Value:
- Calories 206
- Total Fat 0.6 g
- Saturated Fat 0.1 g
- Cholesterol 12 mg
- Sodium 510 mg
- Total Carbohydrate 40.3 g
- Dietary Fiber 15 g
- Protein 11.4 g

Chapter 6: Salad Recipes
Kale & Avocado Salad

Preparation Time: 15 minutes; Cooking Time: 0 minutes; Servings: 4
Ingredients:
Salad
- 6 cups kale, chopped
- 1 cup blueberries, sliced in half
- 1 avocado, sliced into cubes
- 1 cup cherry tomatoes, sliced in half
- ½ cup goat cheese, crumbled

Dressing
- ¼ cup olive oil
- 3 tablespoons lemon juice
- 1 teaspoon Dijon mustard
- 1 teaspoon honey
- 1 tablespoon chives, chopped
- Salt to taste

Method:
1. Toss the salad ingredients in a large bowl.
2. Add the dressing ingredients to a food processor.
3. Pulse until smooth.
4. Pour the dressing over the salad and serve.

Nutritional Value:
- Calories 368
- Total Fat 29 g
- Saturated Fat 5 g
- Cholesterol 10 mg
- Sodium 674 mg
- Total Carbohydrate 21 g
- Dietary Fiber 8 g
- Protein 10 g

Chicken Salad with Yogurt

Preparation Time: 20 minutes; Cooking Time: 6 minutes; Servings: 4
Ingredients:
- 2 tablespoons olive oil
- 1 lb. chicken breast fillet, skinned
- Salt and pepper to taste
- 2 cups broccoli florets, steamed
- 3 tablespoons white balsamic vinegar
- ½ cup yogurt
- 1 tablespoon water
- 2 tablespoons shallots, minced
- 1 cup celery, chopped
- 2 cups grapes, sliced in half
- Chopped scallions

Method:
1. Pour oil into a pan over medium heat.
2. Season chicken with salt and pepper.
3. Cook chicken for 3 minutes per side.
4. Place on a cutting board and chop.
5. Let cool and transfer to a serving bowl.
6. Stir in the rest of the ingredients.
7. Chill before serving.

Nutritional Value:
- Calories 408
- Total Fat 15 g
- Saturated Fat 3 g
- Cholesterol 87 mg
- Sodium 547 mg
- Total Carbohydrate 35 g
- Dietary Fiber 4 g
- Protein 33 g

Broccoli & Pasta Salad

Preparation Time: 15 minutes; Cooking Time: 0 minutes; Servings: 4
Ingredients:

- ¾ cup mayonnaise
- 1 teaspoon lemon juice
- 1 teaspoon lemon zest
- 1 teaspoon dried oregano
- Salt to taste
- 1 onion, chopped
- 4 cups cooked macaroni pasta
- ½ cup red bell pepper, chopped
- 6 cups broccoli florets, steamed
- 2 tablespoons parsley, chopped
- 2 tablespoons basil, chopped

Method:
1. Add the mayo, lemon juice, lemon zest, oregano and salt in a bowl. Mix well.
2. In a salad bowl, combine the rest of the ingredients.
3. Pour the dressing into the salad and mix before serving.

Nutritional Value:
- Calories 222
- Total Fat 13.7 g
- Saturated Fat 2.1 g
- Cholesterol 7 mg
- Sodium 250 mg
- Total Carbohydrate 21.9 g
- Dietary Fiber 3.6 g
- Protein 5.2 g

Cucumber & Tomato Salad

Preparation Time: 10 minutes; Cooking Time: 0 minutes; Servings: 5

Ingredients:
- 2 tablespoons olive oil
- 2 tablespoons red-wine vinegar
- Salt to taste
- 3 cups watercress
- 2 tomatoes, diced
- 1 cucumber, diced
- 2 tablespoons fresh mint leaves, chopped

Method:
1. Combine all the ingredients in a bowl and serve.

Nutritional Value:
- Calories 73
- Total Fat 5.8 g
- Saturated Fat 0.8 g
- Cholesterol 10 mg
- Sodium 133 mg
- Total Carbohydrate 4.2 g
- Dietary Fiber 1.3 g
- Protein 1.7 g

Citrus Salad

Preparation Time: 15 minutes; Cooking Time: 0 minutes; Servings: 4

Ingredients:
- 1 tablespoon white-wine vinegar
- 2 tablespoons grapeseed oil
- Salt and pepper to taste
- 1 tablespoon honey
- 2 cups arugula
- 3 oranges, sliced
- 1 grapefruit, sliced

Method:
1. Mix the vinegar, oil, salt, pepper and honey in a bowl. Mix well.
2. Arrange the arugula in a serving platter.
3. Top with the oranges and grapefruit.
4. Drizzle with the vinaigrette.

Nutritional Value:
- Calories 181
- Total Fat 8 g
- Saturated Fat 0.5 g
- Cholesterol 2 mg
- Sodium 127 mg
- Total Carbohydrate 20 g
- Dietary Fiber 4 g
- Protein 2.2 g

Spinach Salad with Sweet Potatoes

Preparation Time: 10 minutes; Cooking Time: 0 minutes; Servings: 4

Ingredients:

Dressing
- 5 tablespoons olive oil
- ½ cup basil leaves
- 1 tablespoon shallot, chopped
- 3 tablespoons cider vinegar
- 2 teaspoons whole-grain mustard
- Salt and pepper to taste

Salad
- 10 cups baby spinach
- 1 sweet potato, sliced into cubes and roasted
- 15 oz. cannellini beans, rinsed and drained
- 1 cup red bell pepper, chopped
- ¼ cup pecans, toasted and chopped

Method:
1. Add all the dressing ingredients to a glass jar with lid.
2. Shake to blend well.
3. Toss the salad ingredients in a bowl.
4. Pour the dressing into the salad and mix.

Nutritional Value:
- Calories 415
- Total Fat 23.6 g
- Saturated Fat 2.9 g
- Cholesterol 10 mg
- Sodium 564 mg
- Total Carbohydrate 44.3 g
- Dietary Fiber 14.7 g
- Protein 11.8 g

Shrimp Salad

Preparation Time: 15 minutes; Cooking Time: 0 minutes; Servings: 4

Ingredients:
- 4 cups lettuce
- 2 cups cucumber, sliced
- 2 tomatoes, sliced
- 1 ¼ lb. shrimp, peeled, deveined and steamed
- ¼ cup olive oil
- ¼ cup lemon juice
- 4 cloves garlic, minced
- 10 sprigs fresh thyme
- Salt and pepper to taste

Method:
1. Add the lettuce to a serving platter.
2. Top with the cucumber, tomatoes and shrimp.
3. Combine the remaining ingredients in a bowl. Mix well.
4. Serve salad with the dressing.

Nutritional Value:
- Calories 290
- Total Fat 15.1 g
- Saturated Fat 2.2 g
- Cholesterol 228 mg
- Sodium 322 mg
- Total Carbohydrate 10.2 g
- Dietary Fiber 2 g
- Protein 30.5 g

Vibrant Fruit Salad

Preparation Time: 20 minutes; Cooking Time: 0 minutes; Servings: 12

Ingredients:
- 2 cups grapes, sliced
- 2 cups peaches, sliced
- 2 cups melon, sliced
- 2 cups strawberries, sliced
- 3 tablespoons lime juice
- 3 teaspoons lime zest
- 1 tablespoon honey
- ¼ cup coconut flakes, toasted

Method:
1. Toss the fruits in a salad bowl.
2. Mix the lime juice, lime zest and honey.
3. Pour this into the salad.
4. Sprinkle coconut flakes on top.
5. Chill before serving.

Nutritional Value:
- Calories 65
- Total Fat 1.3 g
- Saturated Fat 1.1 g
- Cholesterol 2 mg
- Sodium 20 mg
- Total Carbohydrate 13 g
- Dietary Fiber 1.6 g
- Protein 1 g

Spinach & Strawberry Salad

Preparation Time: 15 minutes; Cooking Time: 0 minutes; Servings: 4

Ingredients:
- 1 tablespoon olive oil
- 1 tablespoon cider vinegar
- 2 tablespoons light mayonnaise
- 1 teaspoon sugar
- 1 teaspoon poppy seeds
- Salt and pepper to taste
- 5 oz. baby spinach
- 1 cup strawberries, sliced
- ¼ cup almonds, toasted and sliced

Method:
1. Mix the olive oil, vinegar, mayo, sugar and poppy seeds in a glass jar with lid.
2. Shake to blend well.
3. Toss the baby spinach and strawberries in a bowl.
4. Sprinkle almonds on top.
5. Drizzle with the dressing.

Nutritional Value:
- Calories 154
- Total Fat 13.3 g
- Saturated Fat 1.8 g
- Cholesterol 4 mg
- Sodium 228 mg
- Total Carbohydrate 7.1 g
- Dietary Fiber 2.6 g
- Protein 2.5 g

Strawberry, Avocado & Spinach Salad

Preparation Time: 10 minutes; Cooking Time: 0 minutes; Serving: 1

Ingredients:
- 3 cups baby spinach
- ¼ onion, chopped
- ½ cup strawberries, sliced
- ¼ medium avocado, diced
- 2 tablespoons walnut, toasted and chopped
- 2 tablespoons light vinaigrette

Method:
1. Combine all the ingredients in a bowl and serve.

Nutritional Value:
- Calories 296
- Total Fat 18 g
- Saturated Fat 2 g
- Cholesterol 0 mg
- Sodium 195 mg
- Total Carbohydrate 27 g
- Dietary Fiber 10.3 g
- Protein 8.2 g

Arugula Salad with Citrus

Preparation Time: 15 minutes; Cooking Time: 0 minutes; Servings: 4
Ingredients:

- 3 cups arugula
- 2 tangerines, sliced
- 1 orange, sliced
- 1 avocado, chopped
- 2 tablespoons lime juice
- 2 tablespoons olive oil
- 1 tablespoon tarragon, chopped
- Salt to taste

Method:
1. Arrange the arugula in a serving platter.
2. Top with the citrus fruits and avocado.
3. In a bowl, mix the rest of the ingredients.
4. Pour the dressing over the salad and serve.

Nutritional Value:
- Calories 183
- Total Fat 14.6 g
- Saturated Fat 2.1 g
- Cholesterol 0 mg
- Sodium 154 mg
- Total Carbohydrate 14 g
- Dietary Fiber 5 g
- Protein 2 g

Spinach & Apple Salad

Preparation Time: 10 minutes; Cooking Time: 0 minutes; Servings: 4

Ingredients:
- 4 cups baby spinach
- 1 apple, sliced thinly
- 1 cup chicken, cooked and shredded
- 2 tablespoons walnuts, toasted and chopped
- 4 tablespoons light vinaigrette

Method:
1. Arrange the spinach in a serving plate.
2. Top with the apple slices and chicken.
3. Sprinkle walnuts on top.
4. Drizzle with the vinaigrette.

Nutritional Value:
- Calories 49
- Total Fat 16.7 g
- Saturated Fat 3.6 g
- Cholesterol 50 mg
- Sodium 567 mg
- Total Carbohydrate 26.1 g
- Dietary Fiber 3.3 g
- Protein 23 g

Green Bean Salad

Preparation Time: 25 minutes; Cooking Time: 0 minutes; Servings: 4

Ingredients:
- 4 cups green beans, trimmed, sliced and steamed
- 4 tablespoons light mayo
- Parmesan cheese, grated
- Turkey bacon slices, cooked crisp and crumbled

Method:
1. Chill beans in the refrigerator for at least 15 minutes.
2. Stir mayo into the beans.
3. Sprinkle with the Parmesan cheese and crumbled bacon.

Nutritional Value:
- Calories 227
- Total Fat 14 g
- Saturated Fat 4 g
- Cholesterol 12 mg
- Sodium 128 mg
- Total Carbohydrate 20 g
- Dietary Fiber 4 g
- Protein 28 g

Garden Salad

Preparation Time: 15 minutes; Cooking Time: 0 minutes; Servings: 4

Ingredients:
- 4 cups Romaine lettuce
- 1 cup cucumber, sliced
- 1 cup tomato, sliced
- Parmesan cheese, grated
- Low-sodium ranch dressing

Method:
1. Toss the lettuce, cucumber and tomatoes in a bowl.
2. Sprinkle cheese on top.
3. Drizzle with the dressing.

Nutritional Value:
- Calories 228
- Total Fat 12 g
- Saturated Fat 1 g
- Cholesterol 0 mg
- Sodium 124 mg
- Total Carbohydrate 8 g
- Dietary Fiber 4 g
- Protein 10 g

Watermelon & Tomato Salad with Feta

Preparation Time: 15 minutes; Cooking Time: 0 minutes; Servings: 6

Ingredients:

Dressing
- 2 tablespoons olive oil
- 1 ½ tablespoons red-wine vinegar
- Salt and pepper to taste

Salad
- 3 cups Romaine lettuce, chopped
- 1 cup grape tomatoes, sliced in half
- 1 cup yellow bell pepper, chopped
- 1 cup watermelon, sliced into cubes
- 2 teaspoons fresh mint leaves, chopped
- 2 tablespoons fresh parsley, chopped
- 15 olives, sliced
- ½ cup feta cheese, crumbled

Method:
1. Whisk the dressing ingredients in a bowl.
2. Toss the salad ingredients in a larger bowl.
3. Pour in the dressing and toss to combine.

Nutritional Value:
- Calories 130
- Total Fat 10 g
- Saturated Fat 2.6 g
- Cholesterol 11 mg
- Sodium 368 mg
- Total Carbohydrate 7.6 g
- Dietary Fiber 1.8 g
- Protein 3 g

Grapefruit & Fennel Salad

Preparation Time: 10 minutes; Cooking Time: 0 minutes; Servings: 4

Ingredients:
- 1 tablespoon olive oil
- 1 teaspoon Dijon mustard
- 1 teaspoon honey
- Salt and pepper to taste
- 1 grapefruit, sliced
- 1 apple, sliced thinly
- 1 bulb fennel, sliced thinly
- 1 tablespoon sunflower seeds, toasted

Method:
1. Mix oil, mustard, honey, salt and pepper in a bowl.
2. Toss the rest of the ingredients in a salad bowl.
3. Pour in the dressing and serve.

Nutritional Value:
- Calories 130
- Total Fat 6.1 g
- Saturated Fat 0.5 g
- Cholesterol 10 mg
- Sodium 206 mg
- Total Carbohydrate 18 g

- Dietary Fiber 4 g
- Protein 1.8 g

Potato Salad with Cucumber

Preparation Time: 30 minutes; Cooking Time: 0 minutes; Servings: 8

Ingredients:
- 1 lb. potatoes, sliced into cubes and boiled
- 2 tablespoons white balsamic vinegar
- 6 oz. plain nonfat yogurt
- 1 tablespoon honey
- 1 tablespoon yellow mustard
- 1 onion, chopped
- 2 cups cucumber, chopped
- 1 tablespoon fresh dill, chopped
- Salt and pepper to taste

Method:
1. Combine all the ingredients in a bowl.
2. Chill for 15 minutes before serving.

Nutritional Value:
- Calories 107
- Total Fat 2 g
- Saturated Fat 0.8 g
- Cholesterol 48 mg
- Sodium 129 mg
- Total Carbohydrate 17 g
- Dietary Fiber 1.6 g
- Protein 5.3 g

Asparagus Salad

Preparation Time: 10 minutes; Cooking Time: 0 minutes; Servings: 2

Ingredients:
- 8 oz. asparagus, steamed and sliced
- 2 tablespoons orange juice
- 2 teaspoons olive oil
- ½ teaspoon Dijon mustard
- Salt and pepper to taste

Method:
1. Toss the asparagus in the mixture of the remaining ingredients.

Nutritional Value:
- Calories 74
- Total Fat 5 g
- Saturated Fat 1 g
- Cholesterol 0 mg
- Sodium 177 mg
- Total Carbohydrate 8 g
- Dietary Fiber 2 g
- Protein 2 g

Spinach & Peach Salad

Preparation Time: 15 minutes; Cooking Time: 0 minutes; Servings: 4

Ingredients:
- 6 cups baby spinach
- 1 peach, sliced thinly
- 3 tablespoons feta cheese, crumbled
- 1 tablespoon walnuts, toasted and chopped
- 1 tablespoon olive oil
- 2 tablespoons white-wine vinegar
- 2 teaspoons water
- 1 tablespoon shallot, chopped
- 1 teaspoon honey mustard
- Salt to taste

Method:
1. Arrange the spinach in a serving plate.
2. Top with the peach slices.
3. Sprinkle feta and walnuts on top.
4. In a glass jar with lid, combine the remaining ingredients.
5. Shake to blend.
6. Pour mixture over the salad and serve.

Nutritional Value:

- Calories 99
- Total Fat 5.8 g
- Saturated Fat 1.1 g
- Cholesterol 2 mg
- Sodium 234 mg
- Total Carbohydrate 7.8 g
- Dietary Fiber 2.7 g
- Protein 4 g

Corn & Raspberry Salad

Preparation Time: 10 minutes; Cooking Time: 0 minutes; Servings: 6
Ingredients:
- 3 tablespoons lime juice
- 1 tablespoon olive oil
- Salt and pepper to taste
- 3 cups corn kernels
- ¼ cup scallions, chopped
- 2 cups raspberries, sliced

Method:
1. Toss all the ingredients in a bowl and serve.

Nutritional Value:
- Calories 116
- Total Fat 6.5 g
- Saturated Fat 0.9 g
- Cholesterol 0 mg
- Sodium 205 mg
- Total Carbohydrate 15 g
- Dietary Fiber 4.6 g
- Protein 2.4 g

Chapter 7: Vegetarian Recipes

Basil Pesto

Preparation Time: 15 minutes; Cooking Time: 0 minutes; Servings: 4
Ingredients:
- 2 cups fresh basil leaves
- ¼ cup Parmesan cheese, grated
- ¼ cup toasted walnuts, chopped
- 1 clove garlic, minced
- Salt and pepper to taste
- ¼ cup olive oil
- 4 cups zucchini noodles

Method:
1. Add all ingredients except zucchini noodles to a food processor.
2. Blend until fully combined.
3. Toss the zucchini noodles in the sauce
4. Serve immediately.

Nutritional Value:
- Calories 234
- Total Fat 29 g
- Saturated Fat 4 g
- Cholesterol 4 mg
- Sodium 411 mg
- Total Carbohydrate 37 g
- Dietary Fiber 8 g
- Protein 12 g

Kale & Avocado with Blueberries

Preparation Time: 15 minutes; Cooking Time: 0 minutes; Servings: 4
Ingredients:
- 1 avocado, sliced into cubes
- 6 cups kale, chopped
- 1 cup blueberries, sliced in half
- 2 oz. crumbled goat cheese
- ¼ cup almonds, toasted and chopped
- Salt to taste

Method:
1. Combine avocado, kale and blueberries in a bowl.
2. Sprinkle goat cheese and almonds on top.
3. Season with salt.

Nutritional Value:
- Calories 168
- Total Fat 19 g
- Saturated Fat 3 g
- Cholesterol 2 mg
- Sodium 456 mg
- Total Carbohydrate 12 g
- Dietary Fiber 8 g
- Protein 10 g

Potato with Green Beans

Preparation Time: 30 minutes; Cooking Time: 0 minutes; Servings: 6
Ingredients:
- 8 oz. baby potatoes, boiled
- 12 oz. green beans, trimmed and steamed
- ¼ cup onion, chopped
- ¼ cup fresh dill, chopped
- 2 tablespoons olive oil
- 2 tablespoons white-wine vinegar
- 2 teaspoons Dijon mustard
- Salt and pepper to taste

Method:
1. Toss the potatoes, green beans and onion in a bowl.
2. Sprinkle dill on top.
3. Combine the rest of the ingredients.
4. Drizzle olive oil mixture over the potato mixture.
5. Mix and serve.

Nutritional Value:
- Calories 126
- Total Fat 7 g
- Saturated Fat 1 g
- Cholesterol 93 mg
- Sodium 160 mg
- Total Carbohydrate 11 g
- Dietary Fiber 2 g
- Protein 5 g

Green Beans with Crispy Garlic

Preparation Time: 15 minutes; Cooking Time: 15 minutes; Servings: 6
Ingredients:
- 3 tablespoons olive oil, divided
- 4 cloves garlic, sliced thinly
- 1 lb. green beans, trimmed and sliced
- ½ cup water
- Salt to taste
- 1 tablespoon capers, rinsed, drained and chopped
- 1 cup cherry tomatoes, sliced in half
- Chopped parsley

Method:
1. Add half of oil to a pan over medium heat.
2. Cook garlic until golden.
3. Transfer to a plate.
4. Add beans, water and salt to the pan.
5. Simmer for 8 minutes.
6. Stir in the remaining oil, capers and tomatoes.
7. Cook for 2 minutes.
8. Garnish with parsley and crispy garlic.

Nutritional Value:
- Calories 92
- Total Fat 7 g
- Saturated Fat 1 g
- Cholesterol 0 mg
- Sodium 120 mg
- Total Carbohydrate 7 g
- Dietary Fiber 3 g
- Protein 2 g

Balsamic Mushrooms

Preparation Time: 10 minutes; Cooking Time: 10 minutes; Servings: 4
Ingredients:
- 2 tablespoons olive oil
- Salt and pepper to taste
- 1 teaspoon dried marjoram
- 1 lb. mushrooms
- 2 tablespoons balsamic vinegar
- ¼ cup Parmesan cheese, grated

Method:
1. Preheat your oven to 450 degrees F.
2. Combine oil, salt, pepper and marjoram in a bowl.
3. Toss mushrooms in this mixture.
4. Spread on a baking pan and roast for 10 to 12 minutes.
5. Drizzle with balsamic vinegar and sprinkle with Parmesan cheese.

Nutritional Value:
- Calories 114
- Total Fat 8.5 g
- Saturated Fat 1.9 g
- Cholesterol 4 mg
- Sodium 238 mg
- Total Carbohydrate 5.5 g
- Dietary Fiber 1.3 g
- Protein 5.5 g

Veggie Wraps

Preparation Time: 30 minutes; Cooking Time: 0 minutes; Servings: 4
Ingredients:

- 4 whole-wheat tortillas
- 8 lettuce leaves
- 14 oz. tofu, sliced into planks and baked until golden
- 6 radishes, sliced thinly
- 1 cup carrot, shredded
- 2 tablespoons scallions, chopped
- ¼ cup orange juice
- ¼ cup tahini
- 1 tablespoon reduced-sodium soy sauce
- 1 tablespoon lime juice
- 1 clove garlic, minced
- 1 tablespoon fresh ginger, minced
- Salt to taste

Method:
1. Top the tortillas with lettuce, tofu, radish, carrot and scallions.
2. In a bowl, mix the rest of the ingredients.
3. Drizzle mixture over the veggies.
4. Roll up the tortillas and serve.

Nutritional Value:
- Calories 385
- Total Fat 20 g
- Saturated Fat 3 g
- Cholesterol 272 mg
- Sodium 660 mg
- Total Carbohydrate 37 g
- Dietary Fiber 5 g
- Protein 18 g

Eggs with Corn & Black Beans

Preparation Time: 15 minutes; Cooking Time: 7 minutes; Servings: 4

Ingredients:
- 2 tablespoons olive oil
- 1 onion, diced
- 4 cloves garlic, chopped
- 1 red bell pepper, diced
- ½ cup corn kernels
- 1 teaspoon dried oregano
- 1 teaspoon ground cumin
- 1 teaspoon red-wine vinegar
- 15 oz. black beans, rinsed and drained
- Salt to taste
- 4 eggs, poached
- 2 tablespoons feta cheese, crumbled
- ¼ cup cilantro, chopped

Method:
1. Pour oil into a pan over medium heat.
2. Cook onion, garlic, red bell pepper and corn kernels for 5 minutes.
3. Season with oregano and cumin.
4. Stir in vinegar, beans and salt.
5. Cook for 2 minutes
6. Serve the bean and corn mixture with eggs.
7. Sprinkle cheese and cilantro on top.

Nutritional Value:
- Calories 284
- Total Fat 14 g
- Saturated Fat 3 g
- Cholesterol 189 mg
- Sodium 569 mg
- Total Carbohydrate 26 g
- Dietary Fiber 7 g
- Protein 14 g

Tofu & Veggie Wrap

Preparation Time: 15 minutes; Cooking Time: 15 minutes; Servings: 4

Ingredients:
- 14 oz. tofu, sliced into strips
- Garlic powder to taste
- 4 tablespoons olive oil
- 4 spinach tortillas
- 4 cups lettuce, shredded
- 1 cup carrots, sliced into sticks
- 1 cup cucumber, sliced into sticks
- 1 yellow onion, sliced thinly

- Yogurt

Method:
1. Marinate tofu in garlic powder for 15 minutes.
2. Pour oil into a pan over medium heat.
3. Cook tofu until golden and crispy.
4. Arrange lettuce, tofu strips, carrots, cucumber and onion on top of the spinach tortillas.
5. Drizzle with yogurt.
6. Roll up the spinach tortillas and serve.

Nutritional Value:
- Calories 302
- Total Fat 10 g
- Saturated Fat 2 g
- Cholesterol 0 mg
- Sodium 450 mg
- Total Carbohydrate 28 g
- Dietary Fiber 5 g
- Protein 17 g

Potato Curry

Preparation Time: 15 minutes; Cooking Time: 20 minutes; Servings: 4

Ingredients:
- 3 tablespoons vegetable oil
- 1 onion, diced
- 3 cloves garlic, minced
- 1 lb. potatoes, sliced into cubes and steamed
- Salt to taste
- 2 teaspoons curry powder
- 14 oz. canned diced tomatoes
- 1 cup water
- ½ teaspoon garam masala

Method:
1. Pour oil into a pot over medium heat.
2. Cook onion, garlic and potatoes for 5 minutes.
3. Sprinkle with salt and curry powder.
4. Cook for 1 minute.
5. Pour in tomatoes and water.
6. Season with garam masala.
7. Simmer for 10 minutes.

Nutritional Value:
- Calories 321
- Total Fat 11.6 g
- Saturated Fat 1.1 g
- Cholesterol 0 mg
- Sodium 533 mg
- Total Carbohydrate 46.5 g
- Dietary Fiber 8 g
- Protein 9 g

Mashed Parsnip

Preparation Time: 15 minutes; Cooking Time: 30 minutes; Servings: 6

Ingredients:
- Water
- 2 lb. parsnips, sliced into cubes
- ½ cup almond milk
- ½ cup butter
- Salt to taste

Method:
1. Fill your pot with water.
2. Boil parsnips for 30 minutes or until tender.
3. Let cool.
4. Transfer to a food processor.
5. Pulse until smooth.
6. Stir in the rest of the ingredients.

Nutritional Value:

- Calories 168
- Total Fat 9.5 g
- Saturated Fat 4 g
- Cholesterol 20 mg
- Sodium 325 mg
- Total Carbohydrate 20 g
- Dietary Fiber 5.6 g
- Protein 1.5 g

Mashed Cauliflower & Potatoes

Preparation Time: 10 minutes; Cooking Time: 30 minutes; Servings: 6

Ingredients:
- 1 lb. potatoes, sliced into cubes
- Water
- 1 lb. cauliflower florets, steamed
- 2 tablespoons butter
- 3 tablespoons sour cream
- Salt and pepper to taste
- Chopped chives

Method:
1. Fill a pot with water.
2. Boil the potatoes until tender.
3. Drain and transfer to a food processor.
4. Add the cauliflower, butter, sour cream, salt and pepper.
5. Process until pureed.
6. Sprinkle with chives.

Nutritional Value:
- Calories 126
- Total Fat 5.2 g
- Saturated Fat 3.1 g
- Cholesterol 14 mg
- Sodium 354 mg
- Total Carbohydrate 15 g
- Dietary Fiber 2 g
- Protein 3.2 g

Salsa Stuffed Potatoes

Preparation Time: 15 minutes; Cooking Time: 1 hour; Servings: 4

Ingredients:
- 4 large potatoes
- ½ cup salsa
- 15 oz. pinto beans, cooked
- ½ cup avocado, chopped

Method:
1. Poke the potatoes with a fork.
2. Bake in the oven at 425 degrees F for 1 hour.
3. Let cool.
4. On a cutting board, slice the potatoes in the middle but not all the way through.
5. Stuff the potatoes with the salsa, beans and avocado.

Nutritional Value:
- Calories 324
- Total Fat 8 g
- Saturated Fat 1.2 g
- Cholesterol 0 mg
- Sodium 422 mg
- Total Carbohydrate 56.7 g
- Dietary Fiber 11 g
- Protein 9 g

Veggie Stew

Preparation Time: 20 minutes; Cooking Time: 8 hours; Servings: 6

Ingredients:
- 2 cups vegetable broth
- 1 onion, chopped
- 15 oz. cannellini beans, rinsed and drained
- 42 oz. canned tomatoes
- 12 oz. baby potatoes, sliced
- 2 teaspoons dried oregano
- Salt and pepper to taste

Method:

1. Combine all ingredients in a slow cooker.
2. Cover the pot.
3. Cook on low for 8 hours.
4. Serve warm.

Nutritional Value:
- Calories 407
- Total Fat 10 g
- Saturated Fat 1.6 g
- Cholesterol 0 mg
- Sodium 829 mg
- Total Carbohydrate 62.8 g
- Dietary Fiber 12.4 g
- Protein 15 g

Grilled Tomatoes & Eggplant

Preparation Time: 15 minutes; Cooking Time: 10 minutes; Servings: 4

Ingredients:
- 4 eggplants, sliced in half
- 4 tablespoons olive oil
- Salt to taste
- 1 lb. tomatoes, chopped
- 2 teaspoons fresh oregano, chopped
- 1 clove garlic, grated
- Pepper to taste
- ½ cup fresh basil, chopped
- Crumbled cheese

Method:
1. Coat eggplant with oil.
2. Season with salt.
3. Mix the rest of the ingredients except cheese in a bowl.
4. Grill the eggplant for 3 minutes per side.
5. Spread the tomato mixture on top.
6. Sprinkle with cheese and serve.

Nutritional Value:
- Calories 354
- Total Fat 20.6 g
- Saturated Fat 5.4 g
- Cholesterol 16 mg
- Sodium 404 mg
- Total Carbohydrate 39 g
- Dietary Fiber 8.4 g
- Protein 6.8 g

Vegetable Lasagna

Preparation Time: 30 minutes; Cooking Time: 40 minutes; Servings: 4

Ingredients:
- 1 tablespoon olive oil
- 1 onion, chopped
- 3 cloves garlic, sliced
- 8 oz. mushrooms, sliced
- Salt and pepper to taste
- 14 oz. canned diced tomatoes
- 8 cups baby spinach
- 8 oz. lasagna noodles, cooked according to package directions
- ¾ cup ricotta cheese

Method:
1. Add oil to a pan over medium heat.
2. Cook onion, garlic and mushrooms for 4 minutes.
3. Season with salt and pepper.
4. Pour in canned tomatoes.
5. Simmer for 20 minutes.
6. Stir in spinach and cook for 1 minute.
7. Arrange lasagna noodles in a baking pan.
8. Top with the mushroom mixture and cheese.
9. Repeat layers until ingredients are used.
10. Bake in the oven at 350 degrees F for 15 minutes.

Nutritional Value:
- Calories 338
- Total Fat 8.6 g
- Saturated Fat 3 g
- Cholesterol 14 mg
- Sodium 493 mg
- Total Carbohydrate 53 g
- Dietary Fiber 8 g
- Protein 17 g

Zucchini Lasagna

Preparation Time: 30 minutes; Cooking Time: 30 minutes; Servings: 4

Ingredients:
- 1 tablespoon olive oil
- 1 onion, diced
- 1 clove garlic, minced
- 1 cup canned diced tomatoes
- 1 cup mushrooms
- 2 zucchini, sliced into long thin strips
- 1 cup cheddar cheese
- Salt and pepper to taste

Method:
1. Pour oil into a pan over medium heat.
2. Cook onion and garlic for 2 minutes.
3. Add mushrooms and tomatoes and simmer for 10 minutes.
4. Transfer to a bowl.
5. Arrange zucchini strips in a baking pan.
6. Top with mushroom mixture and cheese.
7. Repeat layers.
8. Season with salt and pepper.
9. Bake in the oven until cheese has melted.

Nutritional Value:
- Calories 212
- Total Fat 12 g
- Saturated Fat 2 g
- Cholesterol 6 mg
- Sodium 112 mg
- Total Carbohydrate 32 g
- Dietary Fiber 5 g
- Protein 14 g

Veggie Burgers

Preparation Time: 20 minutes; Cooking Time: 10 minutes; Servings: 4

Ingredients:
- 15 oz. chickpeas
- 2 tablespoons red beet, grated
- ⅔ cup ground walnuts
- 3 tablespoons potato starch
- 1 ½ cups quinoa, cooked
- Salt and pepper to taste
- 2 tablespoons vegetable oil

Method:
1. Combine all ingredients except oil in a bowl.
2. Mix well.
3. Form patties from the mixture.
4. Pour oil into a pan over medium heat.
5. Cook patties for 5 minutes per side.
6. Serve with rice or burger buns.

Nutritional Value:
- Calories 498
- Total Fat 23.5 g
- Saturated Fat 2.2 g
- Cholesterol 0 mg
- Sodium 787 mg
- Total Carbohydrate 60.8 g
- Dietary Fiber 9.7 g
- Protein 14 g

Spicy Tomato Pasta

Preparation Time: 20 minutes; Cooking Time: 1 hour; Servings: 8

Ingredients:
- 5 tomatoes, diced
- Water
- Salt to taste
- 2 tablespoons olive oil
- 3 shallots, chopped
- 3 cloves garlic, chopped
- 14 oz. crushed tomatoes
- ¼ cup arugula, chopped
- 2 teaspoons fresh oregano, chopped
- 1 lb. angel hair pasta, cooked
- Parmesan cheese, grated

Method:
1. Boil the tomatoes in a pot of water over medium heat for 40 minutes.
2. Transfer to a bowl.
3. Mash the tomatoes.
4. Pour oil into a pan over medium heat.
5. Add mashed tomatoes and the rest of the ingredients except pasta and Parmesan cheese.
6. Mix well.
7. Cook for 10 minutes.
8. Toss in pasta and sprinkle with cheese.

Nutritional Value:
- Calories 305
- Total Fat 7.3 g
- Saturated Fat 0.8 g
- Cholesterol 0 mg
- Sodium 361 mg
- Total Carbohydrate 52.5 g
- Dietary Fiber 7.3 g
- Protein 9.4 g

Garlic Carrots with Pistachios & Spices

Preparation Time: 15 minutes; Cooking Time: 30 minutes; Servings: 6

Ingredients:
- 2 lb. carrots
- 4 cloves garlic, peeled
- 3 sprigs fresh thyme
- 3 tablespoons olive oil
- Salt and pepper to taste
- ¼ cup pistachios, chopped
- 1 teaspoon ground cumin
- 1 teaspoon ground coriander

Method:
1. Preheat your oven to 400 degrees F.
2. Add carrots to a baking pan.
3. Drizzle with oil, thyme and garlic.
4. Season with salt.
5. Roast for 30 minutes.
6. Sprinkle with pistachios and spices.

Nutritional Value:
- Calories 160
- Total Fat 10 g
- Saturated Fat 1.4 g
- Cholesterol 0 mg
- Sodium 240 mg
- Total Carbohydrate 15 g
- Dietary Fiber 4 g
- Protein 2.8 g

Grilled Broccoli

Preparation Time: 10 minutes; Cooking Time: 10 minutes; Servings: 4

Ingredients:
- 6 cups broccoli florets, steamed
- 1 tablespoon olive oil
- 1 tablespoon lemon juice
- ½ teaspoon ground cumin

- ½ teaspoon smoked paprika
- Salt and pepper to taste
- 1 cup Greek yogurt

Method:
1. Mix olive oil, lemon juice, cumin, paprika, salt and pepper in a bowl.
2. Toss the broccoli in the mixture. Thread the broccoli onto skewers.
3. Grill for 3 to 4 minutes per side.
4. Serve with yogurt.

Nutritional Value:
- Calories 115
- Total Fat 6.4 g
- Saturated Fat 1.7 g
- Cholesterol 6 mg
- Sodium 338 mg
- Total Carbohydrate 10.5 g
- Dietary Fiber 3.9 g
- Protein 7.9 g

Green Beans with Rosemary & Garlic

Preparation Time: 15 minutes; Cooking Time: 10 minutes; Servings: 8

Ingredients:
- 3 tablespoons olive oil
- 3 tablespoons avocado oil
- 1 sprig rosemary
- 2 cloves garlic, crushed
- 2 cups shallot, chopped
- Salt and pepper to taste
- 2 lb. green beans, trimmed, sliced and steamed
- ¾ teaspoon Dijon mustard
- 2 tablespoons white-wine vinegar
- 2 teaspoons lemon juice
- ¼ teaspoon lemon zest

Method:
1. Pour the oils into a pan over medium heat.
2. Cook rosemary and garlic for 2 minutes.
3. Discard rosemary.
4. Add shallots to the pan.
5. Season with salt.
6. Add the oil mixture to a food processor and stir in the rest of the ingredients.
7. Pulse until smooth.
8. Toss the steamed green beans in the dressing.

Nutritional Value:
- Calories 151
- Total Fat 10.7 g
- Saturated Fat 1.3 g
- Cholesterol 0 mg
- Sodium 167 mg
- Total Carbohydrate 13.4 g
- Dietary Fiber 2.9 g
- Protein 2.7 g

Grilled Zucchini with Avocado Salsa

Preparation Time: 10 minutes; Cooking Time: 10 minutes; Servings: 4

Ingredients:
- 2 zucchini, sliced in half lengthwise
- 2 tablespoons olive oil, divided
- Salt and pepper to taste
- 1 cup avocado, cubed
- 2 tablespoons white-wine vinegar

Method:
1. Brush zucchini with half of olive oil.
2. Season with salt and pepper.
3. Grill for 3 minutes per side.
4. In a bowl, toss avocado in vinegar and remaining oil.
5. Sprinkle with salt and pepper.
6. Serve grilled zucchini with avocado salsa.

Nutritional Value:
- Calories 312
- Total Fat 19 g
- Saturated Fat 5 g
- Cholesterol 10 mg
- Sodium 301 mg
- Total Carbohydrate 13 g
- Dietary Fiber 5 g
- Protein 8 g

Mango & Cucumber Relish

Preparation Time: 5 minutes; Cooking Time: 0 minutes; Servings: 4

Ingredients:
- 2 cups mango, sliced into cubes
- 1 cucumber, chopped
- 1 onion, chopped
- 1 tablespoon white wine vinegar
- Salt and pepper to taste

Method:
1. Combine all ingredients in a bowl.
2. Serve with grilled meat or any main course.

Nutritional Value:
- Calories 109
- Total Fat 10 g
- Saturated Fat 2 g
- Cholesterol 0 mg
- Sodium 120 mg
- Total Carbohydrate 15 g
- Dietary Fiber 4 g
- Protein 4 g

Lettuce Cups

Preparation Time: 15 minutes; Cooking Time: 0 minutes; Servings: 4

Ingredients:
- 1 cup cucumber, chopped
- 1 cup tomato, chopped
- 1 tablespoon lemon juice
- 1 tablespoon mustard
- 1 tablespoon light mayo
- ½ teaspoon garlic powder
- 4 large lettuce leaves

Method:
1. In a bowl, mix all the ingredients except the lettuce leaves.
2. Place lettuce leaves in muffin cups.
3. Top with the cucumber mixture.
4. Refrigerate until ready to serve.

Nutritional Value:
- Calories 43
- Total Fat 5 g
- Saturated Fat 0 g
- Cholesterol 0 mg
- Sodium 119 mg
- Total Carbohydrate 13 g
- Dietary Fiber 4 g
- Protein 8 g

Tofu Kebab

Preparation Time: 15 minutes; Cooking Time: 10 minutes; Servings: 4

Ingredients:
- 3 tablespoons olive oil
- 14 oz. tofu, sliced into cubes
- ½ zucchini, sliced into chunks
- 16 cherry tomatoes
- Garlic mayo sauce

Method:
1. Pour oil into a pan over medium heat.
2. Cook tofu until golden.
3. Drain and let cool.
4. Thread alternately onto skewers.

5. Grill for 1 to 2 minutes per side.
6. Serve with garlic mayo sauce.

Nutritional Value:
- Calories 88
- Total Fat 6 g
- Saturated Fat 0 g
- Cholesterol 0 mg
- Sodium 90 mg
- Total Carbohydrate 13 g
- Dietary Fiber 3 g
- Protein 2 g

Stuffed Zucchini

Preparation Time: 20 minutes; Cooking Time: 15 minutes; Servings: 4

Ingredients:
- 4 zucchini, sliced in half lengthwise
- Salt and pepper to taste
- 1 tablespoon olive oil
- 1 onion, chopped
- 8 olives, pitted and chopped
- 1 cup tomatoes, chopped
- 1 tablespoon garlic, chopped
- 1 tablespoon fresh oregano, chopped
- ¾ teaspoon smoked paprika
- ½ cup feta cheese, crumbled

Method:
1. Preheat your oven to 350 degrees F.
2. Scoop the flesh out of the zucchini and chop.
3. Transfer to a bowl.
4. Stir in the rest of the ingredients except cheese.
5. Season the zucchini shells with salt and pepper.
6. Spread the tomato mixture on top of the zucchini shells.
7. Top with cheese.
8. Bake in the oven for 15 minutes.

Nutritional Value:
- Calories 207
- Total Fat 11 g
- Saturated Fat 3.6 g
- Cholesterol 17 mg
- Sodium 458 mg
- Total Carbohydrate 21.6 g
- Dietary Fiber 4.1 g
- Protein 7.7 g

Cinnamon Oats

Preparation Time: 5 minutes; Cooking Time: 5 minutes; Servings: 2

Ingredients:
- 1 teaspoon butter
- 2 teaspoons olive oil
- ½ cup rolled oats
- 1 teaspoon brown sugar
- ⅛ teaspoon nutmeg
- ¼ teaspoon cinnamon

Method:
1. Add butter and oil to a pan over medium heat.
2. Coat the oats with sugar, nutmeg and cinnamon.
3. Add to the pan.
4. Cook while stirring for 4 to 5 minutes.

Nutritional Value:
- Calories 140
- Total Fat 8.1 g
- Saturated Fat 1.8 g
- Cholesterol 5 mg
- Sodium 1 mg
- Total Carbohydrate 15.3 g
- Dietary Fiber 2.2 g
- Protein 2.5 g

Cucumber Salsa

Preparation Time: 15 minutes; Cooking Time: 0 minutes; Servings: 6

Ingredients:
- 1 cup honeydew melon, diced
- 2 cups cucumber, diced
- 1 onion, chopped
- ½ cup fresh cilantro, chopped
- 2 tablespoons fresh juice
- 1 jalapeño pepper, chopped
- 1 teaspoon lime zest, grated
- 1 teaspoon sugar
- 2 teaspoons white-wine vinegar
- Salt to taste

Method:
1. Combine all ingredients in a bowl. Mix well and serve.

Nutritional Value:
- Calories 20
- Total Fat 0.1 g
- Saturated Fat 103 g
- Cholesterol 0 mg
- Sodium 103 mg
- Total Carbohydrate 5.1 g
- Dietary Fiber 0.6 g
- Protein 0.5 g

Sautéed Zucchini

Preparation Time: 10 minutes; Cooking Time: 10 minutes; Servings: 4

Ingredients:
- 1 tablespoon olive oil
- 1 onion, chopped
- 1 lb. zucchini, sliced
- Salt and pepper to taste
- 2 tablespoons butter
- 1 tablespoon lemon juice
- 1 tablespoon fresh chives, chopped

Method:
1. Pour oil into a pan over medium heat.
2. Cook onion and zucchini for 5 minutes.
3. Season with salt and pepper.
4. Mix butter, lemon juice and chives in a bowl.
5. Turn off the heat.
6. Pour the butter mixture into the pan.
7. Mix and serve in bowls.

Nutritional Value:
- Calories 110
- Total Fat 9.7 g
- Saturated Fat 4.2 g
- Cholesterol 15 mg
- Sodium 301 mg
- Total Carbohydrate 5.6 g
- Dietary Fiber 1.4 g
- Protein 1.7 g

Corn & Avocado

Preparation Time: 15 minutes; Cooking Time: 0 minutes; Servings: 6

Ingredients:
- 4 cups corn kernels
- 1 tablespoon olive oil
- 3 tablespoons lime juice
- 1 tablespoon honey
- Salt to taste
- 1 tomato, chopped
- ¼ cup cotija cheese, crumbled
- ¼ cup fresh cilantro, chopped
- 1 avocado, sliced into chunks

Method:
1. Combine all ingredients in a bowl.
2. Serve immediately.

Nutritional Value:
- Calories 218
- Total Fat 16.5 g
- Saturated Fat 2.8 g
- Cholesterol 5 mg
- Sodium 275 mg
- Total Carbohydrate 17.6 g

- Dietary Fiber 3.8 g
- Protein 3.7 g

Chickpea Curry

Preparation Time: 15 minutes; Cooking Time: 35 minutes; Servings: 6

Ingredients:
- 2 tablespoons avocado oil
- 1 onion, chopped
- 2 cloves garlic, minced
- 1 tablespoon ginger, minced
- Salt to taste
- Red pepper flakes
- 1 tablespoon curry powder
- 14 oz. coconut milk
- 1 cup reduced-sodium vegetable stock
- 1 sweet potato, chopped
- 2 tomatoes, chopped
- 2 cups green beans, trimmed and sliced
- 15 oz. chickpeas, rinsed and drained
- 2 tablespoons lime juice
- ½ cup cilantro, chopped

Method:
1. Pour oil into a pan over medium heat.
2. Cook onion, garlic and ginger for 3 minutes.
3. Stir in salt, red pepper flakes and curry powder.
4. Cook for 1 minute.
5. Add the rest of the ingredients.
6. Bring to a boil.
7. Simmer for 30 minutes or until veggies are tender.

Nutritional Value:
- Calories 312
- Total Fat 20.5 g
- Saturated Fat 13 g
- Cholesterol 0 mg
- Sodium 436 mg
- Total Carbohydrate 29.6 g
- Dietary Fiber 7.7 g
- Protein 7.1 g

Cauliflower Parmesan

Preparation Time: 20 minutes; Cooking Time: 40 minutes; Servings: 4

Ingredients:
- Cooking spray
- 2 lb. cauliflower, sliced into steaks
- Salt and pepper to taste
- 1 tablespoon olive oil
- ½ cup onion, chopped
- 2 cloves garlic, crushed and minced
- ¼ cup red wine
- 2 cups canned diced tomatoes
- 1 teaspoon dried Italian seasoning
- 1 cup mozzarella, shredded
- Chopped parsley

Method:
1. Preheat your oven to 450 degrees F.
2. Spray your baking pan with oil.
3. Season cauliflower steaks with salt and pepper.
4. Roast in the oven for 25 minutes.
5. Pour oil into a pan over medium heat.
6. Cook onion and garlic for 2 minutes.
7. Pour in wine and tomatoes.
8. Season with Italian seasoning.
9. Simmer for 10 minutes.
10. Pour mixture on top of the cauliflower steaks.
11. Sprinkle with cheese.
12. Bake in the oven for 10 minutes.
13. Garnish with parsley and serve.

Nutritional Value:
- Calories 111
- Total Fat 4.9 g
- Saturated Fat 2 g
- Cholesterol 9 mg
- Sodium 359 mg
- Total Carbohydrate 11.2 g
- Dietary Fiber 3.3 g
- Protein 6.4 g

Grilled Veggies in Foil Packet

Preparation Time: 30 minutes; Cooking Time: 15 minutes; Servings: 6

Ingredients:
- 1 lb. red bell peppers, sliced
- 2 zucchini, sliced
- 1 lb. asparagus, trimmed and sliced
- 2 tablespoons olive oil
- 3 cloves garlic, minced
- Salt and pepper to taste
- 2 tablespoons butter
- Chopped parsley
- Chopped chives

Method:
1. Preheat your grill.
2. Toss the veggies in oil, garlic, salt and pepper.
3. Place on top of foil sheets.
4. Fold the foil and seal the edges.
5. Grill the foil packet for 4 to 6 minutes per side.
6. In a bowl, mix the butter and herbs.
7. Pour butter mixture over the veggies and serve.

Nutritional Value:
- Calories 126
- Total Fat 8.9 g
- Saturated Fat 3 g
- Cholesterol 10 mg
- Sodium 310 mg
- Total Carbohydrate 10 g
- Dietary Fiber 3.6 g
- Protein 3.4 g

Roasted Mushrooms with Butter & Parmesan

Preparation Time: 20 minutes; Cooking Time: 20 minutes; Servings: 4

Ingredients:
- 2 tablespoons olive oil
- Salt and pepper to taste
- 1 tablespoon chopped fresh thyme
- 1 cup onion, sliced
- 1 lb. mushrooms, sliced in half
- 1 tablespoon butter
- 2 tablespoons Parmesan cheese, grated

Method:
1. Preheat your oven to 450 degrees F.
2. In a bowl, combine oil, salt, pepper and thyme.
3. Coat the onion and mushrooms with this mixture.
4. Transfer to a baking pan.
5. Roast for 15 minutes.
6. Add butter to a pan over medium heat.
7. Stir in Parmesan and cook for 1 minute.
8. Pour the butter mixture over the mushrooms and serve.

Nutritional Value:
- Calories 138
- Total Fat 10.8 g
- Saturated Fat 3.2 g
- Cholesterol 10 mg
- Sodium 198 mg
- Total Carbohydrate 8 g
- Dietary Fiber 2 g
- Protein 4.8 g

Garlic Butter Mushrooms

Preparation Time: 10 minutes; Cooking Time: 10 minutes; Servings: 4
Ingredients:
- 2 tablespoons butter
- 1 tablespoon olive oil
- 1 lb. mushrooms, sliced
- Salt and pepper to taste
- 5 cloves garlic, minced
- Chopped parsley

Method:
1. Add oil and butter to a pan over medium heat.
2. Cook mushrooms for 8 minutes.
3. Stir in the garlic and cook for 2 minutes.
4. Garnish with parsley and serve.

Nutritional Value:
- Calories 110
- Total Fat 9.6 g
- Saturated Fat 4 g
- Cholesterol 15 mg
- Sodium 226 mg
- Total Carbohydrate 4.7 g
- Dietary Fiber 1.3 g
- Protein 3.8 g

Pasta Salad with Pesto

Preparation Time: 15 minutes; Cooking Time: 0 minutes; Servings: 8
Ingredients:
- 2 cups basil leaves
- ½ cup olive oil
- 5 cloves garlic, minced
- ¾ cup Parmesan cheese, grated
- 1 cup walnuts, chopped
- ½ cup light mayo
- 1 lb. whole-wheat penne pasta, cooked
- Salt and pepper to taste

Method:
1. Add basil, oil, garlic, cheese and walnuts in the food processor.
2. Pulse until smooth.
3. Mix mayo and pesto.
4. Toss the cooked penne in the mixture.
5. Season with salt and pepper.
6. Chill before serving.

Nutritional Value:
- Calories 497
- Total Fat 24.5 g
- Saturated Fat 4.1 g
- Cholesterol 6 mg
- Sodium 461 mg
- Total Carbohydrate 58.8 g
- Dietary Fiber 10 g
- Protein 16 g

Beet Burger

Preparation Time: 15 minutes; Cooking Time: 30 minutes; Servings: 6
Ingredients:
- 1 cup beet, grated
- ½ cup onion, diced
- 1 cup carrot, grated
- 3 tablespoons whole-wheat flour
- ½ cup Parmesan cheese, grated
- 1 teaspoon low-sodium soy sauce
- 2 tablespoons fresh parsley, chopped
- 1 egg, beaten
- Salt to taste
- 1 tablespoon olive oil

Method:
1. Preheat your oven to 375 degrees F.
2. Combine all the ingredients.
3. Form patties from the mixture.

4. Bake the patties in the oven for 30 minutes.

Nutritional Value:
- Calories 205
- Total Fat 13.2 g
- Saturated Fat 2.6 g
- Cholesterol 37 mg
- Sodium 430 mg
- Total Carbohydrate 16 g
- Dietary Fiber 3.8 g
- Protein 7.5 g

Kale with Grapes

Preparation Time: 15 minutes; Cooking Time: 0 minutes; Servings: 4

Ingredients:
- 2 tablespoons olive oil
- 3 tablespoons lemon juice
- 1 tablespoon honey
- Salt and pepper to taste
- 8 oz. kale, torn
- ½ tablespoon pepitas, toasted
- 1 cup grapes, sliced in half
- ¼ cup cheddar cheese, crumbled

Method:
1. Combine olive oil, lemon juice, honey, salt and pepper in a bowl.
2. Stir in the kale. Coat evenly with the sauce.
3. Top with the remaining ingredients and serve.

Nutritional Value:
- Calories 249
- Total Fat 17.5 g
- Saturated Fat 3.6 g
- Cholesterol 7 mg
- Sodium 224 mg
- Total Carbohydrate 19.2 g
- Dietary Fiber 3.4 g
- Protein 8.9 g

Black Rice with Tofu & Asparagus

Preparation Time: 20 minutes; Cooking Time: 20 minutes; Servings: 4

Ingredients:
- 14 oz. tofu, sliced into cubes
- Garlic powder
- 2 tablespoons olive oil
- 4 cups cooked hot black rice
- 2 cups asparagus, steamed
- 2 cups tomatoes, chopped

Method:
1. Coat tofu with garlic powder.
2. Marinate for 10 minutes.
3. Pour oil into a pan over medium heat.
4. Cook the tofu cubes until golden.
5. Divide the black rice among 4 bowls.
6. Top with the tofu, asparagus and tomatoes.
7. Serve immediately.

Nutritional Value:
- Calories 577
- Total Fat 37 g
- Saturated Fat 14 g
- Cholesterol 0 mg
- Sodium 815 mg
- Total Carbohydrate 49 g
- Dietary Fiber 7.6 g
- Protein 18 g

Cheesy Baked Potato

Preparation Time: 20 minutes; Cooking Time: 10 minutes; Servings: 8

Ingredients:
- 4 potatoes, sliced in half and boiled
- 2 tablespoons olive oil
- Salt and pepper to taste
- 1 cup cheddar cheese, shredded
- Sour cream

Method:
1. Scoop the potato flesh and place in a bowl.
2. Stir in the olive oil, salt and pepper.
3. Top with the cheese.
4. Broil in the oven until cheese has melted.
5. Serve with sour cream.

Nutritional Value:
- Calories 141
- Total Fat 5.9 g
- Saturated Fat 1.9 g
- Cholesterol 7 mg
- Sodium 197 mg
- Total Carbohydrate 18.8 g
- Dietary Fiber 1.4 g
- Protein 3.8 g

Chapter 8: Side Dish Recipes

Orange Broccoli Rabe

Preparation Time: 15 minutes; Cooking Time: 15 minutes; Servings: 8

Ingredients:
- 2 oranges, sliced in half
- 1 lb. broccoli rabe, trimmed
- 1 tablespoon orange juice
- Salt and pepper to taste
- 2 tablespoons toasted sesame oil
- 1 tablespoon sesame seeds

Method:
1. Add orange slices to a pan over medium heat.
2. Cook for 5 minutes.
3. Transfer to a plate.
4. Put broccoli rabe to the same pan.
5. Cook for 8 minutes.
6. Add orange juice, salt, pepper and oil to a bowl.
7. Toss the cooked broccoli rabe in the mixture.
8. Garnish with sesame seeds.

Nutritional Value:
- Calories 59
- Total Fat 4.4 g
- Saturated Fat 0.6 g
- Cholesterol 0 mg
- Sodium 164 mg
- Total Carbohydrate 4.1 g
- Dietary Fiber 1.6 g
- Protein 3 g

Baked Zucchini Rounds with Herbed Cream Dip

Preparation Time: 15 minutes; Cooking Time: 30 minutes; Servings: 6

Ingredients:
- Cooking spray
- 12 oz. zucchini, sliced into rounds
- 1 tablespoon water
- 2 eggs
- 1 cup breadcrumbs
- Pepper to taste
- 2 teaspoons Old Bay seasoning
- ¼ cup yogurt
- 2 tablespoons mayonnaise
- 1 tablespoon lemon juice
- ½ teaspoon garlic powder
- Salt to taste
- ¼ cup chopped mixed herbs (chives, parsley and tarragon)

Method:
1. Preheat your oven to 425 degrees F.
2. Spray your baking pan with oil.
3. Combine water and eggs in another bowl.
4. Mix breadcrumbs, pepper and Old Bay seasoning in a bowl.
5. Dip zucchini in the first and second bowls.
6. Arrange on the baking pan.
7. Bake for 30 minutes.
8. In a bowl, mix the remaining ingredients.
9. Serve zucchini rounds with dip.

Nutritional Value:
- Calories 84
- Total Fat 4.9 g
- Saturated Fat 0.9 g
- Cholesterol 30 mg
- Sodium 237 mg
- Total Carbohydrate 7.1 g
- Dietary Fiber 1.2 g
- Protein 3.6 g

Baked Potato Stuffed with Salmon

Preparation Time: 20 minutes; Cooking Time: 1 hour; Servings: 4
Ingredients:
- 4 large potatoes
- ½ cup low-fat sour cream
- 4 oz. salmon flakes
- ½ cup red onion, sliced thinly
- 1 cup tomato, chopped
- 4 teaspoons chives, chopped

Method:
1. Poke the potatoes with fork.
2. Bake in the oven at 425 degrees F for 1 hour.
3. Place on a cutting board.
4. Let cool.
5. Slice the potatoes but not all the way through.
6. Scoop out some of the flesh and mix with the remaining ingredients.
7. Stuff the potatoes with the mixture.

Nutritional Value:
- Calories 256
- Total Fat 5.1 g
- Saturated Fat 2.6 g
- Cholesterol 18 mg
- Sodium 231 mg
- Total Carbohydrate 42.9 g
- Dietary Fiber 3 g
- Protein 11 g

Parmesan Spiralized Onions

Preparation Time: 30 minutes; Cooking Time: 30 minutes; Servings: 8
Ingredients:
- Cooking spray
- 2 onions, spiralized
- 2 tablespoons olive oil
- Salt and pepper to taste
- ¼ cup Parmesan cheese, grated

Method:
1. Preheat your oven to 425 degrees F.
2. Spray your pan with oil.
3. Coat onions with oil.
4. Sprinkle with salt, pepper and Parmesan cheese.
5. Transfer to the pan.
6. Bake for 30 minutes.

Nutritional Value:
- Calories 102
- Total Fat 4.7 g
- Saturated Fat 1 g
- Cholesterol 2 mg
- Sodium 231 mg
- Total Carbohydrate 12 g
- Dietary Fiber 2.2 g
- Protein 3 g

Roasted Mushrooms with Shallots

Preparation Time: 10 minutes; Cooking Time: 20 minutes; Servings: 4
Ingredients:
- 2 cups shallots, sliced
- 1 lb. mixed mushrooms
- 2 tablespoons olive oil
- Salt and pepper to taste
- 1 tablespoon fresh thyme, chopped
- 1 tablespoon red wine

Method:
1. Preheat your oven to 450 degrees F.
2. Coat shallots and mushrooms in oil, salt, pepper and thyme.
3. Arrange in a baking pan.

4. Roast in the oven for 15 minutes.
5. Stir in the wine and roast for another 5 minutes.

Nutritional Value:
- Calories 178
- Total Fat 7.3 g
- Saturated Fat 1 g
- Cholesterol 0 mg
- Sodium 163 mg
- Total Carbohydrate 20 g
- Dietary Fiber 3.6 g
- Protein 5 g

Grilled Eggplant

Preparation Time: 10 minutes; Cooking Time: 10 minutes; Servings: 4

Ingredients:
- 1 eggplant, sliced lengthwise and then sliced in half
- Garlic salt to taste
- 2 tablespoons olive oil

Method:
1. Preheat your grill.
2. Coat eggplant with oil.
3. Season with garlic salt.
4. Grill for 5 minutes per side.

Nutritional Value:
- Calories 149
- Total Fat 7.3 g
- Saturated Fat 1 g
- Cholesterol 0 mg
- Sodium 148 mg
- Total Carbohydrate 8.3 g
- Dietary Fiber 3.8 g
- Protein 1.4 g

Packet Potatoes

Preparation Time: 30 minutes; Cooking Time: 40 minutes; Servings: 5

Ingredients:
- 1 ½ lb. potatoes, sliced
- 2 cloves garlic, sliced thinly
- 2 tablespoons olive oil
- Salt and pepper to taste

Method:
1. Preheat your grill.
2. Place the potatoes on top of the foil sheet.
3. Sprinkle with the garlic.
4. Drizzle with the olive oil.
5. Season with salt and pepper.
6. Seal the packets.
7. Grill for 40 minutes, turning every 10 minutes.

Nutritional Value:
- Calories 148
- Total Fat 5.8 g
- Saturated Fat 0.8 g
- Cholesterol 0 mg
- Sodium 141 mg
- Total Carbohydrate 22 g
- Dietary Fiber 2.4 g
- Protein 2.7 g

Potato & Bacon Hash

Preparation Time: 15 minutes; Cooking Time: 15 minutes; Servings: 1

Ingredients:
- 1 teaspoon olive oil
- ½ cup zucchini, shredded
- ¾ cup grilled potatoes
- 1 slice turkey bacon, chopped and cooked crispy
- 1 egg, beaten
- Salt and pepper to taste

Method:
1. Pour olive oil into a pan over medium heat.
2. Cook zucchini and potatoes for 3 minutes.
3. Stir in bacon. Pour egg on top.
4. Cook until egg has become firm.
5. Season with salt and pepper.

Nutritional Value:
- Calories 302
- Total Fat 14.2 g
- Saturated Fat 3.4 g
- Cholesterol 186 mg
- Sodium 398 mg
- Total Carbohydrate 30 g
- Dietary Fiber 3.5 g
- Protein 13 g

Mixed Veggies with Lemon

Preparation Time: 10 minutes; Cooking Time: 20 minutes; Servings: 5

Ingredients:
- 2 cloves garlic, sliced thinly
- 2 cups broccoli florets
- 1 cup cauliflower florets
- 1 tablespoon olive oil
- Salt and pepper to taste
- 1 teaspoon dried oregano
- 1 cup zucchini, diced
- 1 red bell peppers, sliced
- 2 teaspoons lemon zest

Method:
1. Preheat your oven to 425 degrees F.
2. Mix garlic, broccoli and cauliflower in a baking pan.
3. Drizzle with olive oil.
4. Season with salt, pepper and dried oregano.
5. Roast for 10 minutes.
6. Stir in the remaining ingredients.
7. Roast for another 10 minutes.

Nutritional Value:
- Calories 52
- Total Fat 3.1 g
- Saturated Fat 0.5 g
- Cholesterol 0 mg
- Sodium 134 mg
- Total Carbohydrate 5.3 g
- Dietary Fiber 1.9 g
- Protein 1.8 g

Pickled Zucchini

Preparation Time: 15 minutes; Cooking Time: 10 minutes; Servings: 8

Ingredients:
- 8 sprigs fresh dill
- 2 zucchini, sliced into thin strips
- ¾ cup water
- ¾ cup vinegar
- 1 clove garlic, crushed and minced
- 1 tablespoon sugar
- ¼ teaspoon red pepper flakes

Method:
1. Add dill and zucchini to a glass jar with lid.
2. Add the remaining ingredients to a pan over medium heat.
3. Bring to a boil.
4. Let cool.
5. Pour into the jar.
6. Let sit for 20 minutes.

Nutritional Value:
- Calories 8
- Total Fat 0.2 g

- Saturated Fat 0 g
- Cholesterol 0 mg
- Sodium 40 mg
- Total Carbohydrate 1.5 g
- Dietary Fiber 0.4 g
- Protein 0.5 g

Squash & Zucchini with Anchovy Paste

Preparation Time: 15 minutes; Cooking Time: 18 minutes; Servings: 6

Ingredients:
- ¼ cup olive oil
- 4 cloves garlic, crushed
- ¼ teaspoon red pepper flakes
- ½ teaspoon anchovy paste
- 1 lb. zucchini, sliced
- 1 lb. squash, sliced
- Salt to taste
- 1 teaspoon dried oregano

Method:
1. Pour olive oil into a pan.
2. Add garlic, red pepper flakes and anchovy paste.
3. Cook for 3 minutes, stirring.
4. Stir in zucchini and squash.
5. Season with salt and oregano.
6. Cook for 15 minutes.

Nutritional Value:
- Calories 140
- Total Fat 12.7 g
- Saturated Fat 1.8 g
- Cholesterol 0 mg
- Sodium 202 mg
- Total Carbohydrate 5.7 g
- Dietary Fiber 1.6 g
- Protein 2 g

Spicy Root Veggies

Preparation Time: 15 minutes; Cooking Time: 30 minutes; Servings: 6

Ingredients:
- 1 onion, chopped
- 1 cup carrot, sliced
- 1 cup parsnip, sliced
- 3 cups squash, sliced
- 1 tablespoon olive oil
- 1 teaspoon cayenne pepper
- Salt and pepper to taste

Method:
1. Preheat your oven to 400 degrees F.
2. Combine all the root vegetables in a baking pan.
3. Drizzle with olive oil.
4. Season with cayenne pepper, salt and pepper.
5. Roast for 30 minutes, stirring halfway through.
6. Serve warm.

Nutritional Value:
- Calories 106
- Total Fat 3.7 g
- Saturated Fat 0.5 g
- Cholesterol 0 mg
- Sodium 162 mg
- Total Carbohydrate 18.5 g
- Dietary Fiber 5.3 g
- Protein 1.5 g

Green Beans with Garlic & Mushrooms

Preparation Time: 10 minutes; Cooking Time: 10 minutes; Servings: 8

Ingredients:
- Water
- 2 lb. green beans, trimmed and sliced
- 2 tablespoons olive oil
- 8 cloves garlic, crushed and minced
- 12 oz. mushrooms
- Garlic salt to taste

Method:
1. Fill a pot with water.
2. Bring to a boil.
3. Boil beans for 5 minutes.
4. Drain the beans.
5. Pour oil into a pan over medium heat.
6. Add the garlic and mushrooms.
7. Cook for 5 minutes.
8. Add the beans and season with garlic salt.

Nutritional Value:
- Calories 74
- Total Fat 3.1 g
- Saturated Fat 0.5 g
- Cholesterol 0 mg
- Sodium 185 mg
- Total Carbohydrate 11 g
- Dietary Fiber 3.6 g
- Protein 3.3 g

Zucchini with Couscous

Preparation Time: 15 minutes; Cooking Time: 15 minutes; Servings: 6

Ingredients:
- 1 teaspoon olive oil
- 1 onion, sliced into rings
- 1 clove garlic, crushed and minced
- 1 cup low-sodium chicken broth
- 12 oz. zucchini, sliced
- Salt to taste
- Cooked couscous

Method:
1. Pour oil into a pan over medium heat.
2. Cook onion and garlic for 6 minutes.
3. Pour in the broth.
4. Bring to a boil.
5. Stir in zucchini and salt.
6. Cook for 4 minutes.
7. Serve zucchini with couscous.

Nutritional Value:
- Calories 134
- Total Fat 1.4 g
- Saturated Fat 0.1 g
- Cholesterol 0 mg
- Sodium 223 mg
- Total Carbohydrate 26 g
- Dietary Fiber 4.7 g
- Protein 6.4 g

Mashed Veggies

Preparation Time: 20 minutes; Cooking Time: 30 minutes; Servings: 4

Ingredients:
- 1 sweet potato, sliced into cubes
- 2 carrots, sliced
- 1 onion, sliced
- 2 cloves garlic, sliced
- 4 teaspoons olive oil
- Salt and pepper to taste
- 3 tablespoons almond milk

Method:
1. Preheat your oven to 425 degrees F.
2. Add all the vegetables to a baking pan.
3. Coat with oil.
4. Bake in the oven for 30 minutes.
5. Transfer veggies to a food processor.
6. Stir in the rest of the ingredients.

7. Pulse until pureed.

Nutritional Value:
- Calories 114
- Total Fat 4.6 g
- Saturated Fat 0.7 g
- Cholesterol 0 mg
- Sodium 202 mg
- Total Carbohydrate 17 g
- Dietary Fiber 2.9 g
- Protein 1.7 g

Zucchini & Squash with Green Chili

Preparation Time: 10 minutes; Cooking Time: 15 minutes; Servings: 6

Ingredients:
- 2 teaspoons olive oil
- 2 zucchini, sliced
- 2 squash, sliced
- 1 onion, sliced
- 2 tomatoes, chopped
- 4 oz. green chili
- 2 teaspoons oregano, chopped
- Salt and pepper to taste

Method:
1. Add oil to a pan over medium heat.
2. Cook onion, squash and zucchini for 10 minutes.
3. Stir in tomatoes and green chili.
4. Season with salt, pepper and oregano.
5. Serve warm.

Nutritional Value:
- Calories 49
- Total Fat 1.8 g
- Saturated Fat 0.3 g
- Cholesterol 0 mg
- Sodium 112 mg
- Total Carbohydrate 7.8 g
- Dietary Fiber 2.3 g
- Protein 1.9 g

Peas with Celery

Preparation Time: 15 minutes; Cooking Time: 15 minutes; Servings: 8

Ingredients:
- 1 tablespoon olive oil
- 1 onion, chopped
- ½ cup celery, chopped
- 20 oz. peas
- ¼ cup celery leaves, chopped
- Salt and pepper to taste

Method:
1. Pour oil into a pan over medium heat.
2. Cook onion for 5 minutes.
3. Stir in celery and cook for 3 minutes.
4. Add peas and cook for 5 minutes.
5. Stir in celery leaves.
6. Season with salt and pepper.
7. Serve warm.

Nutritional Value:
- Calories 82
- Total Fat 1.9 g
- Saturated Fat 0.3 g
- Cholesterol 0 mg
- Sodium 221 mg
- Total Carbohydrate 12 g
- Dietary Fiber 4.7 g
- Protein 4.3 g

Mustard & Parsley Potatoes

Preparation Time: 30 minutes; Cooking Time: 30 minutes; Servings: 4

Ingredients:
- 4 lb. potatoes, sliced
- 3 tablespoons olive oil

- Salt and pepper to taste
- 2 teaspoons dry mustard
- ¼ cup parsley, chopped

Method:
1. Preheat your oven to 450 degrees F.
2. Coat the potatoes with oil.
3. Season with salt and pepper.
4. Sprinkle with mustard and parsley.
5. Roast in the oven for 30 minutes, stirring halfway through.

Nutritional Value:
- Calories 155
- Total Fat 4 g
- Saturated Fat 0.5 g
- Cholesterol 0 mg
- Sodium 156 mg
- Total Carbohydrate 27.5 g
- Dietary Fiber 3.8 g
- Protein 3.5 g

Ginger & Miso Kale

Preparation Time: 15 minutes; Cooking Time: 0 minutes; Servings: 6

Ingredients:
- 2 tablespoons olive oil
- 2 tablespoons rice vinegar
- 1 tablespoon lime juice
- ½ teaspoon lemon zest
- 4 cups kale, chopped, steamed
- 2 teaspoons miso
- 1 clove garlic, minced
- 1 teaspoon ginger, grated
- 2 tablespoons cashews, chopped

Method:
1. Combine all the ingredients in a serving bowl.

Nutritional Value:
- Calories 86
- Total Fat 5.2 g
- Saturated Fat 0.4 g
- Cholesterol 0 mg
- Sodium 104 mg
- Total Carbohydrate 8 g
- Dietary Fiber 1.6 g
- Protein 2.8 g

Collard Greens with Mushrooms

Preparation Time: 15 minutes; Cooking Time: 20 minutes; Servings: 4

Ingredients:
- ¼ teaspoon ground cumin
- ¾ teaspoon smoked paprika
- 1 cup reduced-sodium vegetable broth
- Salt and pepper to taste
- 2 tablespoons olive oil
- 4 cloves garlic, minced
- 5 oz. mushrooms, chopped
- 15 oz. collard greens, chopped
- 2 tablespoons cider vinegar

Method:
1. Mix cumin, paprika, broth, salt and pepper in a pot over medium heat.
2. Bring to a boil.
3. Reduce heat and simmer for 1 minute.
4. Pour oil into a pan over medium heat.
5. Cook garlic and mushrooms for 5 minutes.
6. Pour reserved mixture into the pan.
7. Add collard greens and vinegar.
8. Cook for 10 more minutes.

Nutritional Value:
- Calories 120
- Total Fat 7.7 g
- Saturated Fat 1 g
- Cholesterol 0 mg

- Sodium 227 mg
- Total Carbohydrate 10.7 g
- Dietary Fiber 6 g
- Protein 4.5 g

Mashed Potato Casserole

Preparation Time: 15 minutes; Cooking Time: 15 minutes; Servings: 2
Ingredients:
- 2 cups mashed potato
- 1 cup shredded cheese
- ½ cup reduced-sodium turkey bacon bits, cooked crispy

Method:
1. Preheat your oven to 350 degrees F.
2. Spread mashed potato in a baking pan.
3. Top with cheese and bacon.
4. Bake in the oven for 15 minutes.

Nutritional Value:
- Calories 212
- Total Fat 10 g
- Saturated Fat 3 g
- Cholesterol 27 mg
- Sodium 108 mg
- Total Carbohydrate 15 g
- Dietary Fiber 3 g
- Protein 24 g

Zucchini Fries with Buttermilk Dip

Preparation Time: 30 minutes; Cooking Time: 15 minutes; Servings: 8
Ingredients:
Zucchini Fries
- Cooking spray
- ½ cup whole-wheat flour
- ¼ cup reduced-fat buttermilk
- 2 eggs, beaten
- ½ cup whole-wheat breadcrumbs
- Salt and pepper to taste
- 1 lb. zucchini, sliced into strips

Dip
- 6 oz. nonfat yogurt
- ¼ cup nonfat buttermilk
- 2 tablespoons fresh chives, chopped
- 1 tablespoon parsley, chopped
- 2 teaspoons dill, chopped
- 2 cloves garlic, minced
- ½ teaspoon onion powder
- Pepper to taste

Method:
1. Preheat your oven to 450 degrees F.
2. Spray your baking pan with oil.
3. Put the flour in a bowl.
4. Mix the milk and eggs in a second bowl.
5. In the third bowl, combine breadcrumbs, salt and pepper.
6. Dip the zucchini in the first, second and third bowls.
7. Arrange in a single layer in the baking pan.
8. Bake in the oven for 15 minutes, turning halfway through.
9. Combine the ingredients for the dip.
10. Serve fries with dip.

Nutritional Value:
- Calories 94
- Total Fat 1 g
- Saturated Fat 0.2 g
- Cholesterol 1 mg
- Sodium 123 mg
- Total Carbohydrate 15.3 g
- Dietary Fiber 2.1 g
- Protein 5.7 g

Roasted Veggies with Gremolata

Preparation Time: 30 minutes; Cooking Time: 40 minutes; Servings: 8

Ingredients:

Roasted Vegetables
- 1 squash, sliced into cubes
- Olive oil for drizzling
- Salt to taste
- 2 red bell peppers, sliced into strips
- 2 cups broccoli florets
- 4 cups cauliflower florets
- 2 tablespoons orange juice
- ½ teaspoon orange zest
- 2 tablespoons lemon juice
- 1 clove garlic, minced
- Pepper to taste

Gremolata
- 2 tablespoons fresh parsley, chopped
- 2 tablespoons scallions, chopped
- 2 tablespoons tomatoes
- 2 tablespoons almonds, chopped

Method:
1. Preheat your oven to 375 degrees F.
2. Spread squash in a baking pan.
3. Drizzle with oil.
4. Season with salt.
5. Roast for 20 minutes.
6. Stir in the rest of the veggies.
7. Roast for another 20 minutes.
8. Mix olive oil, orange juice, orange zest, lemon juice, garlic and pepper in a bowl. Set aside.
9. In another bowl, mix the gremolata ingredients.
10. Coat the roasted veggies with the orange juice mixture and sprinkle with the gremolata.

Nutritional Value:
- Calories 100
- Total Fat 4.3 g
- Saturated Fat 0.6 g
- Cholesterol 0 mg
- Sodium 182 mg
- Total Carbohydrate 15 g
- Dietary Fiber 3.4 g
- Protein 2.5 g

Apples & Pea Pods

Preparation Time: 10 minutes; Cooking Time: 15 minutes; Servings: 8

Ingredients:
- 2 teaspoons vegetable oil
- 3 slices turkey bacon
- 3 apples, sliced
- 2 leeks, chopped
- 4 cups pea pods, trimmed
- Salt and pepper to taste

Method:
1. Pour oil into a pan over medium heat.
2. Cook turkey bacon until crispy.
3. Stir in apples and leeks.
4. Cook for 4 minutes.
5. Add peas and cook for 3 minutes.
6. Season with salt and pepper.
7. Serve on the side of main course.

Nutritional Value:
- Calories 78
- Total Fat 2 g
- Saturated Fat 0 g
- Cholesterol 4 mg
- Sodium 115 mg
- Total Carbohydrate 11 g
- Dietary Fiber 2 g
- Protein 2 g

Roasted Mixed Mushrooms

Preparation Time: 20 minutes; Cooking Time: 20 minutes; Servings: 6
Ingredients:
- 1 lb. mixed mushrooms, sliced
- 6 cloves garlic, sliced thinly
- 2 tablespoons olive oil
- 2 teaspoons balsamic vinegar
- 2 teaspoons Worcestershire sauce
- Salt and pepper to taste
- 2 tablespoons Italian parsley, chopped
- 1 teaspoon dried oregano, crushed

Method:
1. Preheat your oven to 400 degrees F.
2. Arrange mushrooms in the baking pan.
3. Stir in garlic and the rest of the ingredients.
4. Roast for 20 minutes.
5. Serve warm.

Nutritional Value:
- Calories 65
- Total Fat 5 g
- Saturated Fat 1 g
- Cholesterol 0 mg
- Sodium 124 mg
- Total Carbohydrate 4 g
- Dietary Fiber 1 g
- Protein 4 g

Steamed Carrots & Cabbage

Preparation Time: 15 minutes; Cooking Time: 20 minutes; Servings: 8
Ingredients:
- 2 teaspoons olive oil
- 1 cup carrots, sliced
- 1 green bell pepper, sliced into strips
- 5 cups cabbage, sliced
- Salt and pepper to taste
- Water

Method:
1. Pour oil into a pan over medium heat.
2. Cook the carrots for 5 minutes.
3. Stir in the rest of the ingredients.
4. Cook for 15 minutes.

Nutritional Value:
- Calories 36
- Total Fat 1.3 g
- Saturated Fat 0.2 g
- Cholesterol 0 mg
- Sodium 168 mg
- Total Carbohydrate 6 g
- Dietary Fiber 2.3 g
- Protein 1.3 g

Baked Potato with Cheese & Broccoli

Preparation Time: 15 minutes; Cooking Time: 30 minutes; Servings: 8
Ingredients:
- 4 large potatoes
- 1 cup low-fat milk
- 2 tablespoons whole-wheat flour
- 1 cup broccoli florets, chopped
- Salt and pepper to taste
- ½ cup reduced-sodium cheddar cheese
- Chives, chopped

Method:
1. Poke the potatoes with a fork.
2. Bake in the oven for 1 hour.
3. Let cool and set aside.
4. Pour milk into a pan and simmer for 10 minutes.
5. Stir in the flour.

6. Add the broccoli and cook for 10 minutes.
7. Slice the potatoes in half but not all the way through.
8. Scoop out some of the flesh and stir into the broccoli.
9. Season with salt and pepper.
10. Stuff the potatoes with the broccoli mixture.
11. Top with the cheese.
12. Bake in the oven until cheese has melted.
13. Sprinkle with chives.

Nutritional Value:
- Calories 137
- Total Fat 3.1 g
- Saturated Fat 1.8 g
- Cholesterol 9 mg
- Sodium 148 mg
- Total Carbohydrate 22.2 g
- Dietary Fiber 2.3 g
- Protein 5 g

Potatoes with Rosemary

Preparation Time: 15 minutes; Cooking Time: 25 minutes; Servings: 8

Ingredients:
- 1 lb. potatoes, sliced
- 2 tablespoons olive oil
- Salt and pepper to taste
- 1 teaspoon fresh rosemary, chopped
- 3 cloves garlic, minced
- ½ cup Kalamata olives, chopped
- 1 oz. Parmesan cheese, grated

Method:
1. Preheat your oven to 450 degrees F.
2. Spray your baking pan with oil.
3. In a bowl, mix the olive oil, salt, pepper and rosemary.
4. Coat the potatoes with this mixture.
5. Spread in the baking pan.
6. Bake for 20 minutes.
7. Stir in the rest of the ingredients.
8. Bake for 5 minutes.

Nutritional Value:
- Calories 103
- Total Fat 5 g
- Saturated Fat 1 g
- Cholesterol 2 mg
- Sodium 208 mg
- Total Carbohydrate 11 g
- Dietary Fiber 2 g
- Protein 3 g

Honey Balsamic Parsnips & Carrots

Preparation Time: 15 minutes; Cooking Time: 10 minutes; Servings: 10

Ingredients:
- 3 parsnips, sliced
- 8 carrots, sliced
- Water
- 1 tablespoon vegetable oil
- 1 tablespoon honey
- 2 tablespoons balsamic vinegar
- ¼ teaspoon ground nutmeg

Method:
1. Add parsnips and carrots in a pan with water over medium heat.
2. Boil for 7 minutes.
3. Drain and put the veggies back to the pan.
4. Add the oil.
5. Cook for 2 minutes.
6. In a bowl, mix the honey, vinegar and nutmeg.

7. Stir into the pan.
8. Cook for 1 minute.

Nutritional Value:
- Calories 67
- Total Fat 1.1 g
- Saturated Fat 0.2 g
- Cholesterol 0 mg
- Sodium 42 mg
- Total Carbohydrate 14 g
- Dietary Fiber 3.3 g
- Protein 0.9 g

Balsamic Squash & Beans

Preparation Time: 15 minutes; Cooking Time: 25 minutes; Servings: 8

Ingredients:
- 2 tablespoons olive oil
- 1 onion, sliced into wedges
- 2 cloves garlic, minced
- 1 lb. green beans, trimmed
- Salt and pepper to taste
- 4 squash, sliced
- ¼ cup balsamic vinegar

Method:
1. Preheat your oven to 450 degrees F.
2. Drizzle oil over onion, garlic, and green beans.
3. Spread in a pan.
4. Season with salt and pepper.
5. Roast in the oven for 8 minutes.
6. Add squash and roast for another 7 minutes.
7. Boil balsamic vinegar in a pan over medium heat.
8. Reduce heat and simmer for 10 minutes.
9. Pour vinegar over the veggies and serve.

Nutritional Value:
- Calories 90
- Total Fat 3.6 g
- Saturated Fat 0.5 g
- Cholesterol 0 mg
- Sodium 45 mg
- Total Carbohydrate 13 g
- Dietary Fiber 2.7 g
- Protein 1.9 g

Lemon Mustard Baby Veggies

Preparation Time: 10 minutes; Cooking Time: 5 minutes; Servings: 8

Ingredients:
- 1 tablespoon olive oil
- 2 tablespoons fresh lemon juice
- 1 teaspoon Dijon-style mustard
- 2 tablespoons water
- ½ teaspoon lemon zest
- 2 teaspoons fresh basil, chopped
- 1 clove garlic, minced
- 12 cherry tomatoes
- 1 lb. baby zucchini
- 1 lb. baby carrots
- Water

Method:
1. Pour oil, lemon juice, mustard, water, lemon zest and basil into a glass jar with lid.
2. Shake to blend well. Set aside.
3. Cook veggies in a pan with water over medium heat for 3 minutes.
4. Drain and coat with the mixture.

Nutritional Value:
- Calories 57
- Total Fat 2 g
- Saturated Fat 0.3 g
- Cholesterol 0 mg
- Sodium 190 mg
- Total Carbohydrate 9 g
- Dietary Fiber 2 g
- Protein 2 g

Cheesy Acorn Squash

Preparation Time: 10 minutes; Cooking Time: 35 minutes; Servings: 6
Ingredients:
- 1 tablespoon vegetable oil
- 1 lb. squash, sliced
- 1 teaspoon fresh sage, chopped
- Salt and pepper to taste
- ¼ teaspoon ground nutmeg
- ¼ cup Parmesan cheese, grated

Method:
1. Preheat your oven to 350 degrees F.
2. Add squash to a baking pan.
3. Coat the squash with oil.
4. Sprinkle with salt, pepper and nutmeg.
5. Roast for 30 minutes.
6. Sprinkle with cheese.
7. Roast for another 5 minutes.

Nutritional Value:
- Calories 86
- Total Fat 3 g
- Saturated Fat 1 g
- Cholesterol 2 mg
- Sodium 171 mg
- Total Carbohydrate 15 g
- Dietary Fiber 2 g
- Protein 2 g

Roasted Carrots with Honey

Preparation Time: 10 minutes; Cooking Time: 20 minutes; Servings: 4
Ingredients:
- 1 lb. carrots, sliced
- 2 teaspoons olive oil
- Salt and pepper to taste
- Honey for drizzling

Method:
1. Preheat your oven to 425 degrees F.
2. Spray your pan with oil.
3. Coat the carrots with olive oil.
4. Season with salt and pepper.
5. Spread in the baking pan.
6. Roast for 20 minutes.
7. Drizzle with honey and serve as side dish

Nutritional Value:
- Calories 56
- Total Fat 1.9 g
- Saturated Fat 1.8 g
- Cholesterol 0.3 mg
- Sodium 193 mg
- Total Carbohydrate 9.7 g
- Dietary Fiber 2.8 g
- Protein 0.9 g

Parmesan Leeks

Preparation Time: 15 minutes; Cooking Time: 30 minutes; Servings: 4
Ingredients:
- 4 leeks, trimmed
- ¼ cup whole-wheat breadcrumbs
- 3 tablespoons light butter
- 3 tablespoons Parmesan cheese, grated
- ¼ cup parsley, chopped

Method:
1. Preheat your oven to 350 degrees F.
2. Spread the leeks in the baking pan.
3. In a bowl, mix the remaining ingredients.

4. Bake in the oven for 30 minutes.

Nutritional Value:
- Calories 162
- Total Fat 5.3 g
- Saturated Fat 2.2 g
- Cholesterol 6 mg
- Sodium 199 mg
- Total Carbohydrate 22.7 g
- Dietary Fiber 2.5 g
- Protein 6 g

Zucchini Fritters

Preparation Time: 15 minutes; Cooking Time: 10 minutes; Servings: 2

Ingredients:
- 2 cups zucchini, shredded
- ½ cup red bell pepper, chopped
- ½ white onion, chopped
- 3 tablespoons multi-grain crackers, crushed
- 1 egg, beaten
- Pinch garlic powder
- Salt and pepper to taste
- 1 tablespoon olive oil
- ¼ cup nonfat Greek yogurt

Method:
1. Mix all the ingredients except oil and yogurt in a bowl.
2. Form patties from the mixture.
3. Pour the oil into a pan over medium heat.
4. Cook the fritters for 3 to 5 minutes per side.
5. Serve with yogurt.

Nutritional Value:
- Calories 110
- Total Fat 10 g
- Saturated Fat 2 g
- Cholesterol 200 mg
- Sodium 360 mg
- Total Carbohydrate 20.8 g
- Dietary Fiber 2.4 g
- Protein 9 g

Roasted Brussels Sprouts with Parmesan Cheese

Preparation Time: 10 minutes; Cooking Time: 20 minutes; Servings: 4

Ingredients:
- 1 lb. Brussels sprouts, sliced in half
- 2 teaspoons olive oil
- Garlic salt to taste
- Parmesan cheese, grated

Method:
1. Preheat your oven to 425 degrees F.
2. Spray your pan with oil.
3. Coat the Brussels sprouts with oil.
4. Season with garlic salt.
5. Spread in the baking pan.
6. Roast for 20 minutes.
7. Sprinkle with Parmesan cheese before serving.

Nutritional Value:
- Calories 59
- Total Fat 2 g
- Saturated Fat 0.3 g
- Cholesterol 0 mg
- Sodium 149 mg
- Total Carbohydrate 9.2 g
- Dietary Fiber 3.9 g
- Protein 3.5 g

Baked Beans with Bacon

Preparation Time: 20 minutes; Cooking Time: 6 hours; Servings: 12

Ingredients:
- Cooking spray
- 1 onion, chopped

- 3 cloves garlic, minced
- ½ cup celery, chopped
- 50 oz. navy beans, rinsed and drained
- ½ cup low-sodium tomato juice
- ½ cup unsalted tomato sauce
- ½ cup brown sugar
- 1 tablespoon cider vinegar
- ½ cup low-sugar ketchup
- 1 teaspoon dry mustard
- Salt to taste
- 4 slices turkey bacon, chopped and cooked crispy

Method:
1. Spray your slow cooker with oil.
2. Add all the ingredients except turkey bacon to a pot.
3. Mix well.
4. Cover the pot and cook on low for 6 hours.
5. Serve topped with crispy bacon bits.

Nutritional Value:
- Calories 143
- Total Fat 2 g
- Saturated Fat 0.7 g
- Cholesterol 2 mg
- Sodium 189 mg
- Total Carbohydrate 24.5 g
- Dietary Fiber 5.8 g
- Protein 6.4 g

Spicy Brussels Sprouts

Preparation Time: 10 minutes; Cooking Time: 10 minutes; Servings: 4
Ingredients:
- 1 lb. Brussels sprouts, trimmed
- 1 tablespoon olive oil
- Salt and pepper to taste
- ½ teaspoon chili powder
- ½ teaspoon lemon zest
- 1 teaspoon lemon juice

Method:
1. Preheat your oven to 400 degrees F.
2. Coat Brussels sprouts with olive oil, salt, pepper, chili powder, lemon zest and lemon juice.
3. Spread in a baking pan.
4. Roast for 10 minutes.

Nutritional Value:
- Calories 44
- Total Fat 3.6 g
- Saturated Fat 0.5 g
- Cholesterol 0 mg
- Sodium 89 mg
- Total Carbohydrate 2.6 g
- Dietary Fiber 1.1 g
- Protein 0.9 g

Sautéed Spinach

Preparation Time: 5 minutes; Cooking Time: 5 minutes; Servings: 4
Ingredients:
- 2 teaspoons olive oil
- 2 cloves garlic, sliced
- 2 teaspoons lemon zest
- 1 lb. baby spinach
- ¼ cup low-sodium chicken broth
- Salt to taste

Method:
1. Add oil to a pan over medium heat.
2. Cook garlic and lemon zest for 30 seconds.
3. Add spinach and broth.
4. Season with salt.
5. Cook for 3 minutes and serve.

Nutritional Value:
- Calories 50
- Total Fat 2.7 g

- Saturated Fat 0.4 g
- Cholesterol 0 mg
- Sodium 198 mg
- Total Carbohydrate 4.8 g
- Dietary Fiber 2.6 g
- Protein 3.5 g

Smoky Mashed Potatoes

Preparation Time: 15 minutes; Cooking Time: 30 minutes; Servings: 8

Ingredients:
- 4 lb. potatoes, peeled and sliced into cubes
- 3 tablespoons light and unsalted butter
- 1 cup almond milk
- 2 teaspoons dried thyme
- 4 cloves garlic, minced
- 1 ½ teaspoons smoked paprika
- Salt to taste

Method:
1. Add potatoes, butter, milk, thyme and garlic in a pot.
2. Cover and cook for 30 minutes.
3. Transfer to a food processor along with paprika and salt.
4. Process until smooth.

Nutritional Value:
- Calories 272
- Total Fat 7.4 g
- Saturated Fat 4.6 g
- Cholesterol 20 mg
- Sodium 427 mg
- Total Carbohydrate 48 g
- Dietary Fiber 7.1 g
- Protein 4.7 g

Chapter 9: Appetizers and Snacks Recipes

Cauliflower Gnocchi with Marinara Dip

Preparation Time: 10 minutes; Cooking Time: 20 minutes; Servings: 8

Ingredients:
- 20 oz. cauliflower gnocchi
- 3 tablespoons olive oil
- ½ cup Parmesan cheese, grated
- 2 tablespoons parsley, chopped
- 1 cup marinara sauce

Method:
1. Coat cauliflower gnocchi in oil.
2. Bake in the oven at 350 degrees F for 20 minutes.
3. Sprinkle with Parmesan cheese and parsley.
4. Serve with marinara sauce.

Nutritional Value:
- Calories 159
- Total Fat 9 g
- Saturated Fat 1.9 g
- Cholesterol 4 mg
- Sodium 163 mg
- Total Carbohydrate 14 g
- Dietary Fiber 3.6 g
- Protein 3 g

Goat Cheese Crostini

Preparation Time: 15 minutes; Cooking Time: 25 minutes; Servings: 15

Ingredients:
- ¼ cup honey
- 8 oz. figs, diced
- ¼ cup orange juice
- ¼ cup lemon juice
- 1 teaspoon fresh rosemary, minced
- 3 tablespoons water
- Salt and pepper to taste
- 30 whole-wheat baguette
- 1 tablespoon olive oil
- 6 oz. goat cheese

Method:
1. Mix honey, figs, orange juice, lemon juice, rosemary, water, salt and pepper in a pan over medium heat.
2. Simmer for 15 minutes.
3. Spread mixture on top of baguette slices.
4. Add to a baking pan.
5. Bake in the oven at 375 degrees F for 10 minutes.
6. Top with goat cheese and serve.

Nutritional Value:
- Calories 137
- Total Fat 3.6 g
- Saturated Fat 1.8 g
- Cholesterol 5 mg
- Sodium 183 mg
- Total Carbohydrate 22.9 g
- Dietary Fiber 1 g
- Protein 4 g

Black Bean Dip

Preparation Time: 20 minutes; Cooking Time: 5 minutes; Servings: 18

Ingredients:

Dip
- 1 tablespoon lime juice
- 15 oz. refried black beans
- 1 clove garlic, grated
- ½ teaspoon ground cumin
- ½ teaspoon chili powder
- Salt to taste

Toppings
- ¼ cup onion, chopped
- ¼ cup fresh cheese, crumbled

- 1 avocado, diced
- 2 tablespoons pickled jalapeño, diced
- ½ cup tomato, chopped
- Chopped cilantro

Method:
1. Simmer dip ingredients in a pan over medium heat for 5 minutes.
2. Spread the mixture in a baking pan.
3. Top with the topping ingredients and serve.

Nutritional Value:
- Calories 58
- Total Fat 2.9 g
- Saturated Fat 0.5 g
- Cholesterol 2 mg
- Sodium 107 mg
- Total Carbohydrate 6.2 g
- Dietary Fiber 2.2 g
- Protein 2.4 g

Cheesy Apple Bites

Preparation Time: 10 minutes; Cooking Time: 10 minutes; Servings: 24
Ingredients:
- Cooking spray
- 1 pie crust
- ¼ cup apple butter
- ½ cup cheddar cheese, shredded
- 24 thin apple slices

Method:
1. Preheat your oven to 450 degrees F.
2. Spray your muffin pan with oil.
3. Cut circles on the dough using a cookie cutter.
4. Press the circles into muffin cups.
5. Bake for 5 minutes.
6. Top with the apple butter, cheese and apple slices.
7. Bake for another 5 minutes.
8. Let cool and serve warm.

Nutritional Value:
- Calories 51
- Total Fat 2.9 g
- Saturated Fat 1.2 g
- Cholesterol 0 mg
- Sodium 49 mg
- Total Carbohydrate 5.5 g
- Dietary Fiber 0.2 g
- Protein 0.8 g

Baked Cheesy Broccoli

Preparation Time: 20 minutes; Cooking Time: 15 minutes; Servings: 8
Ingredients:
- Cooking spray
- ¾ cup broccoli, steamed and chopped
- ¼ teaspoon onion powder
- ½ teaspoon garlic powder
- Pepper to taste
- ¾ cup cheddar cheese, shredded

Method:
1. Preheat your oven to 350 degrees F.
2. Spray your muffin pan with oil.
3. Season broccoli with onion powder, garlic powder and pepper.
4. Divide into the muffin cups.
5. Top with the cheese.
6. Bake for 15 minutes.
7. Let cool before serving.

Nutritional Value:
- Calories 87
- Total Fat 4.2 g
- Saturated Fat 2 g
- Cholesterol 32 mg

- Sodium 209 mg
- Total Carbohydrate 7.8 g
- Dietary Fiber 0.9 g
- Protein 4.6 g

Grilled Figs with Goat Cheese & Honey

Preparation Time: 10 minutes; Cooking Time: 6 minutes; Servings: 4
Ingredients:
- 2 teaspoons honey
- 1 tablespoon low-fat milk
- ½ teaspoon fresh thyme, chopped
- ¼ cup goat cheese, crumbled
- 12 fresh figs
- Cooking spray
- Salt to taste

Method:
1. Preheat your grill.
2. Combine the honey, milk, thyme and goat cheese in a bowl.
3. Spray figs with oil.
4. Spread mixture on top of figs.
5. Grill for 3 minutes per side.
6. Sprinkle with salt and serve.

Nutritional Value:
- Calories 109
- Total Fat 4 g
- Saturated Fat 2 g
- Cholesterol 0 mg
- Sodium 167 mg
- Total Carbohydrate 17 g
- Dietary Fiber 2 g
- Protein 3 g

Deviled Eggs with Rosemary

Preparation Time: 15 minutes; Cooking Time: 0 minutes; Servings: 12
Ingredients:
- 6 hard-boiled eggs, sliced in half
- ½ teaspoon dried rosemary
- ¼ cup mayonnaise
- 1 tablespoon mustard
- Salt to taste

Method:
1. Scoop the yolks from the hard-boiled eggs.
2. Mash the egg yolks in a bowl.
3. Stir in the rest of the ingredients.
4. Add a scoop of mixture on top of the egg whites.

Nutritional Value:
- Calories 69
- Total Fat 5.9 g
- Saturated Fat 1.3 g
- Cholesterol 95 mg
- Sodium 110 mg
- Total Carbohydrate 0.4 g
- Dietary Fiber 0.1 g
- Protein 3.2 g

Rainbow Salsa

Preparation Time: 30 minutes; Cooking Time: 0 minutes; Servings: 8
Ingredients:
- ½ cup onion, diced
- 1 red bell peppers, chopped
- 1 yellow bell pepper, chopped
- 1 green bell pepper, chopped
- 1 cup mango, diced
- 2 cups peaches, chopped
- Chopped cilantro
- 2 tablespoons lemon juice
- Garlic salt to taste

Method:
1. Combine all the ingredients in a bowl.

2. Serve with nacho chips.

Nutritional Value:
- Calories 46
- Total Fat 0.3 g
- Saturated Fat 0.1 g
- Cholesterol 0 mg
- Sodium 74 mg
- Total Carbohydrate 11.3 g
- Dietary Fiber 1.5 g
- Protein 0.9 g

Spicy Pecans

Preparation Time: 15 minutes; Cooking Time: 1 hour; Servings: 20

Ingredients:
- 1 egg white
- 1 tablespoon water
- 6 tablespoons white sugar
- Salt to taste
- ¼ teaspoon ground allspice
- ¼ teaspoon ground cloves
- ¼ teaspoon ground nutmeg
- 4 cups pecans, sliced in half

Method:
1. Preheat your oven to 275 degrees F.
2. Combine all the ingredients in a bowl.
3. Coat pecans evenly with the spices.
4. Spread pecans in the baking pan.
5. Bake for 30 minutes.
6. Stir and bake for another 30 minutes.
7. Let cool before serving.

Nutritional Value:
- Calories 151
- Total Fat 14 g
- Saturated Fat 1.2 g
- Cholesterol 0 mg
- Sodium 51 mg
- Total Carbohydrate 6 g
- Dietary Fiber 1.9 g
- Protein 2 g

Tomato Dip

Preparation Time: 20 minutes; Cooking Time: 5 hours; Servings: 10

Ingredients:
- 15 oz. tomato sauce
- 15 oz. canned diced tomatoes
- 1 onion, chopped
- ½ cup tomato paste
- 2 teaspoons dried oregano
- 2 cloves garlic, minced
- 1 teaspoon granulated sugar
- Pinch cayenne pepper
- Vegetable dippers

Method:
1. Combine all ingredients except vegetable dippers in the slow cooker.
2. Cook on low for 5 hours.
3. Let cool and transfer to a bowl.
4. Serve with vegetable dippers.

Nutritional Value:
- Calories 68
- Total Fat 0.6 g
- Saturated Fat 0.1 g
- Cholesterol 0 mg
- Sodium 94 mg
- Total Carbohydrate 14 g
- Dietary Fiber 3.8 g
- Protein 2 g

Chives Dip

Preparation Time: 5 minutes; Cooking Time: 0 minutes; Servings: 16

Ingredients:

- 1 tub vegetable oil spread
- 1 teaspoon fresh chives, chopped
- ½ teaspoon lemon zest
- Pepper to taste

Method:
1. Combine all ingredients in a bowl.
2. Chill until ready to serve.

Nutritional Value:
- Calories 26
- Total Fat 3 g
- Saturated Fat 1 g
- Cholesterol 0 mg
- Sodium 30 mg
- Total Carbohydrate 10 g
- Dietary Fiber 3 g
- Protein 15 g

Tuna Canapes

Preparation Time: 10 minutes; Cooking Time: 0 minutes; Servings: 6

Ingredients:
- 1 onion, chopped
- 5 oz. tuna flakes
- 3 oz. low-fat cream cheese
- 2 teaspoons olive oil
- 2 tablespoon chives, chopped
- ½ teaspoon liquid smoke
- ½ teaspoon Worcestershire sauce
- 1 teaspoon low-sodium Old Bay Seasoning
- 24 whole wheat crackers
- 1 cup cucumber, chopped

Method:
1. Mix all ingredients except crackers and cucumber in a bowl.
2. Spread mixture on top of crackers.
3. Top with chopped cucumber and serve.

Nutritional Value:
- Calories 112
- Total Fat 5.6 g
- Saturated Fat 2 g
- Cholesterol 21 mg
- Sodium 160 mg
- Total Carbohydrate 8.5 g
- Dietary Fiber 0.6 g
- Protein 7.4 g

Wasabi Snack Mix

Preparation Time: 15 minutes; Cooking Time: 30 minutes; Servings: 14

Ingredients:
- 2 cups mini pretzel sticks
- 2 ½ cups rice and corn cereal
- ¾ cup almonds
- 1 cup wasabi dried peas
- 1 tablespoon low-sodium soy sauce
- 2 tablespoons rice vinegar
- ¼ cup light butter
- ¼ teaspoon cayenne pepper
- ½ teaspoon ground ginger

Method:
1. Preheat your oven to 300 degrees F.
2. Mix all ingredients in a bowl.
3. Transfer to a baking pan.
4. Bake for 30 minutes.
5. Let cool before serving.

Nutritional Value:
- Calories 126
- Total Fat 6.6 g
- Saturated Fat 1.7 g
- Cholesterol 4 mg
- Sodium 211 mg
- Total Carbohydrate 15.2 g
- Dietary Fiber 1.7 g
- Protein 3.3 g

Spicy Appetizer Mix

Preparation Time: 15 minutes; Cooking Time: 30 minutes; Servings: 14

Ingredients:
- 3 tablespoons vegetable oil
- 2 cups whole-wheat melba toast rounds, sliced
- 2 cups corn cereal
- 3 tablespoons honey
- 1 teaspoon smoked paprika
- 3 tablespoons low-sodium Worcestershire sauce
- 1 cup chipotle-flavored chickpeas
- 1 teaspoon hot sauce
- 1 cup unsalted pistachios

Method:
1. Mix all ingredients in a bowl.
2. Transfer to a baking pan.
3. Bake in the oven at 375 degrees F for 30 minutes.
4. Stir and let cool.

Nutritional Value:
- Calories 148
- Total Fat 6 g
- Saturated Fat 1 g
- Cholesterol 0 mg
- Sodium 195 mg
- Total Carbohydrate 20 g
- Dietary Fiber 2 g
- Protein 4 g

Roasted Vegetable Spread

Preparation Time: 20 minutes; Cooking Time: 40 minutes; Servings: 9

Ingredients:
- 2 red bell peppers, sliced in half
- 1 lb. tomatoes, sliced into wedges
- 3 cloves garlic, peeled
- 1 onion, sliced in wedges
- 2 tablespoons olive oil
- Salt and pepper to taste
- 2 tablespoons balsamic vinegar
- 2 teaspoons fresh thyme, chopped
- ¼ cup fresh basil, chopped

Method:
1. Preheat your oven to 425 degrees F.
2. Toss the vegetables in olive oil and season with salt and pepper.
3. Roast in the oven for 40 minutes.
4. Transfer to a food processor.
5. Stir in the rest of the ingredients.

Nutritional Value:
- Calories 57
- Total Fat 3.3 g
- Saturated Fat 0.4 g
- Cholesterol 0 mg
- Sodium 113 mg
- Total Carbohydrate 6.5 g
- Dietary Fiber 1.5 g
- Protein 1.1 g

Sugar Snap Peas with Dip

Preparation Time: 5 minutes; Cooking Time: 5 minutes; Servings: 6

Ingredients:
- 3 cups sugar snap peas
- Water
- 1 cup honey mustard sauce

Method:
1. Boil sugar snap peas in a pot of water for 5 minutes.
2. Drain and let cool.
3. Serve with dip.

Nutritional Value:
- Calories 20
- Total Fat 0 g
- Saturated Fat 0 g
- Cholesterol 0 mg
- Sodium 10 mg
- Total Carbohydrate 4 g
- Dietary Fiber 1 g
- Protein 1 g

Pumpkin & Avocado Salsa

Preparation Time: 15 minutes; Cooking Time: 0 minutes; Servings: 2

Ingredients:
- 1 cup pumpkin puree
- 1 tomato, chopped
- 1 avocado, chopped
- 1 onion, chopped
- 1 tablespoon fresh cilantro, chopped
- 1 tablespoon lime juice
- 1 clove garlic, minced
- 2 tablespoons hot sauce
- Salt to taste

Method:
1. Combine all the ingredients in a bowl.
2. Serve with vegetable dippers.

Nutritional Value:
- Calories 45
- Total Fat 2.7 g
- Saturated Fat 0.4 g
- Cholesterol 0 mg
- Sodium 23 mg
- Total Carbohydrate 5.4 g
- Dietary Fiber 2.4 g
- Protein 0.9 g

Chicken Wings

Preparation Time: 10 minutes; Cooking Time: 6 hours; Servings: 12

Ingredients:
- 24 chicken wings
- ¼ cup water
- 1 tablespoon lime juice
- ¾ teaspoon ground ginger
- 2 tablespoons low-sodium soy sauce
- ½ cup natural peanut butter
- Red pepper flakes
- 2 cloves garlic, minced

Method:
1. Add chicken to a slow cooker.
2. Pour in water and lime juice.
3. Add ground ginger.
4. Cover the pot.
5. Cook on low for 6 hours.
6. In a pan over medium heat, cook soy sauce, peanut butter, red pepper flakes and garlic.
7. Coat the chicken wings in the sauce and serve.

Nutritional Value:
- Calories 102
- Total Fat 6.4 g
- Saturated Fat 1.3 g
- Cholesterol 15 mg
- Sodium 160 mg
- Total Carbohydrate 3 g
- Dietary Fiber 0.6 g
- Protein 8.6 g

Roasted Pears with Bacon

Preparation Time: 15 minutes; Cooking Time: 15 minutes; Servings: 12

Ingredients:
- 4 ripe pears, sliced
- 6 slices turkey bacon
- 2 tablespoons balsamic vinegar

Method:

1. Wrap turkey bacon around pear slices.
2. Arrange pears in a baking pan.
3. Bake for 15 minutes.
4. Drizzle with balsamic vinegar.

Nutritional Value:
- Calories 51
- Total Fat 0.8 g
- Saturated Fat 0.3 g
- Cholesterol 6 mg
- Sodium 189 mg
- Total Carbohydrate 9.7 g
- Dietary Fiber 1.8 g
- Protein 2.2 g

Zucchini Rolls

Preparation Time: 15 minutes; Cooking Time: 0 minutes; Servings: 10

Ingredients:
- 1 cup low-fat cream cheese
- ¼ cup Parmesan cheese, grated
- ¼ cup basil, chopped
- 1 ½ teaspoons Italian seasoning
- 1 clove garlic, grated
- Pepper to taste
- 3 zucchinis, sliced into long strips

Method:
1. Put all the ingredients except zucchini in a bowl.
2. Mix well.
3. Spread mixture on top of zucchini and roll it up.

Nutritional Value:
- Calories 77
- Total Fat 5 g
- Saturated Fat 3 g
- Cholesterol 6 mg
- Sodium 132 mg
- Total Carbohydrate 4.6 g
- Dietary Fiber 1.1 g
- Protein 3.7 g

Bruschetta with Cranberry & Pomegranate

Preparation Time: 40 minutes; Cooking Time: 15 minutes; Servings: 16

Ingredients:
- ½ cup cranberries, chopped
- ¾ cup pomegranate seeds
- 1 teaspoon orange zest
- 2 tablespoons sugar
- Salt to taste
- 16 baguette slices
- Cooking spray
- Pepper to taste
- Brie cheese, shredded
- 1 tablespoon fresh basil, chopped

Method:
1. In a bowl, mix cranberries, pomegranate seeds, orange zest, sugar and salt.
2. Cover and chill in the refrigerator for 30 minutes.
3. Preheat your oven to 350 degrees F.
4. Arrange bread slices in the baking pan.
5. Spray with oil.
6. Season with pepper.
7. Bake for 8 minutes.
8. Top with cheese.
9. Bake for 5 minutes.
10. Top with reserved mixture and basil.
11. Serve.

Nutritional Value:
- Calories 77
- Total Fat 3.5 g
- Saturated Fat 1.5 g
- Cholesterol 8 mg

- Sodium 114 mg
- Total Carbohydrate 8.4 g
- Dietary Fiber 0.2 g
- Protein 2.2 g

Mushrooms with Pesto

Preparation Time: 10 minutes; Cooking Time: 25 minutes; Servings: 12
Ingredients:
- 12 large button mushroom caps
- ½ cup pesto
- ¼ cup breadcrumbs

Method:
1. Preheat your oven to 350 degrees F.
2. Add mushrooms to a baking pan.
3. Top with the pesto and breadcrumbs.
4. Bake for 25 minutes.

Nutritional Value:
- Calories 45
- Total Fat 3.2 g
- Saturated Fat 0.8 g
- Cholesterol 2 mg
- Sodium 56 mg
- Total Carbohydrate 2.5 g
- Dietary Fiber 0.4 g
- Protein 1.8 g

Chicken Fingers

Preparation Time: 20 minutes; Cooking Time: 25 minutes; Servings: 4
Ingredients:
- Cooking spray
- ½ cup almonds, crushed
- ¼ cup whole-wheat flour
- 1 ½ teaspoons paprika
- ½ teaspoon garlic powder
- ½ teaspoon dry mustard
- Salt and pepper to taste
- 1 teaspoon olive oil
- 1 lb. chicken strips

Method:
1. Preheat your oven to 425 degrees F.
2. Add all ingredients except chicken and oil to a food processor.
3. Pulse until fully combined.
4. Coat the chicken strips with the mixture.
5. Drizzle with the oil.
6. Arrange in a baking pan.
7. Bake in the oven for 25 minutes or until golden and crispy.

Nutritional Value:
- Calories 184
- Total Fat 6.6 g
- Saturated Fat 1.1 g
- Cholesterol 63 mg
- Sodium 147 mg
- Total Carbohydrate 4.4 g
- Dietary Fiber 1.3 g
- Protein 26 g

Spicy Cauliflower

Preparation Time: 15 minutes; Cooking Time: 20 minutes; Servings: 6
Ingredients:
- 8 cups cauliflower florets
- 2 tablespoons olive oil
- Salt to taste
- 1 tablespoon lemon juice
- 1 tablespoon melted butter
- 3 tablespoons hot sauce

Method:
1. Preheat your oven to 450 degrees F.
2. Spray your baking pan with oil.

3. Toss the cauliflower in salt and oil.
4. Spread on the baking pan.
5. Roast in the oven for 15 minutes.
6. Mix the lemon juice, butter and hot sauce.
7. Drizzle over the cauliflower.
8. Roast for another 5 minutes.
9. Serve warm.

Nutritional Value:
- Calories 99
- Total Fat 7 g
- Saturated Fat 2 g
- Cholesterol 5 mg
- Sodium 288 mg
- Total Carbohydrate 8 g
- Dietary Fiber 3 g
- Protein 3 g

Onion Rings

Preparation Time: 15 minutes; Cooking Time: 10 minutes; Servings: 6
Ingredients:
- 2 onions, sliced into rings
- ¾ cup all-purpose flour
- 2 teaspoons baking powder
- 3 eggs, beaten
- 2 cups breadcrumbs
- 1 tablespoon Old Bay seasoning
- Cooking spray

Method:
1. Preheat your oven to 450 degrees F.
2. Dip the onion rings in a mixture of flour and baking powder.
3. Dip in eggs.
4. Dredge with breadcrumbs season with Old Bay seasoning.
5. Spray with oil.
6. Bake in the oven for 10 minutes.

Nutritional Value:
- Calories 175
- Total Fat 3 g
- Saturated Fat 0.9 g
- Cholesterol 70 mg
- Sodium 558 mg
- Total Carbohydrate 29 g
- Dietary Fiber 2 g
- Protein 7 g

Chips & Salsa

Preparation Time: 15 minutes; Cooking Time: 0 minutes; Servings: 4
Ingredients:
- Low-sodium nacho chips
- 1 white onion, chopped
- ½ cup fresh cilantro, chopped
- 1 teaspoon lime zest, grated
- 2 cups cucumber, chopped
- 1 jalapeño pepper, chopped
- 2 tablespoons lemon juice
- Salt to taste

Method:
1. Place nacho chips in a serving plate.
2. In a bowl, combine the rest of the ingredients.
3. Serve nachos with salsa.

Nutritional Value:
- Calories 20
- Total Fat 0.1 g
- Saturated Fat 0 g
- Cholesterol 0 mg
- Sodium 103 mg
- Total Carbohydrate 5 g
- Dietary Fiber 0.6 g
- Protein 0.5 g

Zucchini Chips

Preparation Time: 15 minutes; Cooking Time: 20 minutes; Servings: 8
Ingredients:
- 1 lb. zucchini, sliced into rounds
- ½ cup cornstarch
- 4 egg whites, beaten
- 2 cups breadcrumbs
- Cooking spray
- Salt to taste
- ¼ cup mayonnaise
- ¾ cup sour cream
- 2 teaspoons fresh dill, chopped
- 1 ½ tablespoons fresh chives, chopped
- 2 teaspoons lemon juice

Method:
1. Dip zucchini in cornstarch then in eggs.
2. Dredge with breadcrumbs.
3. Spray zucchini with oil.
4. Bake in the oven at 375 degrees F for 15 to 20 minutes.
5. In a bowl, mix the rest of the ingredients.
6. Serve zucchini chips with dip.

Nutritional Value:
- Calories 218
- Total Fat 10.6 g
- Saturated Fat 3 g
- Cholesterol 14 mg
- Sodium 347 mg
- Total Carbohydrate 25.2 g
- Dietary Fiber 1.1 g
- Protein 5.1 g

Cheesy Deviled Eggs

Preparation Time: 30 minutes; Cooking Time: 0 minutes; Servings: 24
Ingredients:
- 12 hard-boiled eggs, peeled and sliced in half
- ¼ cup mayonnaise
- ½ cup cheddar cheese, shredded
- 2 tablespoons scallions, chopped
- 2 tablespoons pimientos, chopped
- Salt and pepper to taste
- Pinch garlic powder

Method:
1. Scoop out the yolks from the eggs.
2. Place egg yolks in a bowl.
3. Stir in the rest of the ingredients.
4. Place a spoonful of the mixture on top of the egg whites and serve.

Nutritional Value:
- Calories 61
- Total Fat 4.9 g
- Saturated Fat 1.5 g
- Cholesterol 96 mg
- Sodium 78 mg
- Total Carbohydrate 0.4 g
- Dietary Fiber 2 g
- Protein 3.7 g

Pickle Chips

Preparation Time: 15 minutes; Cooking Time: 15 minutes; Servings: 6
Ingredients:
- 16 oz. dill pickle chips (low-sodium)
- ½ cup all-purpose flour
- 2 eggs, beaten
- 1 cup panko breadcrumbs
- 1 tablespoon mustard
- ¼ cup mayonnaise
- 1 teaspoon lemon juice
- ½ teaspoon smoked paprika

Method:
1. Dip the pickle chips in flour.

2. Dip into the eggs.
3. Dredge with breadcrumbs.
4. Bake in the oven at 350 degrees F for 15 minutes.
5. Mix the rest of the ingredients in a bowl.
6. Serve pickle chips with dip.

Nutritional Value:
- Calories 177
- Total Fat 9.1 g
- Saturated Fat 1.6 g
- Cholesterol 66 mg
- Sodium 409 mg
- Total Carbohydrate 18.6 g
- Dietary Fiber 2.1 g
- Protein 5.6 g

Spinach Feta Dip & Crackers

Preparation Time: 10 minutes; Cooking Time: 0 minutes; Servings: 8

Ingredients:
- ¾ cup feta cheese, crumbled
- 2 oz. low-fat cream cheese
- 2 cups spinach, chopped
- 1 clove garlic, grated
- ½ cup fresh dill sprigs
- ½ cup low-fat sour cream
- Pepper to taste
- Whole-wheat crackers

Method:
1. Combine all ingredients in a food processor.
2. Pulse until smooth.
3. Serve with whole-wheat crackers.

Nutritional Value:
- Calories 75
- Total Fat 5.9 g
- Saturated Fat 3.9 g
- Cholesterol 22 mg
- Sodium 174 mg
- Total Carbohydrate 2.3 g
- Dietary Fiber 0.2 g
- Protein 3 g

Turkey Nachos

Preparation Time: 30 minutes; Cooking Time: 4 hours; Servings: 6

Ingredients:
- 1 ½ lb. turkey breast fillet
- Pepper to taste
- 2 tablespoons lime juice
- 2 tablespoons chili powder
- 1 teaspoon ground cumin
- 1 tablespoon honey
- 3 cloves garlic, minced
- 1 ½ cups pico de gallo
- ½ cup fresh cilantro, chopped
- 6 oz. baked tortilla chips
- 2 oz. Mexican cheese, crumbled

Method:
1. Sprinkle turkey with pepper.
2. Place in a slow cooker.
3. Stir in the rest of the ingredients except chips and cheese.
4. Cover the pot and cook on low for 4 hours.
5. Shred the turkey.
6. Return to the pot and stir.
7. Place chips in a serving plate.
8. Sprinkle shredded turkey mixture on top.
9. Top with cheese.

Nutritional Value:
- Calories 297
- Total Fat 9 g
- Saturated Fat 2 g
- Cholesterol 0 mg

- Sodium 600 mg
- Total Carbohydrate 26 g
- Dietary Fiber 5 g
- Protein 29 g

Caprese Skewers

Preparation Time: 15 minutes; Cooking Time: 0 minutes; Servings: 8

Ingredients:
- 24 cherry tomatoes
- 48 mozzarella cheese balls
- 2 peaches, sliced
- 24 basil leaves
- 2 tablespoons balsamic glaze

Method:
1. Thread tomatoes, mozzarella, peaches and basil onto skewers.
2. Drizzle with balsamic glaze.

Nutritional Value:
- Calories 79
- Total Fat 4 g
- Saturated Fat 2 g
- Cholesterol 0 mg
- Sodium 263 mg
- Total Carbohydrate 6 g
- Dietary Fiber 1 g
- Protein 4 g

Antipasto Skewers

Preparation Time: 15 minutes; Cooking Time: 0 minutes; Servings: 12

Ingredients:
- 6 red bell pepper, sliced
- 12 slices salami, sliced in half and cooked
- 24 basil leaves
- 24 black olives
- 1 teaspoon chopped rosemary
- 2 teaspoons white wine vinegar
- 3 teaspoons olive oil

Method:
1. Thread red bell pepper, salami, basil leaves and olives onto skewers.
2. In a bowl, mix rosemary, vinegar and oil.
3. Drizzle over the skewers and serve.

Nutritional Value:
- Calories 96
- Total Fat 7 g
- Saturated Fat 2 g
- Cholesterol 0 mg
- Sodium 205 mg
- Total Carbohydrate 6 g
- Dietary Fiber 1 g
- Protein 3 g

Beet Hummus

Preparation Time: 15 minutes; Cooking Time: 0 minutes; Servings: 12

Ingredients:
- 1 lb. roasted red beets
- 15 oz. chickpeas, rinsed and drained
- 6 tablespoons olive oil
- ¼ cup lemon juice
- ¼ cup tahini
- Salt to taste
- 1 ½ teaspoons ground cumin
- ⅛ teaspoon cayenne pepper

Method:
1. Add all the ingredients to a food processor.
2. Pulse until smooth.
3. Serve with veggie strips or crackers.

Nutritional Value:
- Calories 146
- Total Fat 10 g
- Saturated Fat 1 g
- Cholesterol 0 mg
- Sodium 240 mg
- Total Carbohydrate 12 g

- Dietary Fiber 3 g
- Protein 3 g

Cocoa Pumpkin Seeds

Preparation Time: 10 minutes; Cooking Time: 40 minutes; Servings: 8
Ingredients:
- 2 tablespoons coconut oil
- 2 tablespoons cocoa powder
- 2 cups pumpkin seeds
- ¼ cup sugar
- Salt to taste

Method:
1. Preheat your oven to 300 degrees F.
2. Mix all the ingredients in a bowl.
3. Spread on a baking sheet.
4. Bake for 40 minutes.
5. Let cool before serving.

Nutritional Value:
- Calories 238
- Total Fat 17.5 g
- Saturated Fat 6.4 g
- Cholesterol 0 mg
- Sodium 24 mg
- Total Carbohydrate 11.1 g
- Dietary Fiber 3.5 g
- Protein 9.3 g

Buffalo Wings

Preparation Time: 15 minutes; Cooking Time: 35 minutes; Servings: 4
Ingredients:
- 1 ½ teaspoons paprika
- ½ teaspoon onion powder
- ½ teaspoon garlic powder
- Pepper to taste
- 3 lb. chicken wings
- ½ cup Buffalo hot sauce
- 2 tablespoons butter

Method:
1. Preheat your oven to 200 degrees F.
2. Mix paprika, onion powder and garlic powder in a bowl.
3. Coat chicken wings evenly with the mixture.
4. Bake in the oven for 30 minutes.
5. Mix butter and hot sauce in a pan over medium heat.
6. Simmer for 5 minutes.
7. Dip the wings in the mixture before serving.

Nutritional Value:
- Calories 302
- Total Fat 17.3 g
- Saturated Fat 5.9 g
- Cholesterol 92 mg
- Sodium 1277 mg
- Total Carbohydrate 6.5 g
- Dietary Fiber 1.9 g
- Protein 29 g

Garlic Olives

Preparation Time: 5 minutes; Cooking Time: 5 minutes; Servings: 4
Ingredients:
- ¼ cup olive oil
- 2 cloves garlic, crushed
- 1 teaspoon lemon zest
- Red pepper flakes
- 1 cup olives

Method:
1. Combine all the ingredients in a pan.
2. Simmer for 5 minutes.

Nutritional Value:
- Calories 94
- Total Fat 9.4 g
- Saturated Fat 0.8 g
- Cholesterol 0 mg
- Sodium 280 mg
- Total Carbohydrate 1.5 g
- Dietary Fiber 0.8 g
- Protein 0.3 g

Stuffed Mushrooms

Preparation Time: 15 minutes; Cooking Time: 15 minutes; Servings: 10

Ingredients:
- Cooking spray
- 10 mushrooms buttons
- Salt and pepper to taste
- ¼ cup whole-wheat breadcrumbs
- 4 oz. cream cheese
- 2 tablespoons parsley, chopped

Method:
1. Spray mushrooms with oil and season with salt and pepper.
2. Mix breadcrumbs, cream cheese and parsley in a bowl.
3. Stuff the mixture into the mushrooms.
4. Bake in the oven at 350 degrees F for 15 minutes.

Nutritional Value:
- Calories 75
- Total Fat 4 g
- Saturated Fat 2 g
- Cholesterol 0 mg
- Sodium 184 mg
- Total Carbohydrate 7 g
- Dietary Fiber 1 g
- Protein 4 g

Cauliflower Nachos

Preparation Time: 15 minutes; Cooking Time: 20 minutes; Servings: 4

Ingredients:
- 8 cups cauliflower florets, sliced
- 3 tablespoons avocado oil
- Salt to taste
- ¾ teaspoon chili powder
- ¾ teaspoon ground cumin
- ¾ teaspoon onion powder
- Chopped tomatoes
- Chopped avocado
- Sour cream
- Salsa

Method:
1. Coat cauliflower with oil.
2. Season with salt and spices.
3. Bake in the oven at 400 degrees F for 20 minutes.
4. Top with tomatoes and avocado.
5. Serve with sour cream and salsa.

Nutritional Value:
- Calories 487
- Total Fat 28 g
- Saturated Fat 6.6 g
- Cholesterol 79 mg
- Sodium 484 mg
- Total Carbohydrate 27 g
- Dietary Fiber 11 g
- Protein 35 g

Garlic Chicken Wings

Preparation Time: 15 minutes; Cooking Time: 30 minutes; Servings: 8

Ingredients:
- 2 lb. chicken wings
- ½ cup all-purpose flour
- 2 tablespoons garlic powder
- 2 teaspoons ground pepper
- 3 eggs, beaten
- 1 ½ cups panko breadcrumbs
- 1 ¼ cups Parmesan cheese, grated
- Cooking spray

Method:
1. Preheat your oven to 400 degrees F.
2. Mix flour, garlic powder and pepper in a bowl.
3. Dip chicken wings in this mixture.
4. Dip in the egg and dredge with breadcrumbs.
5. Sprinkle with Parmesan cheese.
6. Spray with oil.
7. Bake in the oven for 30 minutes.

Nutritional Value:
- Calories 221
- Total Fat 11.6 g
- Saturated Fat 3.9 g
- Cholesterol 122 mg
- Sodium 242 mg
- Total Carbohydrate 12.4 g
- Dietary Fiber 0.4 g
- Protein 16 g

Chapter 10: Drinks Recipes

Pineapple & Strawberry Smoothie

Preparation Time: 10 minutes; Cooking Time: 0 minutes; Serving: 1

Ingredients:
- 1 cup strawberries
- 1 cup pineapple, chopped
- ¾ cup almond milk
- 1 tablespoon almond butter

Method:
1. Add all ingredients to a blender.
2. Blend until smooth.
3. Add more almond milk until it reaches your desired consistency.
4. Chill before serving.

Nutritional Value:
- Calories 255
- Total Fat 11.1 g
- Saturated Fat 1.1 g
- Cholesterol 0 mg
- Sodium 168 mg
- Total Carbohydrate 39 g
- Dietary Fiber 7.8 g
- Protein 5.6 g

Green Smoothie

Preparation Time: 10 minutes; Cooking Time: 0 minutes; Serving: 1

Ingredients:
- 1 cup vanilla almond milk (unsweetened)
- ¼ ripe avocado, chopped
- 1 cup kale, chopped
- 1 banana
- 2 teaspoons honey
- 1 tablespoon chia seeds
- 1 cup ice cubes

Method:
1. Combine all the ingredients in a blender.
2. Process until creamy.

Nutritional Value:
- Calories 343
- Total Fat 14.2 g
- Saturated Fat 1.6 g
- Cholesterol 0 mg
- Sodium 199 mg
- Total Carbohydrate 54.7 g
- Dietary Fiber 12.1 g
- Protein 5.9 g

Berry Smoothie With Mint

Preparation Time: 5 minutes; Cooking Time: 0 minutes; Servings: 2

Ingredients:
- ¼ cup orange juice
- ½ cup blueberries
- ½ cup blackberries
- 1 cup reduced-fat plain kefir
- 1 tablespoon honey
- 2 tablespoons fresh mint leaves

Method:
1. Add all the ingredients to a blender.
2. Blend until smooth.

Nutritional Value:
- Calories 137
- Total Fat 1 g
- Saturated Fat 1 g
- Cholesterol 5 mg
- Sodium 64 mg
- Total Carbohydrate 27 g
- Dietary Fiber 4 g
- Protein 6 g

Berry & Spinach Smoothie

Preparation Time: 5 minutes; Cooking Time: 0 minutes; Servings: 4

Ingredients:
- 2 cups strawberries
- 1 cup raspberries
- 1 cup blueberries
- 1 cup fresh baby spinach leaves
- 1 cup pomegranate juice
- 3 tablespoons milk powder (unsweetened)

Method:
1. Mix all the ingredients in a blender.
2. Blend until smooth.
3. Chill before serving.

Nutritional Value:
- Calories 118
- Total Fat 0.7 g
- Saturated Fat 0.2 g
- Cholesterol 10 mg
- Sodium 37 mg
- Total Carbohydrate 25.7 g
- Dietary Fiber 5 g
- Protein 4.6 g

Banana, Cauliflower & Berry Smoothie

Preparation Time: 5 minutes; Cooking Time: 0 minutes; Servings: 2

Ingredients:
- 2 cups almond milk (unsweetened)
- 1 cup banana, sliced
- ½ cup blueberries
- ½ cup blackberries
- 1 cup cauliflower rice
- 2 teaspoons maple syrup

Method:
1. Pour almond milk into a blender.
2. Stir in the rest of the ingredients.
3. Process until smooth.
4. Chill before serving.

Nutritional Value:
- Calories 149
- Total Fat 3 g
- Saturated Fat 0.1 g
- Cholesterol 0 mg
- Sodium 184 mg
- Total Carbohydrate 29 g
- Dietary Fiber 5 g
- Protein 3 g

Peach & Apricot Smoothie

Preparation Time: 10 minutes; Cooking Time: 0 minutes; Serving: 1

Ingredients:
- 1 cup almond milk (unsweetened)
- 1 teaspoon honey
- ½ cup apricots, sliced
- ½ cup peaches, sliced
- ½ cup carrot, chopped
- 1 teaspoon vanilla extract

Method:
1. Mix milk and honey.
2. Pour into a blender.
3. Add the apricots, peaches and carrots.
4. Stir in the vanilla.
5. Blend until smooth.

Nutritional Value:
- Calories 153
- Total Fat 2.6 g
- Saturated Fat 0.1 g
- Cholesterol 0 mg

- Sodium 173 mg
- Total Carbohydrate 30 g
- Dietary Fiber 5.3X g
- Protein 32.6 g

Peanut Butter Smoothie with Blueberries

Preparation Time: 5 minutes; Cooking Time: 0 minutes; Servings: 2

Ingredients:
- 2 tablespoons creamy peanut butter
- 1 cup vanilla almond milk (unsweetened)
- 6 oz. soft silken tofu
- ½ cup grape juice
- 1 cup blueberries
- Crushed ice

Method:
1. Mix all the ingredients in a blender.
2. Process until smooth.

Nutritional Value:
- Calories 247
- Total Fat 10.5 g
- Saturated Fat 1.7 g
- Cholesterol 0 mg
- Sodium 243 mg
- Total Carbohydrate 30 g
- Dietary Fiber 2.8 g
- Protein 10.7 g

Banana & Strawberry Smoothie

Preparation Time: 5 minutes; Cooking Time: 0 minutes; Servings: 8

Ingredients:
- 1 banana, sliced
- 4 cups fresh strawberries, sliced
- 1 cup ice cubes
- 6 oz. yogurt
- 1 kiwi fruit, sliced

Method:
1. Add banana, strawberries, ice cubes and yogurt in a blender.
2. Blend until smooth.
3. Garnish with kiwi fruit slices and serve.

Nutritional Value:
- Calories 54
- Total Fat 0.5 g
- Saturated Fat 0.2 g
- Cholesterol 1 mg
- Sodium 15 mg
- Total Carbohydrate 11.8 g
- Dietary Fiber 1.8 g
- Protein 1.7 g

Tropical Smoothie

Preparation Time: 1 hour and 5 minutes; Cooking Time: 0 minutes; Servings: 4

Ingredients:
- 1 banana, sliced
- 1 cup mango, sliced
- 1 cup pineapple, sliced
- 1 cup peaches, sliced
- 6 oz. nonfat coconut yogurt
- Pineapple wedges

Method:
1. Freeze the fruit slices for 1 hour.
2. Transfer to a blender.
3. Stir in the rest of the ingredients except pineapple wedges.
4. Process until smooth.
5. Garnish with pineapple wedges.

Nutritional Value:
- Calories 102
- Total Fat 0.6 g
- Saturated Fat 0.3 g
- Cholesterol 0 mg

- Sodium 37 mg
- Total Carbohydrate 22.6 g
- Dietary Fiber 2 g
- Protein 2.5 g

Watermelon & Cantaloupe Smoothie

Preparation Time: 10 minutes; Cooking Time: 0 minutes; Servings: 2
Ingredients:
- 2 cups watermelon, sliced
- 1 cup cantaloupe, sliced
- ½ cup nonfat yogurt
- ¼ cup orange juice

Method:
1. Add all the ingredients to a blender.
2. Blend until creamy and smooth.
3. Chill before serving.

Nutritional Value:
- Calories 114
- Total Fat 1.3 g
- Saturated Fat 0.7 g
- Cholesterol 4 mg
- Sodium 57 mg
- Total Carbohydrate 22.7 g
- Dietary Fiber 1.2 g
- Protein 4.8 g

Cantaloupe & Papaya Smoothie

Preparation Time: 10 minutes; Cooking Time: 0 minutes; Serving: 1
Ingredients:
- ¾ cup low-fat milk
- ½ cup papaya, chopped
- ½ cup cantaloupe, chopped
- ½ cup mango, cubed
- 4 ice cubes
- Lime zest

Method:
1. Pour milk into a blender.
2. Add the chopped fruits and ice cubes.
3. Blend until smooth.
4. Garnish with lime zest and serve.

Nutritional Value:
- Calories 207
- Total Fat 3.9 g
- Saturated Fat 2.3 g
- Cholesterol 15 mg
- Sodium 107 mg
- Total Carbohydrate 38.4 g
- Dietary Fiber 3.8 g
- Protein 7.7 g

Avocado Green Smoothie

Preparation Time: 5 minutes; Cooking Time: 0 minutes; Servings: 2
Ingredients:
- 1 cup almond milk
- 1 stalk celery, minced
- 1 apple, sliced
- 1 ripe banana, sliced
- 1 ripe avocado, sliced
- 1 teaspoon ginger, grated
- 2 cups spinach
- 8 ice cubes

Method:
1. Combine all the ingredients in a blender.
2. Blend until smooth.
3. Chill in the refrigerator and serve.

Nutritional Value:
- Calories 307
- Total Fat 17.2 g
- Saturated Fat 2.3 g
- Cholesterol 0 mg
- Sodium 144 mg
- Total Carbohydrate 40.3 g

- Dietary Fiber 12.2 g
- Protein 4.6 g

Peach, Strawberry & Green Tea Smoothie

Preparation Time: 10 minutes; Cooking Time: 0 minutes; Servings: 4

Ingredients:
- 1 cup green tea
- 1 ½ teaspoons honey
- 1 cup peaches, sliced
- 1 cup strawberries, sliced

Method:
1. Let green tea cool.
2. Transfer to a blender.
3. Add honey, peaches and strawberries.
4. Blend until smooth.

Nutritional Value:
- Calories 147
- Total Fat 0.6 g
- Saturated Fat 0 g
- Cholesterol 0 mg
- Sodium 6 mg
- Total Carbohydrate 37 g
- Dietary Fiber 5.4 g
- Protein 2.5 g

Peach & Nectarine Smoothie

Preparation Time: 5 minutes; Cooking Time: 0 minutes; Servings: 2

Ingredients:
- 1 cup nectarine, sliced
- 1 cup peaches, sliced
- 1 cup nonfat almond milk
- 6 oz. nonfat yogurt
- 1 cup ice cubes

Method:
1. Put all the ingredients in a blender.
2. Blend until smooth.

Nutritional Value:
- Calories 102
- Total Fat 0.6 g
- Saturated Fat 0.5 g
- Cholesterol 4 mg
- Sodium 50 mg
- Total Carbohydrate 20.4 g
- Dietary Fiber 1.7 g
- Protein 4.6 g

Carrot & Orange Smoothie

Preparation Time: 10 minutes; Cooking Time: 15 minutes; Servings: 4

Ingredients:
- 1 cup carrots, sliced
- Water
- ½ teaspoon orange zest
- 1 cup orange juice
- Orange peel curls

Method:
1. In a pan over medium heat, boil the carrots in water for 15 minutes.
2. Drain and let cool.
3. Transfer to a blender.
4. Add orange zest and orange juice.
5. Blend well.
6. Garnish with orange peel curls.

Nutritional Value:
- Calories 55
- Total Fat 3 g
- Saturated Fat 0 g
- Cholesterol 0 mg
- Sodium 98 mg
- Total Carbohydrate 13 g

- Dietary Fiber 1 g
- Protein 1 g

Grapefruit & Pineapple Smoothie

Preparation Time: 5 minutes; Cooking Time: 0 minutes; Servings: 2
Ingredients:
- 1 cup plain coconut water
- 1 grapefruit, sliced
- 1 cup spinach, chopped
- 1 cup pineapple, diced
- 1 cup grapefruit juice
- 1 cup ice

Method:
1. Put all the ingredients in a blender.
2. Blend until frothy.

Nutritional Value:
- Calories 102
- Total Fat 0.2 g
- Saturated Fat 0 g
- Cholesterol 0 mg
- Sodium 102 mg
- Total Carbohydrate 25.2 g
- Dietary Fiber 2.9 g
- Protein 2 g

Avocado & Raspberry Smoothie

Preparation Time: 5 minutes; Cooking Time: 0 minutes; Servings: 2
Ingredients:
- 1 avocado, pitted and sliced
- ¾ cup orange juice
- ¾ cup raspberry juice
- ½ cup raspberries

Method:
1. Add all the ingredients to a blender.
2. Process until smooth.
3. Chill before serving.

Nutritional Value:
- Calories 218
- Total Fat 10.7 g
- Saturated Fat 1.5 g
- Cholesterol 0 mg
- Sodium 12 mg
- Total Carbohydrate 30.5 g
- Dietary Fiber 5.6 g
- Protein 2.4 g

Strawberry, Watermelon & Lime Shake

Preparation Time: 10 minutes; Cooking Time: 0 minutes; Servings: 2
Ingredients:
- 1 cup watermelon, chopped
- 2 cups strawberries, sliced
- 2 teaspoons lime juice
- 1 cup nonfat yogurt

Method:
1. Add watermelon, strawberries, lime juice and yogurt to a blender.
2. Blend until smooth.
3. Chill before serving.

Nutritional Value:
- Calories 152
- Total Fat 2.2 g
- Saturated Fat 1.3 g
- Cholesterol 7 mg
- Sodium 90 mg
- Total Carbohydrate 28 g
- Dietary Fiber 3.4 g
- Protein 7.5 g

Honeydew Melon Smoothie

Preparation Time: 5 minutes; Cooking Time: 0 minutes; Serving: 2
Ingredients:

- 1 cup honeydew melon, chopped
- 1 cup cantaloupe, chopped
- 1 cup watermelon, chopped
- ¼ cup avocado, chopped
- 1 tablespoon honey

Method:
1. Mix the ingredients using a blender.
2. Process until smooth.
3. Chill before serving.

Nutritional Value:
- Calories 161
- Total Fat 7.8 g
- Saturated Fat 1.1 g
- Cholesterol 0 mg
- Sodium 36 mg
- Total Carbohydrate 24.3 g
- Dietary Fiber 5 g
- Protein 5 g

Orange Lemon Juice

Preparation Time: 5 minutes; Cooking Time: 0 minutes; Serving: 1
Ingredients:
- 1 orange, sliced into 2
- 1 lemon, sliced into 2
- 1 tablespoon honey
- 2 glasses water

Method:
1. Use a juicer to squeeze juice from orange and lemon.
2. Transfer to drinking glasses.
3. Stir in honey.
4. Pour in water.
5. Mix.
6. Chill before serving.

Nutritional Value:
- Calories 80
- Total Fat 5 g
- Saturated Fat 0 g
- Cholesterol 0 mg
- Sodium 12 mg
- Total Carbohydrate 8 g
- Dietary Fiber 3 g
- Protein 20 g

Pomegranate Cooler

Preparation Time: 5 minutes; Cooking Time: 0 minutes; Servings: 5
Ingredients:
- 1 cup pomegranate juice
- 1 cup lime juice
- ½ cup pineapple chunks
- Ice cubes

Method:
1. Combine all ingredients in a blender.
2. Process until smooth.

Nutritional Value:
- Calories 38
- Total Fat 1 g
- Saturated Fat 0 g
- Cholesterol 0 mg
- Sodium 7 mg
- Total Carbohydrate 9.4 g
- Dietary Fiber 0.2 g
- Protein 0.2 g

Fruit Tea

Preparation Time: 10 minutes; Cooking Time: 4 hours; Servings: 10
Ingredients:
- 1 cinnamon stick, broken into smaller pieces
- 1 tablespoon crystallized ginger, chopped

- 4 cups black tea
- 4 cups orange juice

Method:
1. Place cinnamon sticks on top of cheesecloth.
2. Bring the corners together and tie.
3. Add the tea and juice along with the cinnamon bag to a slow cooker.
4. Cover the pot.
5. Cook on low for 4 hours.
6. Serve in tea cups.

Nutritional Value:
- Calories 45
- Total Fat 0 g
- Saturated Fat 0 g
- Cholesterol 0 mg
- Sodium 11 mg
- Total Carbohydrate 11.1 g
- Dietary Fiber 3 g
- Protein 0.2 g

Cherry & Spinach Smoothie

Preparation Time: 10 minutes; Cooking Time: 0 minutes; Serving: 1

Ingredients:
- ½ cup baby spinach leaves
- 1 cup cherries
- 1 cup plain kefir (low-fat)
- 1 teaspoon ginger, minced
- 1 tablespoon almond butter
- ¼ cup avocado, mashed
- 1 teaspoon chia seeds

Method:
1. Add all ingredients except chia seeds to a blender.
2. Pulse until smooth.
3. Garnish with chia seeds.

Nutritional Value:
- Calories 410
- Total Fat 20.1 g
- Saturated Fat 3.9 g
- Cholesterol 13 mg
- Sodium 169 mg
- Total Carbohydrate 46.6 g
- Dietary Fiber 10.1 g
- Protein 17.4 g

Frozen Lemonade

Preparation Time: 1 hour and 10 minutes; Cooking Time: 10 minutes; Servings: 4

Ingredients:
- ½ cup water
- ½ cup granulated sugar
- 1 teaspoon lemon zest
- ½ cup lemon juice
- 1 cup coconut milk
- 2 cups ice cubes

Method:
1. Simmer water and sugar in a pot over medium heat until sugar has been dissolved.
2. Add lemon zest.
3. Turn off the stove.
4. Steep for 1 hour.
5. Strain the mixture.
6. Add the remaining ingredients to a blender.
7. Process until smooth.
8. Serve drizzled with the syrup.

Nutritional Value:
- Calories 167
- Total Fat 12.1 g
- Saturated Fat 10.7 g
- Cholesterol 0 mg
- Sodium 8 mg
- Total Carbohydrate 16 g

- Dietary Fiber 0.8 g
- Protein 1.3 g

Watermelon Juice

Preparation Time: 5 minutes; Cooking Time: 0 minutes; Servings: 4
Ingredients:
- ¼ cup lime juice
- 6 lb. watermelon, sliced into cubes

Method:
1. Add watermelon to a blender.
2. Process until frothy.
3. Stir in lime juice.
4. Chill before serving.

Nutritional Value:
- Calories 208
- Total Fat 1 g
- Saturated Fat 0.1 g
- Cholesterol 0 mg
- Sodium 7 mg
- Total Carbohydrate 52.6 g
- Dietary Fiber 2.8 g
- Protein 4.2 g

Pineapple Smoothie

Preparation Time: 5 minutes; Cooking Time: 0 minutes; Servings: 2
Ingredients:
- 1 cup pineapple chunks
- 1 cup pineapple-orange juice
- ½ cup yogurt
- ¼ cup water
- 1 cup crushed ice

Method:
1. Mix all the ingredients in a blender.
2. Process until frothy.
3. Serve immediately.

Nutritional Value:
- Calories 154
- Total Fat 0.2 g
- Saturated Fat 0.1 g
- Cholesterol 1 mg
- Sodium 49 mg
- Total Carbohydrate 15.2 g
- Dietary Fiber 1.1 g
- Protein 4 g

Banana & Cranberry Shake

Preparation Time: 5 minutes; Cooking Time: 0 minutes; Servings: 2
Ingredients:
- 1 ripe banana, sliced
- 1 cup cranberries
- 1 cup almond milk
- 1 cup crushed ice

Method:
1. Put the banana, cranberries, almond milk and ice in a blender.
2. Blend until smooth.
3. Serve immediately.

Nutritional Value:
- Calories 117
- Total Fat 0.4 g
- Saturated Fat 0.1 g
- Cholesterol 2 mg
- Sodium 54 mg
- Total Carbohydrate 25.6 g
- Dietary Fiber 3.8 g
- Protein 5 g

Strawberry Frappe

Preparation Time: 5 minutes; Cooking Time: 0 minutes; Serving: 1

Ingredients:
- 1 cup strawberries, sliced
- 1 cup almond milk
- 1 tablespoon honey
- 2 ice cubes

Method:
1. Process strawberries, almond milk, honey and ice cubes in a blender until frothy.
2. Serve right away.

Nutritional Value:
- Calories 152
- Total Fat 1.9 g
- Saturated Fat 1 g
- Cholesterol 8 mg
- Sodium 76 mg
- Total Carbohydrate 29 g
- Dietary Fiber 2.2 g
- Protein 6.2 g

Banana & Coffee Smoothie

Preparation Time: 5 minutes; Cooking Time: 0 minutes; Servings: 2

Ingredients:
- 1 ripe banana, sliced
- 1 ¼ cups almond milk
- 1 tablespoon honey
- ½ cup silken tofu
- 2 teaspoons coffee
- 2 ice cubes
- Cinnamon powder

Method:
1. Add all ingredients except cinnamon powder to a blender.
2. Blend until smooth and frothy.
3. Sprinkle with cinnamon powder and serve.

Nutritional Value:
- Calories 186
- Total Fat 3.7 g
- Saturated Fat 1 g
- Cholesterol 8 mg
- Sodium 93 mg
- Total Carbohydrate 29.8 g
- Dietary Fiber 2.4 g
- Protein 10 g

Strawberry Smoothie With Almonds & Tofu

Preparation Time: 5 minutes; Cooking Time: 0 minutes; Servings: 2

Ingredients:
- 1 cup coconut milk
- 2 tablespoons honey
- 10 strawberries, sliced
- ½ cup silken tofu

Method:
1. Pour milk and honey into a blender.
2. Stir in strawberries and tofu.
3. Process until smooth.

Nutritional Value:
- Calories 171
- Total Fat 3.3 g
- Saturated Fat 0 g
- Cholesterol 0 mg
- Sodium 105 mg
- Total Carbohydrate 20 g
- Dietary Fiber 3 g
- Protein 4.6 g

Mint Melonade

Preparation Time: 1 hour and 15 minutes; Cooking Time: 0 minutes; Servings: 8

Ingredients:
- ½ cup lime juice
- 3 lb. honeydew melon, sliced into cubes
- 6 mint leaves, chopped and divided
- 2 cups soda water

Method:
1. Process lime juice, melon and half of mint leaves in a blender.
2. Transfer to a container and refrigerate for 1 hour.
3. Pour into serving glasses.
4. Pour soda water on top and serve.

Nutritional Value:
- Calories 60
- Total Fat 0.2 g
- Saturated Fat 0.1 g
- Cholesterol 0 mg
- Sodium 45 mg
- Total Carbohydrate 15.4 g
- Dietary Fiber 1.3 g
- Protein 0.9 g

Pear Tea

Preparation Time: 20 minutes; Cooking Time: 20 minutes; Servings: 8

Ingredients:
- 1 cup orange juice
- 3 orange peels
- 3 cups water
- 12 oz. pear nectar
- 1 cinnamon stick
- 1 teaspoon whole cloves
- 6 tea bags

Method:
1. Pour orange juice into a small pot over medium heat.
2. Add water and pear nectar.
3. Wrap cinnamon stick and cloves in cheesecloth and tie with kitchen string.
4. Add to the pot.
5. Bring to a boil.
6. Reduce heat and simmer for 10 minutes.
7. Add tea bag.
8. Turn off heat and steep for 10 minutes.
9. Serve in tea cups.

Nutritional Value:
- Calories 57
- Total Fat 1 g
- Saturated Fat 0 g
- Cholesterol 0 mg
- Sodium 6 mg
- Total Carbohydrate 15 g
- Dietary Fiber 0.5 g
- Protein 0.2 g

Green Tea & Fruit Smoothie

Preparation Time: 5 minutes; Cooking Time: 0 minutes; Servings: 2

Ingredients:
- 1 cup green tea
- 2 cups frozen mixed fruits (unsweetened)
- 1 tablespoon lemon juice
- 1 tablespoon honey

Method:
1. Add all the ingredients to a blender.
2. Blend until smooth.

Nutritional Value:
- Calories 106
- Total Fat 0.3 g
- Saturated Fat 0 g
- Cholesterol 0 mg
- Sodium 3 mg
- Total Carbohydrate 27.4 g
- Dietary Fiber 2.3 g
- Protein 1.4 g

Melon & Kiwi Smoothie with Ginger

Preparation Time: 5 minutes; Cooking Time: 0 minutes; Servings: 2

Ingredients:
- 1 kiwi, chopped
- 1 cup honeydew melon
- 1 banana, sliced
- 2 teaspoons lime juice
- ¼ cup grape juice
- ½ teaspoon minced ginger
- ½ cup ice

Method:
1. Mix all the ingredients in a blender.
2. Pulse until smooth.
3. Serve immediately.

Nutritional Value:
- Calories 132
- Total Fat 0.3 g
- Saturated Fat 0 g
- Cholesterol 0 mg
- Sodium 29 mg
- Total Carbohydrate 34 g
- Dietary Fiber 2.5 g
- Protein 1.1 g

Hawaiian Smoothie

Preparation Time: 10 minutes; Cooking Time: 0 minutes; Servings: 2

Ingredients:
- ½ cup papaya, sliced into cubes
- 1 cup pineapple chunks
- 1 tablespoon lemon juice
- ¼ cup guava nectar
- ½ cup crushed ice

Method:
1. Add the fruits to a blender.
2. Pulse until chopped.
3. Stir in the juice, nectar and ice.
4. Process until smooth.

Nutritional Value:
- Calories 86
- Total Fat 0.2 g
- Saturated Fat 0.1 g
- Cholesterol 0 mg
- Sodium 7 mg
- Total Carbohydrate 22.4 g
- Dietary Fiber 2 g
- Protein 0.7 g

Mango Smoothie with Yogurt

Preparation Time: 5 minutes; Cooking Time: 0 minutes; Servings: 2

Ingredients:
- 1 cup mango, chopped
- ½ cup yogurt
- ⅓ cup peach sorbet
- ¼ cup orange juice

Method:
1. Add mango to a blender.
2. Pulse until finely chopped.
3. Stir in the rest of the ingredients.
4. Blend until smooth.
5. Chill before serving.

Nutritional Value:
- Calories 163
- Total Fat 0.5 g
- Saturated Fat 0.2 g
- Cholesterol 1 mg
- Sodium 43 mg
- Total Carbohydrate 37.3 g

- Dietary Fiber 1.5 g
- Protein 4 g

Vegan Fruit Smoothie

Preparation Time: 5 minutes; Cooking Time: 0 minutes; Servings: 1
Ingredients:
- ¾ cup orange juice
- ½ cup peaches
- ¼ cup silken tofu
- 1 tablespoon honey

Method:
1. Mix all the ingredients in a blender.
2. Blend until smooth.
3. Chill before serving.

Nutritional Value:
- Calories 166
- Total Fat 2.9 g
- Saturated Fat 0.1 g
- Cholesterol 0 mg
- Sodium 27 mg
- Total Carbohydrate 31 g
- Dietary Fiber 3.3 g
- Protein 5.8 g

Watermelon & Turmeric Smoothie

Preparation Time: 10 minutes; Cooking Time: 0 minutes; Servings: 2
Ingredients:
- 3 tablespoons lemon juice
- 4 cups watermelon, sliced into cubes
- 4 teaspoons honey
- 1 teaspoon ginger, minced
- 1 teaspoon ground turmeric
- ½ cup water

Method:
1. Combine all the ingredients in a blender.
2. Process until pureed.
3. Chill before serving.

Nutritional Value:
- Calories 169
- Total Fat 2.9 g
- Saturated Fat 2.1 g
- Cholesterol 0 mg
- Sodium 7 mg
- Total Carbohydrate 38.5 g
- Dietary Fiber 1.8 g
- Protein 2.3 g

Sage Tea

Preparation Time: 10 minutes; Cooking Time: 0 minutes; Serving: 1
Ingredients:
- 10 sage leaves
- 1 cup hot water
- 1 teaspoon honey
- 1 teaspoon lemon juice

Method:
1. Steep the sage leaves in hot water for 5 to 10 minutes.
2. Discard sage leaves.
3. Pour in lemon juice.
4. Stir in honey.
5. Serve while warm.

Nutritional Value:
- Calories 22
- Total Fat 0 g
- Saturated Fat 0 g
- Cholesterol 0 mg
- Sodium 7 mg
- Total Carbohydrate 6.1 g
- Dietary Fiber 1 g
- Protein 2 g

Green Tea with Honey

Preparation Time: 15 minutes; Cooking Time: 20 minutes; Serving: 1

Ingredients:
- 1 lemon peel
- 1 orange peel
- 1 cup hot water
- 1 green tea bag
- 1 teaspoon honey
- 1 lemon slice

Method:
1. Combine fruit peels and hot water in a pan over medium heat.
2. Bring to a boil.
3. Reduce heat and simmer for 10 minutes.
4. Discard fruit peels.
5. Add tea bag to the pot.
6. Turn off heat.
7. Simmer for 5 minutes.
8. Pour mixture into a tea cup.
9. Stir in honey and garnish with lemon slice.

Nutritional Value:
- Calories 16
- Total Fat 0 g
- Saturated Fat 0 g
- Cholesterol 0 mg
- Sodium 8 mg
- Total Carbohydrate 5 g
- Dietary Fiber 0.6 g
- Protein 0.2 g

Chapter 11: Desserts Recipes

Brûléed Oranges

Preparation Time: 10 minutes; Cooking Time: 5 minutes; Servings: 4
Ingredients:
- 4 oranges, sliced into segments
- 1 teaspoon ground cardamom
- 6 teaspoons brown sugar
- 1 cup nonfat Greek yogurt

Method:
1. Preheat your broiler.
2. Arrange orange slices in a baking pan.
3. In a bowl, mix the cardamom and sugar.
4. Sprinkle mixture on top of the oranges. Broil for 5 minutes.
5. Serve oranges with yogurt.

Nutritional Value:
- Calories 168
- Total Fat 4.2 g
- Saturated Fat 1.5 g
- Cholesterol 8 mg
- Sodium 25 mg
- Total Carbohydrate 26.9 g
- Dietary Fiber 2.8 g
- Protein 6.8 g

Pumpkin & Banana Ice Cream

Preparation Time: 10 minutes; Cooking Time: 0 minutes; Servings: 8
Ingredients:
- 15 oz. pumpkin puree
- 4 bananas, sliced and frozen
- 1 teaspoon pumpkin pie spice
- Chopped pecans

Method:
1. Add pumpkin puree, bananas and pumpkin pie spice in a food processor.
2. Pulse until smooth.
3. Chill in the refrigerator.
4. Garnish with pecans.

Nutritional Value:
- Calories 71
- Total Fat 0.4 g
- Saturated Fat 0.2 g
- Cholesterol 0.2 mg
- Sodium 3 mg
- Total Carbohydrate 18 g
- Dietary Fiber 3.1 g
- Protein 1.2 g

Peanut Butter Choco Chip Cookies

Preparation Time: 10 minutes; Cooking Time: 10 minutes; Servings: 15
Ingredients:
- 1 egg
- ½ cup light brown sugar
- 1 cup natural unsweetened peanut butter
- Pinch salt
- ¼ cup dark chocolate chips

Method:
1. Preheat your oven to 375 degrees F.
2. Mix egg, sugar, peanut butter, salt and chocolate chips in a bowl.
3. Form into cookies and place in a baking pan.
4. Bake the cookie for 10 minutes.
5. Let cool before serving.

Nutritional Value:
- Calories 159
- Total Fat 10 g

- Saturated Fat 2 g
- Cholesterol 12 mg
- Sodium 100 mg
- Total Carbohydrate 12 g
- Dietary Fiber 1.3 g
- Protein 4.3 g

Frozen Lemon & Blueberry

Preparation Time: 1 hour and 10 minutes; Cooking Time: 8 minutes; Servings: 12

Ingredients:
- 6 cup fresh blueberries
- 8 sprigs fresh thyme
- ¾ cup light brown sugar
- 1 teaspoon lemon zest
- ¼ cup lemon juice
- 2 cups water

Method:
1. Add blueberries, thyme and sugar in a pan over medium heat.
2. Cook for 6 to 8 minutes.
3. Transfer mixture to a blender.
4. Remove thyme sprigs.
5. Stir in the remaining ingredients.
6. Pulse until smooth.
7. Strain mixture and freeze for 1 hour.

Nutritional Value:
- Calories 78
- Total Fat 0 g
- Saturated Fat 0 g
- Cholesterol 0 mg
- Sodium 4 mg
- Total Carbohydrate 20 g
- Dietary Fiber 1 g
- Protein 3 g

Strawberry & Mango Ice Cream

Preparation Time: 10 minutes; Cooking Time: 0 minutes; Servings: 4

Ingredients:
- 8 oz. strawberries, sliced
- 12 oz. mango, sliced into cubes
- 1 tablespoon lime juice

Method:
1. Add all ingredients in a food processor.
2. Pulse for 2 minutes.
3. Chill before serving.

Nutritional Value:
- Calories 70
- Total Fat 0.5 g
- Saturated Fat 0.1 g
- Cholesterol 0 mg
- Sodium 1 mg
- Total Carbohydrate 17.4 g
- Dietary Fiber 2.5 g
- Protein 1.1 g

Watermelon Sherbet

Preparation Time: 8 hours and 15 minutes; Cooking Time: 0 minutes; Servings: 12

Ingredients:
- 6 cups watermelon, sliced into cubes
- 14 oz. almond milk
- 1 tablespoon honey
- ¼ cup lime juice
- Salt to taste

Method:
1. Freeze watermelon for 4 hours.
2. Add frozen watermelon and other ingredients in a blender.
3. Blend until smooth.
4. Transfer to a container with seal.

5. Seal and freeze for 4 hours.

Nutritional Value:
- Calories 132
- Total Fat 3 g
- Saturated Fat 1.8 g
- Cholesterol 11 mg
- Sodium 91 mg
- Total Carbohydrate 24.5 g
- Dietary Fiber 0.3 g
- Protein 3.1 g

Lemon Custard

Preparation Time: 3 hours and 15 minutes; Cooking Time: 45 minutes; Servings: 6

Ingredients:
- 2 cups nonfat milk
- 2 tablespoons granulated sugar
- 2 sprigs lemon thyme
- 3 eggs, beaten
- 1 teaspoon vanilla
- ⅓ cup lemon curd

Method:
1. Preheat your oven to 325 degrees F.
2. Mix sugar and milk in a pan over medium low heat.
3. Cook while stirring for 5 minutes.
4. Strain the mixture.
5. In a bowl, mix the eggs, vanilla and lemon curd.
6. Add to the milk mixture.
7. Pour into custard cups.
8. Place custard cups in a baking pan filled with hot water.
9. Bake for 40 minutes.
10. Let cool for 1 hour.
11. Chill for 2 hours.

Nutritional Value:
- Calories 117
- Total Fat 0.9 g
- Saturated Fat 0.5 g
- Cholesterol 15 mg
- Sodium 105 mg
- Total Carbohydrate 21 g
- Dietary Fiber 1.8 g
- Protein 5.8 g

Blueberry Pudding

Preparation Time: 15 minutes; Cooking Time: 45 minutes; Servings: 6

Ingredients:
- Cooking spray
- 3 cups nonfat milk
- ¼ teaspoon ground ginger
- ½ teaspoon ground cinnamon
- ⅓ cup brown sugar
- ½ cup cornmeal
- 1 ½ cups fresh blueberries

Method:
1. Preheat your oven to 300 degrees F.
2. Spray your custard cups with oil.
3. Place custard cups in a baking pan.
4. In a pan over medium heat, warm the milk, ginger, cinnamon and sugar.
5. Stir in cornmeal.
6. Reduce heat and cook for 3 minutes or until thickened.
7. Pour mixture into the custard cups and top with blueberries.
8. Bake for 40 minutes.
9. Let cool before serving.

Nutritional Value:
- Calories 165
- Total Fat 2.9 g

- Saturated Fat 1.6 g
- Cholesterol 10 mg
- Sodium 58 mg
- Total Carbohydrate 30.9 g
- Dietary Fiber 1.7 g
- Protein 5.2 g

Vanilla Pudding Pops

Preparation Time: 1 hour and 10 minutes; Cooking Time: 0 minutes; Servings: 8

Ingredients:
- 1 pack nonfat and sugar free vanilla pudding mix
- 2 cups nonfat milk
- 1 teaspoon vanilla
- 1 cup light whipped dessert topping

Method:
1. Mix all the ingredients in a bowl.
2. Pour into popsicle molds.
3. Freeze for 1 hour.

Nutritional Value:
- Calories 72
- Total Fat 1.1 g
- Saturated Fat 1 g
- Cholesterol 1 mg
- Sodium 168 mg
- Total Carbohydrate 13.4 g
- Dietary Fiber 0.4 g
- Protein 2.2 g

Strawberry & Orange Cupcakes

Preparation Time: 30 minutes; Cooking Time: 15 minutes; Servings: 12

Ingredients:
- ¼ cup strawberries, chopped
- 2 tablespoons reduced-sugar orange marmalade
- Cooking spray
- 1 ½ cups all-purpose flour
- ¼ teaspoon baking soda
- 1 teaspoon baking powder
- ¼ teaspoon salt
- ¾ cup nonfat buttermilk
- 1 egg, beaten
- ¼ cup vegetable oil
- ½ cup sugar substitute
- ½ teaspoon orange zest
- 1 teaspoon vanilla

Method:
1. Preheat your oven to 350 degrees F.
2. Mix the strawberries and marmalade in a bowl.
3. Spray your muffin pan with oil.
4. In a bowl, mix the flour, baking soda, baking powder and salt.
5. In another bowl, combine the milk, egg, oil sugar, orange zest and vanilla.
6. Pour this mixture into the first bowl and mix well.
7. Bake for 15 minutes.
8. Let cool before serving.

Nutritional Value:
- Calories 185
- Total Fat 7 g
- Saturated Fat 1.7 g
- Cholesterol 8 mg
- Sodium 156 mg
- Total Carbohydrate 25 g
- Dietary Fiber 0.5 g
- Protein 4 g

Choco Chip Balls

Preparation Time: 1 hour and 30 minutes; Cooking Time: 0 minutes; Servings: 10

Ingredients:
- ½ cup almond butter
- 15 oz. chickpeas, rinsed and drained
- 1 teaspoon vanilla extract
- ¼ cup sugar substitute

- Pinch salt
- ¼ cup dark chocolate chips

Method:
1. Add all ingredients except chocolate chips in a food processor.
2. Pulse until smooth.
3. Transfer to a bowl.
4. Add chocolate chips.
5. Mix well.
6. Form balls from the mixture.
7. Freeze for 1 hour.

Nutritional Value:
- Calories 161
- Total Fat 8.6 g
- Saturated Fat 2.1 g
- Cholesterol 0 mg
- Sodium 145 mg
- Total Carbohydrate 16 g
- Dietary Fiber 2.4 g
- Protein 4.5 g

Baked Rice Pudding

Preparation Time: 30 minutes; Cooking Time: 40 minutes; Servings: 5

Ingredients:
- 1 egg
- 3 egg whites
- 1 teaspoon vanilla
- ¼ cup sugar substitute
- 1 ½ cups almond milk
- ¼ teaspoon ground cardamom
- 2 tablespoons raisins
- ¼ teaspoon orange zest
- ½ cup cooked rice
- Hot water

Method:
1. Mix egg, egg whites, vanilla, sugar substitute and almond milk in a bowl.
2. Beat until fully combined.
3. Add the rest of the ingredients except hot water.
4. Pour mixture into custard cups placed in a baking pan.
5. Pour hot water into the baking pan.
6. Bake in the oven at 325 degrees F for 40 minutes.

Nutritional Value:
- Calories 126
- Total Fat 1.2 g
- Saturated Fat 0.4 g
- Cholesterol 44 mg
- Sodium 84 mg
- Total Carbohydrate 21.6 g
- Dietary Fiber 0.4 g
- Protein 6.6 g

Tiramisu Shots

Preparation Time: 45 minutes; Cooking Time: 0 minutes; Servings: 12

Ingredients:
- 1 pack silken tofu
- 1 oz. dark chocolate, finely chopped
- ¼ cup sugar substitute
- 1 teaspoon lemon juice
- ¼ cup brewed espresso
- Pinch salt
- 24 slices angel food cake
- Cocoa powder (unsweetened)

Method:
1. Add tofu, chocolate, sugar substitute, lemon juice, espresso and salt in a food processor.
2. Pulse until smooth.
3. Add angel food cake pieces into shot glasses.
4. Drizzle with the cocoa powder.
5. Pour the tofu mixture on top.
6. Top with the remaining angel food cake pieces.

7. Chill for 30 minutes and serve.

Nutritional Value:
- Calories 75
- Total Fat 1.8 g
- Saturated Fat 0.3 g
- Cholesterol 0 mg
- Sodium 106 mg
- Total Carbohydrate 12 g
- Dietary Fiber 0.4 g
- Protein 2.9 g

Peanut Butter Cups

Preparation Time: 3 hours and 15 minutes; Cooking Time: 10 minutes; Servings: 6

Ingredients:
- 1 packet plain gelatin
- ¼ cup sugar substitute
- 2 cups nonfat cream
- ½ teaspoon vanilla
- ¼ cup low-fat peanut butter
- 2 tablespoons unsalted peanuts, chopped

Method:
1. Mix gelatin, sugar substitute and cream in a pan.
2. Let sit for 5 minutes.
3. Place over medium heat and cook until gelatin has been dissolved.
4. Stir in vanilla and peanut butter.
5. Pour into custard cups. Chill for 3 hours.
6. Top with the peanuts and serve.

Nutritional Value:
- Calories 171
- Total Fat 5.6 g
- Saturated Fat 1.1 g
- Cholesterol 0 mg
- Sodium 172 mg
- Total Carbohydrate 21 g
- Dietary Fiber 0.6 g
- Protein 6.8 g

Ice Cream Brownie Cake

Preparation Time: 10 hours; Cooking Time: 25 minutes; Servings: 12

Ingredients:
- Cooking spray
- 12 oz. no-sugar brownie mix
- ¼ cup oil
- 2 egg whites
- 3 tablespoons water
- 2 cups sugar-free ice cream

Method:
1. Preheat your oven to 325 degrees F.
2. Spray your baking pan with oil.
3. Mix brownie mix, oil, egg whites and water in a bowl.
4. Pour into the baking pan.
5. Bake for 25 minutes.
6. Let cool.
7. Freeze brownie for 2 hours.
8. Spread ice cream over the brownie.
9. Freeze for 8 hours.

Nutritional Value:
- Calories 198
- Total Fat 10 g
- Saturated Fat 1 g
- Cholesterol 3 mg
- Sodium 118 mg
- Total Carbohydrate 33 g
- Dietary Fiber 4 g
- Protein 3 g

Choco Peppermint Cake

Preparation Time: 15 minutes; Cooking Time: 3 hours; Servings: 18

Ingredients:
- Cooking spray
- ⅓ cup oil
- 15 oz. package chocolate cake mix
- 3 eggs, beaten
- 1 cup water
- ¼ teaspoon peppermint extract

Method:
1. Spray slow cooker with oil.
2. Mix all the ingredients in a bowl.
3. Use an electric mixer on medium speed setting to mix ingredients for 2 minutes.
4. Pour mixture into the slow cooker.
5. Cover the pot and cook on low for 3 hours.
6. Let cool before slicing and serving.

Nutritional Value:
- Calories 185
- Total Fat 7.4 g
- Saturated Fat 2.4 g
- Cholesterol 2 mg
- Sodium 233 mg
- Total Carbohydrate 27 g
- Dietary Fiber 0.7 g
- Protein 3.8 g

Fruit Pizza

Preparation Time: 15 minutes; Cooking Time: 0 minutes; Servings: 8

Ingredients:
- 1 teaspoon maple syrup
- ¼ teaspoon vanilla extract
- ½ cup coconut milk yogurt
- 2 round slices watermelon
- ½ cup blackberries, sliced
- ½ cup strawberries, sliced
- 2 tablespoons coconut flakes (unsweetened)

Method:
1. Mix maple syrup, vanilla and yogurt in a bowl.
2. Spread the mixture on top of the watermelon slice.
3. Top with the berries and coconut flakes.

Nutritional Value:
- Calories 70
- Total Fat 1.6 g
- Saturated Fat 1.2 g
- Cholesterol 0 mg
- Sodium 5 mg
- Total Carbohydrate 14.6 g
- Dietary Fiber 1.5 g
- Protein 1.2 g

Cocoa Popcorn

Preparation Time: 15 minutes; Cooking Time: 10 minutes; Serving: 1

Ingredients:
- 1 ½ tablespoons popcorn kernels
- ½ teaspoon cocoa powder
- ½ teaspoon coconut oil
- ½ teaspoon sugar substitute
- Pinch salt

Method:
1. Pop popcorn kernels according to package directions.
2. In a bowl, mix the remaining ingredients.
3. Coat the popcorn in the cocoa mixture and serve.

Nutritional Value:
- Calories 113
- Total Fat 3.1 g
- Saturated Fat 1.9 g
- Cholesterol 0 mg

- Sodium 146 mg
- Total Carbohydrate 22 g
- Dietary Fiber 5.6 g
- Protein 3.2 g

Chocolate Cookies

Preparation Time: 20 minutes; Cooking Time: 15 minutes; Servings: 18

Ingredients:
- 2 egg whites
- ⅛ teaspoon cream of tartar
- ⅔ cup sugar
- ⅓ cup unsweetened peanut butter
- ½ cup unsalted peanuts, chopped
- 4 oz. dark chocolate
- ½ teaspoon shortening

Method:
1. Preheat your oven to 300 degrees F.
2. Beat egg whites and cream of tartar using a mixer until you see soft peaks forming.
3. Stir in the sugar and beat for a few more seconds.
4. Add peanut butter and peanuts.
5. Form cookies from the mixture and place in a baking pan.
6. Bake for 10 minutes.
7. In a pan over medium heat, melt the chocolate and shortening.
8. Pour over the cookies and serve.

Nutritional Value:
- Calories 115
- Total Fat 6.4 g
- Saturated Fat 1.9 g
- Cholesterol 0 mg
- Sodium 38 mg
- Total Carbohydrate 13.2 g
- Dietary Fiber 1.1 g
- Protein 2.7 g

Orange & Pumpkin Custards

Preparation Time: 30 minutes; Cooking Time: 30 minutes; Servings: 8

Ingredients:
- 2 tablespoons orange juice
- 1 teaspoon vanilla
- ¼ cup raisins
- Cooking spray
- 1 egg, beaten
- 15 oz. pumpkin puree
- ⅓ cup sugar substitute
- 1 teaspoon pumpkin pie spice
- ⅔ cup nonfat milk

Method:
1. In a pan over medium heat, simmer the vanilla and orange juice for 2 minutes.
2. Stir in raisins and turn off heat. Set aside.
3. Preheat your oven to 375 degrees F.
4. Spray your custard cups with oil.
5. In a bowl, mix the remaining ingredients.
6. Pour mixture into custard cups.
7. Pour orange mixture on top.
8. Place custard cups in a baking pan with hot water.
9. Bake in the oven for 30 minutes.
10. Chill before serving.

Nutritional Value:
- Calories 128
- Total Fat 1 g
- Saturated Fat 1 g
- Cholesterol 3 mg
- Sodium 60 mg
- Total Carbohydrate 26 g
- Dietary Fiber 2 g
- Protein 5 g

Apricots & Vanilla Yogurt

Preparation Time: 5 minutes; Cooking Time: 0 minutes; Serving: 1

Ingredients:
- 5 oz. fat-free vanilla yogurt
- 1 cup dried apricots, chopped

Method:
1. Top yogurt with dried apricots.
2. Chill before serving.

Nutritional Value:
- Calories 150
- Total Fat 0.3 g
- Saturated Fat 0.2 g
- Cholesterol 4 mg
- Sodium 50 mg
- Total Carbohydrate 24.9 g
- Dietary Fiber 1.9 g
- Protein 12.8 g

Berry & White Chocolate Pops

Preparation Time: 4 hours and 10 minutes; Cooking Time: 0 minutes; Servings: 8

Ingredients:
- 1 pack no-sugar white chocolate pudding mix
- 2 cups nonfat milk
- 1 cup frozen blueberries, chopped

Method:
1. Cook pudding according to package directions including nonfat milk.
2. Mix well.
3. Pour mixture into popsicle molds with the blueberries.
4. Freeze for 4 hours.

Nutritional Value:
- Calories 44
- Total Fat 0.1 g
- Saturated Fat 0 g
- Cholesterol 1 mg
- Sodium 186 mg
- Total Carbohydrate 8.6 g
- Dietary Fiber 0.4 g
- Protein 2.2 g

Apricot Pizza

Preparation Time: 10 minutes; Cooking Time: 5 minutes; Servings: 4

Ingredients:
- 1 tablespoon apricot preserves (unsweetened)
- 2 tablespoons low-fat cream cheese
- 1 artisan pizza flatbread
- 1 kiwi, sliced thinly
- 1 apricot, sliced thinly
- 2 tablespoons honey

Method:
1. In a bowl, mix apricot preserves and cream cheese.
2. Spread mixture on top of the flatbread.
3. Top with the fruit slices.
4. Grill for 3 to 4 minutes.
5. Drizzle with honey.

Nutritional Value:
- Calories 127
- Total Fat 3.3 g
- Saturated Fat 0.9 g
- Cholesterol 5 mg
- Sodium 89 mg
- Total Carbohydrate 22.9 g
- Dietary Fiber 2 g
- Protein 3.3 g

Choco Pretzels

Preparation Time: 10 minutes; Cooking Time: 5 minutes; Servings: 16
Ingredients:
- 4 oz. dark chocolate
- 16 whole-wheat pretzel sticks
- ½ cup pecans, toasted and chopped

Method:
1. Melt the dark chocolate in a pan.
2. Dip the pretzel sticks in melted chocolate.
3. Sprinkle with pecans.
4. Let sit until chocolate has hardened.

Nutritional Value:
- Calories 79
- Total Fat 4.9 g
- Saturated Fat 1.7 g
- Cholesterol 1 mg
- Sodium 75 mg
- Total Carbohydrate 8.3 g
- Dietary Fiber 0.6 g
- Protein 1.6 g

Vegan Cookies

Preparation Time: 15 minutes; Cooking Time: 15 minutes; Servings: 25
Ingredients:
- 1 cup all-purpose flour
- 1 cup whole-wheat flour
- ⅛ teaspoon salt
- ½ teaspoon baking soda
- ½ tablespoon baking powder
- ½ cup coconut oil
- ¾ cup sugar substitute
- 1 teaspoon vanilla extract
- 4 teaspoons lemon zest
- ⅓ cup water

Method:
1. Combine the flours, salt, baking soda and baking powder in a bowl.
2. In another bowl, mix the sugar and oil using an electric mixer until consistency is light.
3. Stir in vanilla, lemon zest and water.
4. Beat until fully combined.
5. Slowly add the flour mixture.
6. Mix well.
7. Cover the mixture with plastic wrap and refrigerate for 20 to 30 minutes.
8. Preheat your oven to 325 degrees F.
9. Form cookies from the mixture.
10. Place in a cookie sheet.
11. Bake for 15 minutes.

Nutritional Value:
- Calories 49
- Total Fat 2.2 g
- Saturated Fat 1.8 g
- Cholesterol 0 mg
- Sodium 33 mg
- Total Carbohydrate 6.8 g
- Dietary Fiber 0.3 g
- Protein 0.3 g

Roasted Plums

Preparation Time: 15 minutes; Cooking Time: 20 minutes; Servings: 6
Ingredients:
- Cooking spray
- 6 plums, sliced
- ½ cup pineapple juice (unsweetened)
- 1 tablespoon brown sugar
- 2 tablespoons brown sugar
- ¼ teaspoon ground cardamom
- ½ teaspoon ground cinnamon
- ⅛ teaspoon ground cumin

Method:
1. Combine all the ingredients in a baking pan.
2. Roast in the oven at 450 degrees F for 20 minutes.

Nutritional Value:
- Calories 102
- Total Fat 2.7 g
- Saturated Fat 0.8 g
- Cholesterol 4 mg
- Sodium 12 mg
- Total Carbohydrate 18.7 g
- Dietary Fiber 1.4 g
- Protein 2 g

Roasted Mango

Preparation Time: 10 minutes; Cooking Time: 10 minutes; Servings: 4

Ingredients:
- 2 mangoes, sliced
- 2 teaspoons crystallized ginger, chopped
- 2 teaspoons orange zest
- 2 tablespoons coconut flakes (unsweetened)

Method:
1. Preheat your oven to 350 degrees F.
2. Add mango slices in custard cups.
3. Top with the ginger, orange zest and coconut flakes.
4. Bake in the oven for 10 minutes.

Nutritional Value:
- Calories 89
- Total Fat 1.5 g
- Saturated Fat 1.3 g
- Cholesterol 0 mg
- Sodium 14 mg
- Total Carbohydrate 20 g
- Dietary Fiber 2.2 g
- Protein 0.8 g

Berries with Vanilla Yogurt

Preparation Time: 5 minutes; Cooking Time: 0 minutes; Servings: 1

Ingredients:
- ¼ cup nonfat vanilla yogurt
- ¼ cup raspberries, sliced
- 1 gingersnap cookie, broken

Method:
1. Top the yogurt with the raspberries and broken cookie pieces.

Nutritional Value:
- Calories 88
- Total Fat 0.9 g
- Saturated Fat 0.2 g
- Cholesterol 0 mg
- Sodium 62 mg
- Total Carbohydrate 13.7 g
- Dietary Fiber 2.2 g
- Protein 6.5 g

Figs with Honey & Yogurt

Preparation Time: 10 minutes; Cooking Time: 0 minutes; Servings: 2

Ingredients:
- ½ teaspoon vanilla
- 8 oz. nonfat yogurt
- 2 figs, sliced
- 1 tablespoon walnuts, chopped and toasted
- 2 teaspoons honey

Method:
1. Stir vanilla into yogurt.
2. Mix well.
3. Top with the figs and sprinkle with walnuts.
4. Drizzle with honey and serve.

Nutritional Value:
- Calories 157
- Total Fat 4 g
- Saturated Fat 1 g
- Cholesterol 7 mg
- Sodium 80 mg
- Total Carbohydrate 24 g
- Dietary Fiber 2 g
- Protein 7 g

Berries with Creamy Orange Topping

Preparation Time: 10 minutes; Cooking Time: 0 minutes; Servings: 12

Ingredients:
- 1 tablespoon honey
- 2 tablespoons orange juice
- 2 cups blueberries, sliced
- 2 cups raspberries, sliced
- ½ cup light sour cream
- 1 teaspoon orange zest

Method:
1. Mix honey and orange juice in a bowl.
2. Stir in the berries and coat evenly with the mixture.
3. In another bowl, mix sour cream and orange zest.
4. Top the berries with orange cream.

Nutritional Value:
- Calories 64
- Total Fat 1.6 g
- Saturated Fat 1 g
- Cholesterol 3 mg
- Sodium 7 mg
- Total Carbohydrate 12 g
- Dietary Fiber 2 g
- Protein 0.9 g

Baked Apples

Preparation Time: 30 minutes; Cooking Time: 30 minutes; Servings: 4

Ingredients:
- Cooking spray
- 2 apples, sliced
- ½ teaspoon vanilla extract
- ½ teaspoon ground cinnamon
- 4 teaspoons sugar substitute
- Pinch salt
- 3 tablespoons melted butter
- ¼ cup all-purpose flour
- ¼ cup rolled oats
- 2 tablespoons pecans, chopped

Method:
1. Preheat your oven to 400 degrees F.
2. Spray your baking pan with oil.
3. Toss the apples in vanilla.
4. Sprinkle with cinnamon, sugar substitute and salt.
5. Spread in the baking pan.
6. Mix the remaining ingredients in a bowl.
7. Spread on top of the apples.
8. Sprinkle pecans on top.
9. Bake in the oven for 30 minutes.
10. Let cool before slicing and serving.

Nutritional Value:
- Calories 186
- Total Fat 8.8 g
- Saturated Fat 4 g
- Cholesterol 15 mg
- Sodium 119 mg
- Total Carbohydrate 26.7 g
- Dietary Fiber 3.4 g
- Protein 2 g

Berries with Lime Syrup

Preparation Time: 10 minutes; Cooking Time: 5 minutes; Servings: 8

Ingredients:
- 2 lb. mixed frozen berries
- 2 tablespoons lime juice
- 1 tablespoon pure maple syrup
- 1 teaspoon lime zest

Method:
1. Thaw berries.
2. Coat with lime juice, maple syrup and lime zest.
3. Heat through in a pan over medium heat.
4. Serve warm.

Nutritional Value:
- Calories 168
- Total Fat 6.4 g
- Saturated Fat 1.3 g
- Cholesterol 92 mg
- Sodium 36 mg
- Total Carbohydrate 22 g
- Dietary Fiber 4.9 g
- Protein 4 g

Cranberry Pears

Preparation Time: 10 minutes; Cooking Time: 10 minutes; Servings: 6

Ingredients:
- 3 pears, sliced in half and cored
- ½ cup fresh cranberries
- 2 teaspoons honey
- 2 ½ cup cranberry juice

Method:
1. Add pears and cranberries to a baking pan.
2. Toss in honey and cranberry juice.
3. Bake in the oven at 350 degrees F for 10 minutes.
4. Serve warm.

Nutritional Value:
- Calories 90
- Total Fat 1 g
- Saturated Fat 0 g
- Cholesterol 2 mg
- Sodium 24 mg
- Total Carbohydrate 21 g
- Dietary Fiber 3 g
- Protein 2 g

Grilled Peaches

Preparation Time: 5 minutes; Cooking Time: 6 minutes; Servings: 6

Ingredients:
- 1 tablespoon honey
- 1 cup balsamic vinegar
- 2 teaspoons oil
- ⅛ teaspoon ground cinnamon
- 3 peaches, sliced in half and pitted

Method:
1. Mix honey, vinegar, oil and cinnamon in a bowl.
2. Coat the peaches evenly with the mixture.
3. Grill for 3 minutes per side.

Nutritional Value:
- Calories 135
- Total Fat 3.3 g
- Saturated Fat 1.2 g
- Cholesterol 0 mg
- Sodium 42 mg
- Total Carbohydrate 25.2 g
- Dietary Fiber 1.7 g
- Protein 1.5 g

Fruit Salad

Preparation Time: 25 minutes; Cooking Time: 0 minutes; Servings: 6

Ingredients:
- 6 oz. nonfat yogurt
- 8 oz. reduced-fat cream cheese

- 1 tablespoon honey
- 1 teaspoon orange zest
- 1 teaspoon lemon zest
- 3 kiwi, sliced
- 1 cup blueberries, sliced
- 1 mango, sliced into cubes
- 1 orange, sliced

Method:
1. In a bowl, mix yogurt, cream cheese, honey, orange zest and lemon zest.
2. Toss the fruits in a serving bowl.
3. Top with the cream cheese mixture and stir to combine.
4. Chill in the refrigerator for 15 minutes before serving.

Nutritional Value:
- Calories 131
- Total Fat 3.1 g
- Saturated Fat 1.8 g
- Cholesterol 9 mg
- Sodium 102 mg
- Total Carbohydrate 22.9 g
- Dietary Fiber 2.9 g
- Protein 5.3 g

Balsamic Melon

Preparation Time: 2 hours and 15 minutes; Cooking Time: 0 minutes; Servings: 6

Ingredients:
- ½ cup soda water (berry flavored)
- 3 tablespoons white balsamic vinegar
- 4 cups frozen melon balls

Method:
1. In a bowl, mix soda water and vinegar.
2. Coat the melon balls with the mixture.
3. Chill for 2 hours.

Nutritional Value:
- Calories 47
- Total Fat 0.2 g
- Saturated Fat 0 g
- Cholesterol 0 mg
- Sodium 16 mg
- Total Carbohydrate 11 g
- Dietary Fiber 0.8 g
- Protein 0.7 g

Honey Strawberries

Preparation Time: 1 hour and 10 minutes; Cooking Time: 0 minutes; Servings: 4

Ingredients:
- 1 teaspoon honey
- 2 tablespoons orange juice
- 1 tablespoon lemon juice
- ½ teaspoon lemon zest
- 4 cups strawberries, sliced in half

Method:
1. In a bowl, mix the honey, orange juice, lemon juice and lemon zest.
2. Toss the strawberries in the mixture.
3. Chill for 1 hour before serving.

Nutritional Value:
- Calories 66
- Total Fat 0 g
- Saturated Fat 0 g
- Cholesterol 0 mg
- Sodium 2 mg
- Total Carbohydrate 15 g
- Dietary Fiber 3 g
- Protein 1 g

Fruit Kebabs

Preparation Time: 20 minutes; Cooking Time: 0 minutes; Servings: 12

Ingredients:
- 3 apples, sliced
- 1 ½ lb. watermelon, sliced

- ¾ cup blueberries
- ¼ cup orange juice

Method:
1. Thread fruit slices onto skewers.
2. Drizzle with orange juice and serve.

Nutritional Value:
- Calories 52
- Total Fat 0.2 g
- Saturated Fat 0 g
- Cholesterol 0 mg
- Sodium 1 mg
- Total Carbohydrate 13.5 g
- Dietary Fiber 1.8 g
- Protein 0.6 g

Strawberry & Watermelon Pops

Preparation Time: 15 minutes; Cooking Time: 0 minutes; Servings: 6

Ingredients:
- 2 cups watermelon, chopped
- 1 cup strawberries, chopped
- 2 tablespoons sugar substitute
- ¼ cup lime juice
- Pinch salt

Method:
1. Combine all the ingredients in a food processor.
2. Blend until smooth.
3. Pour mixture into popsicle molds.
4. Freeze for 6 hours.

Nutritional Value:
- Calories 57
- Total Fat 0.3 g
- Saturated Fat 0 g
- Cholesterol 0 mg
- Sodium 51 mg
- Total Carbohydrate 14.5 g
- Dietary Fiber 1.6 g
- Protein 0.8 g

Spiced Apples

Preparation Time: 10 minutes; Cooking Time: 0 minutes; Servings: 6

Ingredients:
- 5 apples, sliced thinly
- ¼ cup water
- ½ teaspoon ground cinnamon
- ⅛ teaspoon ground nutmeg
- 2 tablespoons honey

Method:
1. Combine all the ingredients except honey in a pan over medium heat.
2. Bring to a boil.
3. Reduce heat and simmer for 3 minutes.
4. Drizzle with honey before serving.

Nutritional Value:
- Calories 101
- Total Fat 0.3 g
- Saturated Fat 0.1 g
- Cholesterol 0 mg
- Sodium 2 mg
- Total Carbohydrate 26.9 g
- Dietary Fiber 3.8 g
- Protein 0.4 g

Chapter 12: 30-Day Meal plan

Week 1

Sunday
Breakfast: Whole grain pancakes
Lunch: Chicken with kale and sweet potato
Dinner: Grilled lamb and veggies

Monday
Breakfast: Baked banana oatmeal
Lunch: Black rice with tofu and asparagus
Dinner: Grilled curry burgers

Tuesday
Breakfast: Egg peppers with avocado salsa
Lunch: Salmon with sautéed kale
Dinner: Chicken with jerk sauce

Wednesday
Breakfast: Cheesecake toast with kiwi and strawberry
Lunch: Italian beef pasta
Dinner: Oven-fried chicken

Thursday
Breakfast: Yogurt with vanilla and apricots
Lunch: Turkey kebab
Dinner: Sweet and sour pork tenderloin

Friday
Breakfast: Baked oatmeal with cinnamon and pears
Lunch: Pork and rice noodles
Dinner: Chicken with tomatoes and capers

Saturday
Breakfast: Vegan crepe
Lunch: Shredded beef sandwich
Dinner: Garlic salmon

Week 2

Sunday
Breakfast: Toasted bread with goat cheese and beet slices
Lunch: Beef stir fry with bok choy
Dinner: Roasted mushrooms with butter and parmesan

Monday
Breakfast: Cinnamon overnight oatmeal
Lunch: Tofu and veggie wraps
Dinner: Pot roast with mashed potatoes

Tuesday
Breakfast: Egg and veggie muffin
Lunch: Kale and avocado with blueberries
Dinner: Garlic chicken with thyme

Wednesday
Breakfast: Sweet potato hash browns
Lunch: Zucchini lasagna with turkey sausage
Dinner: Chicken with mango chutney

Thursday
Breakfast: Italian breakfast sandwich
Lunch: Grilled veggies in foil packet
Dinner: Moroccan-style pot roast

Friday
Breakfast: Cucumber yogurt
Lunch: Fruit glazed meatballs
Dinner: Cranberry pork medallions

Saturday
Breakfast: Cantaloupe breakfast smoothie in a bowl
Lunch: Chilled cucumber soup with lemon
Dinner: Garlic beef and broccoli

Week 3

Sunday
Breakfast: Oatmeal with pears and ginger

Lunch: Roasted Salmon and asparagus

Dinner: Beef brisket with wine

Monday

Breakfast: Turkey breakfast strata

Lunch: Vegetable Lasagna

Dinner: Pork tenderloin with blackberry

Tuesday

Breakfast: French toast with banana

Lunch: Grilled zucchini with avocado salsa

Dinner: Cinnamon pork tenderloin

Wednesday

Breakfast: Yogurt and granola

Lunch: Rosemary turkey roast

Week 4

Sunday

Breakfast: Scrambled eggs with spinach

Lunch: Chicken thighs with orange and fennel

Dinner: Tomato soup with Italian bread

Monday

Breakfast: Pear salad

Lunch: Barbecue meatball soup

Dinner: Roasted chicken and veggies with hummus

Tuesday

Breakfast: Oatmeal with blueberries

Lunch: Corned beef and cabbage

Dinner: Salmon with pumpkin pie spice

Wednesday

Dinner: Pork chops with grape sauce

Thursday

Breakfast: Baked French toast

Lunch: Seared scallops with lemon

Dinner: Mustard pepper steak

Friday

Breakfast: Breakfast casserole

Lunch: Baked tuna steak with mustard sauce

Dinner: Lamb with apples and onions

Saturday

Breakfast: Banana Choco chip muffins

Lunch: Bacon and green beans

Dinner: Baked chicken with tomato basil

Breakfast: Toasted bread with peaches and pistachios

Lunch: Beef and root veggie soup

Dinner: Sweet and spicy flank steak

Thursday

Breakfast: Waffle with avocado and salsa

Lunch: Cod with caramelized onions

Dinner: Sausage pasta with kale

Friday

Breakfast: Mexican scrambled eggs

Lunch: Salmon chowder

Dinner: Balsamic beef and mushrooms

Saturday

Breakfast: Oatmeal pancakes with fruits

Lunch: Philly chicken sandwich

Dinner: Mexican beef soup

Conclusion

Type 2 diabetes is a life-long disease that can be debilitating and lethal for some. It is also highly preventable. Persistently making healthy choices can help avert diabetes or manage its complications.

It is worth noting that although we can avoid diabetes, some people have higher risks based on their race, family history, prediabetes, and health conditions such as polycystic ovarian syndrome and gestational diabetes.

Eating healthy, getting active, and avoiding smoking is the simple formula for warding off prediabetes and diabetes. If you are diagnosed with type 2 diabetes, you must develop a positive perception of change when you are considering lifestyle adjustments. Keep yourself mentally resilient and practice self-care as often as needed. Do not hesitate to seek support from your doctor, family, and friends.

If you are someone with a family member or friend who is diabetic, you can show your support by encouraging them to reach their goals without being insensitive or pressuring. Reassure them that managing diabetes takes a lot of work and discipline and that all the choices they make, big or small, towards being fit are worth it.

Take the opportunity to live healthily and be their exercise buddy. Who knows, you might end up having a new favorite activity or realize a new appreciation for vegan food. You can also learn about relevant information about their condition, such as signs of low blood sugar, to administer treatment when necessary.

There are many ways to show you care and support them. If you ever find yourself clueless or out of options, it is always a good idea to ask them how you can be of help.

www.ingramcontent.com/pod-product-compliance
Lightning Source LLC
Chambersburg PA
CBHW081356070526
44583CB00020B/2568